ALSO BY JOAN MORRISON

American Mosaic
with Charlotte Fox Zabusky

From Camelot to Kent State

From
Camelot
to
Kent State

The Sixties Experience in the Words of Those Who Lived It

Joan Morrison
Robert K. Morrison

Times
BOOKS

Grateful acknowledgment is made to the following for permission to reprint previously published
material:

  Broken Arrow Music: Excerpts from the lyrics to "Ohio," written by Neil Young. Copyright
© 1970 by Cotillion Music, Inc. Broken Arrow Music. Used by permission. All rights reserved.
  Warner Bros. Music: Excerpt from the lyrics to "The Times They Are A-Changin' " by Bob
Dylan. Copyright © 1963 by Warner Bros. Inc. All rights reserved. Used by permission.

LIBRARY OF CONGRESS CATALOGING-IN-PUBLICATION DATA
Morrison, Joan.
From Camelot to Kent State.
Includes index.
1. United States—History—1960–1970. I. Morrison,
Robert K., 1953– . II. Title.
E841.M67 1987   973.923   87-9978
ISBN 0-8129-1247-0

Designed by Beth Tondreau Design

Manufactured in the United States of America
9 8 7 6 5 4 3 2
First Edition

To R.T.M. and R.L.M
with appreciation fo
their encouragement,
patience, and love.

It is required of a man that he share the action and passion of his time at the peril of being judged not to have lived. Through our great good fortune in our youth, our hearts were touched with fire.
—Supreme Court Justice Oliver Wendell Holmes, Jr.,
Memorial Day Speech, 1884

To everything there is a season . . .
a time to keep silence and a time to speak.
—Ecclesiastes III:1, 7

There's a battle
Outside and it's ragin'.
It'll soon shake your windows
And rattle your walls
For the times they are a-changin'.
—Bob Dylan,
"The Times They Are A-Changin' "

Acknowledgments

We are very grateful to all those who shared their memories and reflections with us, the people whose stories appear here as well as those whose stories could not be included for reasons of space or balance. All of them have added greatly to our understanding of a complex period of history and of the human beings involved in it.

A number of people contributed their time and expertise to this book, especially Virginia Anderson, who, with detectivelike skill, managed to track down for us some very elusive Sixties people; Lisbet Lubar, librarian *extraordinaire*, who always seemed to come up with the right book or article at the moment it was needed; George Goodwin, whose photographic skills brought out the best of a motley collection of home photos, yearbook pictures, and memorabilia from the Sixties; and Barbara Beirne, whose sensitive portraits of a number of Sixties people are scattered throughout this book.

We also want to express our appreciation to John Ware, our literary agent, for his enthusiastic support from the beginning, and to our editors at Times Books, Jonathan Segal and Sarah Trotta, for their encouragement and counsel.

Above all, our heartfelt thanks and admiration for Beverly Smith, our faithful transcriber, who managed to get hundreds of hours of taped interviews onto paper with speed, skill, and good humor. She put in countless long days without complaint, and her comments were always perceptive. It's hard to imagine completing this book without her assistance.

Contents

The Sixties Experience

This is the story of ten years in the life of America—and of fifty-nine men and women who lived through those years. In their own words they describe a decade that shook us all: the struggle for civil rights, the assassinations, war abroad and war at home, a youth-led revolution in music, dress, and values. Some of them recall also the exhilaration of believing that by their actions they could change the course of history. Perhaps they did.

Certainly the world will never be quite the same as it was in that long ago year when it all began. In 1960, there were no Xeroxes, no birth control pills, no legal abortions, no women's liberation movement. No one worried about the destruction of the environment (*Silent Spring* hadn't been published yet), athletes endorsed their favorite brands of cigarettes on television, and drugs were something you bought at the drugstore. High school students looked and dressed like actors in an Andy Hardy movie. Women's magazines focused on "family togetherness." Richard Nixon had announced his first, but not his last, farewell to politics.

In many places in the South, blacks—then politely known as "colored people" or "Negroes"—were routinely denied the right to vote. They went to segregated schools, couldn't eat at public lunch counters, and had to sit in the back of public buses—or stand, even if there were empty seats in the front.

Even then some people were concerned about the dangers of the atomic bomb (but not nuclear power: that was far in the future). Some educators were worried about the effect of television viewing on children. A few scientists were warning us against using up our natural resources. But most people were involved only with their own lives and not very concerned with the world around them. The expectation was that tomorrow would simply follow today and would be pretty much like it.

Then suddenly, the Sixties were upon us. The Chinese have a curse (or a blessing?): "May you live in interesting times." And whatever the Sixties were, they weren't boring. There was a heightened sense of change in both personal and national life, an almost daily pounding of events, shocks, revelations. The predictability of one's own future, or of the future itself, seemed to be eroding away, along with reverence for traditional values and standards. The ground was trembling under our feet, and no one could ignore it.

The decade started, hopefully enough, with the election of John F. Kennedy to the presidency. At his inauguration he called upon Americans to "ask not what your country can do for you, ask rather what you can do for your country." Robert Frost read an inaugural poem, and it seemed to many listeners on that bitterly cold, bright January day that America was entering a decade of intellectual, political, and economic progress. We were going to go to the moon. We were going to end poverty. The arts would flourish.

Young people began flocking to Washington to work in the new agencies, to join the Peace Corps, to be part of that high-minded but somehow fun-filled "New Frontier" that Kennedy had promised during his campaign. It was popular then to work for government; it was the "in" thing to do, and everyone wanted to be in on the action. The cabinet and the higher ranks of the administration were filled by stars from the industrial and academic world—the "best and brightest," as they came to be called. Before long, the glamour and excitement of this new administration under a vigorous young president led to its popular media image as an American Camelot.

But the euphoria didn't last long. There was the Bay of Pigs disaster in Cuba, an embarrassing defeat and capture of thousands of U.S.-aided Cubans trying to overthrow Castro. Kennedy took the blame, and promised reform of the decision-making process. Then in 1962, the Cuban Missile Crisis chilled the world with the shadow of Armageddon. Fortunately the resolution was peaceful, and restraint and wisdom seemed to be the order of the day. The man on the street expressed confidence in our leaders.

In the South, the voter-registration drives and lunch-counter sit-ins were meeting with brutal opposition. There were beatings and murders. But although it was apparent that social progress wouldn't be easy, there was a perception that the federal government was on the right side. As one of the people we interviewed said, "The demonstrators were only helping the government to live up to its own principles." It wasn't yet "us against them," in the sense that "them" was the government.

Fighting the good fight brought its own exhilaration and satisfaction. Hundreds of thousands of listeners were moved to hear Martin Luther King's "I Have a Dream" speech at the culmination of the civil rights march on Washington in 1963. More than one of our narrators describe this moment as a peak experience in their lives.

The assassination of President Kennedy on November 22, 1963, and the subsequent killing of his assassin two days later, was a watershed in the consciousness of the Sixties. An outpouring of sorrow during the days of mourning and a sobering national self-examination followed. Was there something violent about our country? Something uncontrollable, unpredictable?

The feeling of confidence never came back, but in President Johnson's first two years in office, a wide range of civil rights and social programs was passed. The New Frontier became the Great Society, and for a while it seemed that social progress was possible through legislation. Among the bills enacted in 1964 and 1965 were Medicare, Medicaid, the Voting Rights Act, establishment of the National Foundation on the Arts and the Humanities, and a number of federal programs for education and job training.

But even while this legislation was being passed, decisions were being made that would poison our national life for many years to come. Lyndon Johnson had promised in his 1964 campaign against Barry Goldwater that "we are not about to send American boys nine or ten thousand miles away from home to do what Asian boys ought to be doing for themselves." But slowly and surely our involvement in Vietnam was growing. Following two alleged attacks on our naval ships in the Gulf of Tonkin, Congress passed a resolution giving the president virtually unlimited power to act in that region to protect U.S. troops. By the end of 1965, there were 170,000 U.S. servicemen in Vietnam.

Antiwar protests began to spread on campuses across the country. There were "teach-ins" on the war, during which professors and graduate students led discussions on the issues. At first the protests were peaceful: petition signing, candlelit marches, visits to congressmen. But as the war escalated, so did the protests. Television brought Vietnam into everyone's living room. Viewers could see villages burning, villagers weeping, and wounded and dying American soldiers.

The expansion of the air war over Vietnam and the later bombing of North Vietnam fueled the protests. By 1967, there were 464,000 American troops in Vietnam, and antiwar marchers stormed the Pentagon. The smell of tear gas floated across the Washington Mall.

Many young men, because they perceived the war in Vietnam to be immoral, felt justified in using whatever means they could to evade serving in it. From voluntary advisory offices on nearly every campus, they could receive tips on how to lose weight or fake mental illness, how to exaggerate health problems or injuries or even develop them, in order to obtain medical deferments. Thousands fled to Canada, England, or Sweden, where the governments were more sympathetic to their objections to the war. Many others risked jail by burning their draft cards or refusing to register.

There was trouble on the domestic scene, too. The social programs of the Great Society had failed to ease tensions in our inner cities. Hopes had been raised that had not been fulfilled. "Black Power" and militant action began to replace nonviolence as an approach to racial progress. And as the war escalated, the ranks in Vietnam were filled disproportionately by black soldiers. There was widespread despair and anger.

In 1966 and 1967, race riots erupted in a number of major cities: Boston, Cleveland, Detroit, Chicago, Los Angeles, New York, and Baltimore. The "Long Hot Summer" of 1967 ended with a three-day riot in Newark that left twenty-six dead. The dream of social progress "hand in hand together" seemed to be dissolving into an ugly reality. The Kerner Commission Report on the riots warned of "two nations— one black, one white" developing in our country.

Social changes were whizzing past over these years, too. Young men were wearing their hair long, young women were wearing their skirts short, and "The Pill" was making new sexual freedom possible. There was widespread use of marijuana, as well as LSD and other "mind-expanding" drugs, especially on college campuses and in many high schools. "Flower children" adorned with beads drifted barefoot about the country. Parents of many young people could barely stand to look at them, much less to hear about what they are doing. And what was a father who had fought with pride in World War II to think of a son who burned his draft card? The "generation gap" became an abyss.

Many young people were beginning to gather in a sort of substitute family life that came to be known as commune living, perhaps because they felt more at home with their own kind than with their elders. Also, communes provided an inexpensive, simple living arrangement, and the young people of the Sixties disdained the outward signs of material success. The day of the MBA and the "Yuppie" was yet to come—far, far in an unimaginable future.

The women's liberation movement got off to a slow start during this time, perhaps overshadowed by the urgency of the escalating war. Toward the end of the Sixties, many women came together in consciousness-raising groups and began to challenge male leadership roles. But for much of the decade, traditional sex roles were left unaltered, even in the new experimental living arrangements and radical political groups.

At the same time, a highly visible counterculture was developing with its own fashions, cult figures, and celebrations. Gigantic "be-ins" attracted thousands to Central Park in New York and Golden Gate Park in San Francisco. Entire sections of cities—the East Village, the Haight-Ashbury—became enclaves that drew young people from all over the country to join in the excitement.

Shared music seemed to bind the Sixties together in a special new way. Everything was done to music. John Lennon claimed that the Beatles were more popular than Jesus, and a sober Cardinal Cushing said he was right. Outdoor music festivals featured such rock bands as the Grateful Dead, Country Joe and the Fish, Jefferson Airplane, and the Doors, whose lyrics celebrated the new values of the counterculture.

Music can give us clues to what is going on in a society, and during the Sixties much of the music seemed almost like an accompaniment to the action. From the hopeful "We Shall Overcome" of 1960 to the bitter "Ohio" of 1970 only ten years elapsed, but what a world of political idealism, betrayal, and loss lay between. Among the songs of the period were "Where Have All the Flowers Gone?" (1961), "Blowing in the Wind" (1962), "The Times They Are A-Changin' " (1963), "Waist Deep in the Big Muddy" (1967), and the telling dichotomy of 1969's two hits: "Okie from Muskogee" and "Give Peace a Chance."

In 1968, the pot reached the boiling point. The Tet Offensive in Vietnam caught the American military unprepared and brought a sobering realization, even to many former war supporters, that there might be no "light at the end of the tunnel." Suddenly antiwar sentiment became respectable. President Johnson withdrew from the presidential race. Eugene McCarthy and Robert F. Kennedy led antiwar factions within the Democratic Party, and many prominent establishment leaders began to counsel withdrawal of troops from Southeast Asia.

Then came the assassination of Martin Luther King, followed by widespread race riots in over one hundred American cities. The National Guard was called in to police Washington, D.C., and the Capitol building was obscured by smoke from the burning city. In June, on the evening of his victory in the California primary, Robert F. Kennedy was assassinated. People again began asking what kind of country America was.

During the Democratic National Convention that summer in Chicago, millions of television viewers saw police beating unarmed protesters and innocent bystanders. Blood splashed on the floor of the Hilton hotel while the convention was in progress. Walter Cronkite was heard to say, "We are in a police state." An official report later termed the police actions in Chicago a "police riot."

By this time, many were pointing out the contrast between our technological progress, exemplified by our exploration of space and our development of atomic energy, and our rapidly eroding social structure. The glue holding people together—family, patriotism, shared beliefs and standards—seemed to be dissolving. Some were reminded of a line from Yeats's poem *The Second Coming*: "Things fall apart; the center cannot hold."

Over the next year, college disturbances grew. Students were now demanding not only an end to recruiting on campus by ROTC and by the Dow Chemical Company, manufacturer of napalm, but a voice in curriculum and faculty selection, too. A shocked nation saw photographs of black students at Cornell carrying rifles as they ended their occupation of the student union building. On a number of campuses, ROTC buildings were attacked or burned. Activists at the University of Wisconsin blew up an Army research center on their campus one night, inadvertently killing a graduate student who was working late. College administrators across the country reacted in a variety of ways, from negotiating to calling in the police; whatever they did seemed to add to the turmoil.

In the summer of 1969, there was a little breather: the Woodstock festival, a celebration of music and nudity and rain in a green field in upstate New York. And one heady night in July we saw Neil Armstrong step onto the moon.

But the war continued. It seemed endless; some commentators predicted that it could go on for twenty years. News of the massacre of civilians by U.S. soldiers at a tiny village called My Lai shocked the nation. Could American soldiers be the bad guys?

On the fifteenth of October people in communities across the country took part in a national Moratorium on the war in Vietnam—ringing church bells, holding silent vigils, and joining peaceful marches. In Washington, thousands upon thousands of protesters paraded past the White House with candles. Inside, the next moves were being planned.

In the spring of 1970, President Nixon announced an invasion of Cambodia, until then neutral, to find COSVN, the mythical Communist army headquarters. Widespread protests broke out on campuses across the country. At Kent State University in Ohio, after a weekend of turmoil, National Guard soldiers shot four undergraduates dead on a grassy meadow. Ten days later, two black student demonstrators were killed at Jackson State College in Mississippi. Stunned students left campuses all over the country. More than 400 colleges and universities closed early. Nearly 100,000 demonstrators converged on Washington. Then they went home to think and to mourn. The decade that had begun so brightly, with young people flocking to Washington to work for the New Frontier, had ended in blood and bitterness and a deeply divided country. The Sixties were over.

There have been many excellent books on specific aspects of the Sixties: the antiwar movement, the civil rights movement, what went on behind the scenes in Washington, what was going on in Vietnam, the counterculture, the music, the generation gap, the underground press. This book does not attempt to repeat those studies or to cover the entire history of that tumultuous decade—an impossible task in any case— but rather to give some idea of *what it was like to be living then*, to add a human dimension to the black headlines and shocking scenes of those years.

How did it feel to go into the South on a "Freedom Bus," to be teargassed by your own country's soldiers, to take LSD for the first time, to step off a helicopter into a Vietnamese jungle, to take over your college's administration building, to receive a telegram telling you your son had been killed? We wanted to know. We weren't trying to take sides, to judge, to praise, or to apportion blame; we just wanted to get the memories down on tape and into print before they faded.

To gather these stories, we interviewed on tape a wide variety of men and women across the country: old, young, black, white, hawks, doves, war resisters, hard hats, some who went to Vietnam, some who went to Canada. There are a few well-known names in this book, but most of our narrators were members of the rank and file: participants, observers, followers, like most of the rest of us.

Usually we met with them in their own homes, which included an elegant Upper East Side apartment in Manhattan, a walnut farm in California, a commune in Baltimore, and many modest city apartments and comfortable suburban homes. Former activist nun Elizabeth McAlister was interviewed in Alderson Federal Prison, where she was serving a three-year term for attacking an Air Force missile installation. John Lewis, first chairman of the Student Nonviolent Coordinating Committee, was interviewed in Atlanta City Hall, where he was a city councilman—visible proof of how far we have come since the early Sixties, when blacks could not even eat in that building's cafeteria.

We focused on three main topics: What motivated you to act the way you did in the Sixties, what did you actually do, and what are your feelings about those actions now? But, of course, the ramifications of those questions led to many other questions and many other answers. We didn't look for stereotypes, and we didn't find them.

Each of us interviewed approximately half of the narrators, and we shared the work of editing the thousands of pages of transcripts: deleting repetitious material, arranging stories in a chronological form, and focusing on what was significant in each story. Our aim was to present a panorama of life in the Sixties; not a history book, but a book of people living *through* history.

What did we find out? What has happened to the Sixties generation? Well, of course, there is no single answer. Life is complex and so are people. Most of these men and women are in their mid-thirties to early forties now. They've moved into the mainstream, acquired degrees and qualifications, married and produced children. Some of them are still fighting for causes they believe in—preservation of the environment, control of nuclear power, peace in Central America, labor reform, women's rights, minority rights—working, more often than not, within the system. Others, like Candide, are "cultivating their own gardens." If there was any common theme, it was a nostalgia, a sort of yearning wistfulness for the days when something exciting always seemed to be happening, when people thought they could change the future by their actions—when anything was possible.

Hopeful
Beginnings

Harris Wofford

He had worked hard on the Kennedy campaign before the 1960 election, lining up and consolidating support from liberal and civil rights groups. On the day after the election, he was assigned to work with Sargent Shriver on a "talent search" aimed at recruiting the stars of the business and academic worlds for the new administration. Later he served as deputy director of the Peace Corps and still later as president of Bryn Mawr College. He now practices law in Philadelphia.

It was one of those times in our society when it looks as though everything is going to come into focus, when there will be common goals and people will be galvanized as a country to work for those goals. Those moments don't come very often, and people are lucky to be part of them.

As soon as the election was over, Kennedy started this talent search, of which I was a part, to find the so-called "best and brightest" and bring them into the administration. He wanted people like himself; perhaps not exactly like himself, but people that were on balance young and vigorous and *tough*. That was one of the words he liked to use. He wanted them to have a sense of humor and to be committed to public service.

He didn't want people who were bureaucratic, and he certainly didn't want just politicians. We were to scour the country—academia, the professions, business, unions, the party, people who'd been in the campaign—to see who should be called. At the same time that this sort of hunt was going on, people were offering themselves in large numbers because there was excitement in the government, and Washington was a magnet, as it had been with Teddy Roosevelt and with Franklin Roosevelt and with Wilson. So there was a mammoth job of sifting and selecting. And there was a lot of fantastic telephoning back and forth because there wasn't much time till the inauguration.

One of the people we came upon was McNamara, who had just been made president of the Ford Motor Company. There'd been a newspaper article about him, and Sargent Shriver said, "Let's check him out, because I remember all those stories about him as a Whiz Kid at the Pentagon during World War II." We found out that he was in a "great books" discussion group at Ann Arbor, and that he had chosen to live in Ann Arbor instead of wherever it is the car company people live because he wanted to be near the academics. One thing after another made McNamara seem more and more appealing.

We talked to Kennedy about him, and Kennedy said, "Sounds like somebody for either Treasury or Defense. Go out and see him. Offer him either one, but have him come to see me."

It was quite an extraordinary offer to make. I mean, if Kennedy hadn't liked him, I'm sure he could have backed out, but that's what he said. Anyhow, McNamara agreed to fly back and see Kennedy.

Then, at the last minute, Kennedy called up and said, "For God's sake, find out if he's a Catholic. I can't have another Catholic in the cabinet." But we found out he wasn't a Catholic, so that was all right. And McNamara came and saw Kennedy and they hit it off. He agreed to come into the administration, and so did Rusk and Bundy and the others.

In the field of civil rights, which had been my main concern, there was occurring what I had dreamed would someday happen—the combining of popular protests and public power. The federal government was becoming an agent of change. It wasn't all bliss, but the graph was up where I wanted it to go. I'd been on the outside and now I was on the inside. And the Peace Corps, with which I soon became involved, was probably the happiest venture in the government—successful, upbeat, inventive, new. It was a wonderful time.

I think almost everybody I knew was having a ball. In fact some of us have the problem of not letting it be like the perfect school and always looking back on your Old Boy days. The debunking of the

Kennedy era and of the Kennedys has been at least as bad as the overromanticizing—the Camelot stuff. There were flaws in Kennedy and in what was done, but as the world goes, things were moving and they were moving in the right direction. I think the balance is actually struck in the public mind. The common sense American knows that it was a hell of a good time.

. . . The War on Poverty was next and we didn't win it. In some sense we gave it up as the war in Vietnam moved in. I'm the last one to believe that money solves all these problems, but money is part of it, and Vietnam took the resources and the focus. And the underclass in America is still here.

How did it happen? What went wrong? It has been said, you know, that Johnson got us into Vietnam because he was told to do so by the best and brightest—McNamara, Rusk, and Bundy. I think Kennedy erred in picking too many people who were of the bright and sophisticated establishment crew. He didn't like to be bored and they were very witty. But cleverness and wisdom are very different. I've seen it in so many decision-making groups—the bright, the witty, the strong outtalk the wiser voices. It's a continuing problem. In terms of foreign policy it's always easier for the people who talk tough and who talk in terms of military power, and it's always harder for those who are talking a more complex story of ideas and political forces. The brightest are not always the best, or they are not the wisest in many cases. How wrong they could be is one of the great lessons of the Sixties.

Saving
the World

■ **BILL:** We'd both been stirred by the Kennedy inaugural speech—the idea of giving, not getting. And we had the desire to do something for people somewhere in the world. We wanted to do something that would help people directly, with education or with medical aid or some basic part of life.

After we graduated from Grinnell, we got married and taught for a couple of years, and we talked more seriously about going somewhere in the world where we could be of use. A Peace Corps volunteer came to the school where I was teaching in Connecticut and spoke to the students about his experiences in Africa, and going there seemed to me like a really neat thing to do.

We liked the idea of having a grassroots experience and living closely with local people. We decided to apply. We felt we had a good chance to get in, because I was a math teacher and Sue was an English teacher, and we thought that would be a good balance. And we knew that Third World countries needed teachers very badly then. We thought originally of India, but they asked us if we'd be willing to go to Kenya, and we said, "Yes, wherever we're needed."

■ **SUSAN:** My family wasn't too enthusiastic about it when they heard where we were going. They didn't know much about Africa, and they imagined disease and hostility and racial tension and poverty. They didn't like the idea of their only daughter going off to this "dark continent," so to speak. But we were determined. We thought we had something that was needed, and we wanted to use it. And, of course, in our minds the fact that we'd be in a foreign country, someplace that was interesting and different and exciting, was also a factor.

We went into a training program in New York City that lasted for three months. We had one hundred eighty hours in Swahili to enable us to get around in the country and to understand the culture better. And we had training in Kenyan culture, history, politics, government, educational system—everything was new to us.

The country had just gained its independence from Great Britain, and General Kenyatta was president. There was a great amount of hope in Kenya that now that it would have a black parliament and black political leaders, the country was really going to grow. So there were a lot of changes going on there, and the country wanted to improve on many fronts: education, health, production. It seemed we'd be there at the right time.

When we got to the place in Kenya where we were to teach, we were given a little half-of-a-house right on the school compound, which we

Bill and Susan Montfort

*O*ne of the most popular of Kennedy's New Frontier programs was the Peace Corps, which drew many young people to volunteer service in developing countries around the world. Among them were Bill and Susan Montfort. Bill now teaches high-school math and is also faculty adviser for the school's International Relations Club, which every year has raised hundreds of dollars on behalf of Peace Corps projects in Africa. Susan is a counselor in a family planning clinic.

were to share with an African family. It was made of cinderblocks and it had a tile roof. There was no running water. We had to go to a spigot maybe a hundred feet away for cold water, and the toilet facilities were about a hundred feet away, too. There were no screens, and the insects would come in and out all day and all night—big cockroaches and spiders and centipedes and some insects that I couldn't identify. But the hardships were certainly endurable, and we had an advantage in that there were two of us, and we supported each other.

The school where we were assigned was an unusual one. It had been set up by a man of British parentage who was committed to providing a place for youngsters who had been orphaned, or whose families had been in trouble because of the Mau-Mau uprisings, or street children who had run away from home up-country and were getting in trouble with the law.

It was a boarding school for boys aged five to thirteen. For most of the students, it was their one chance to make something of themselves and to get ahead, and we had the feeling that we were helping to train a new generation.

■ **BILL:** I remember the first day in class. There were thirty-five black boys sitting in front of me, all in their school uniforms, and I had, you know, the typical Caucasian reaction: "How am I going to tell them all apart?" But after a few days, they became distinct personalities, distinct names, distinct facial characteristics, head shape, and so on. There was a uniqueness to each person, and they all became individuals to me. I had to get used to them, of course, and they had to get used to me. I had to speak slowly, because they were used to English English; American English sounded different to them and sometimes they couldn't understand it.

I remember one boy told me that the year before he would run six or seven miles to the village school in the early morning, and be so exhausted by the time he got there that it was hard to do the work. And then in the afternoon, of course, he had to do the reverse. He had begun stealing to get the bus fare, because he was so exhausted that he couldn't do his schoolwork. So being able to come to this boarding school was a godsend to him. Both of his parents were dead, and he'd lived with an uncle who wasn't able to help him at all.

Because the school was founded by a Britisher who had been trained in the British school system, the school was run on the lines of a British boarding school.

■ **SUSAN:** Everything was based on the British syllabus, and all the literature was English literature. You know, it was a little difficult teaching

Macbeth to these kids. Shakespearean English is tough enough for kids in *this* country to grasp, and they went through real struggles with it. Their English wasn't all that good to begin with, and they came from a number of different tribes, so they had different accents.

Later on, after I'd been there for a while, I tried to introduce some African poetry and some folk tales from West Africa which were beginning to be published, and I'd have them write their own folk tales and stories that they knew. That was easier for them, and fascinating for me to read.

■ BILL: We were really the first whites who were conversational and friendly with the boys. We invited them into our house and let them cook with us. They showed us how to cook some of their foods, which we'd buy at the market. And we took time to be conversational and got discussions going. It wasn't all up-front lecture, write notes on the board, and "copy this in your notebooks" the way the other teachers had been doing.

On Saturdays we'd take the boys on hikes or on visits to places in Nairobi, or sometimes to their home villages if they weren't too far away. We'd get on a bus with them, with a crowd of smoking men and mothers with crying babies and chickens, old ladies—a little country bus. Almost always we'd be the only whites on the bus. And when we'd get into the small village where the student lived, we'd be given the royal treatment. Even if it was just a mud hut and boiled chicken, they were pleased to have us and to share with us.

■ SUSAN: Whenever there were school holidays, we went on medical projects where we helped vaccinate against smallpox and polio and check for tuberculosis exposure. These projects were in very small villages in remote areas along the coast.

The setup for spreading out the materials to use in the vaccinating would be just a little table under a palm tree somewhere, or sometimes a mud-walled school that had no windows.

The reaction of the local people was interesting. Probably we were the first whites they'd ever seen, in many cases. The kids would rub to see if the white rubbed off our skins. They'd really check that out. And I had long hair at that time, and every once in a while I would feel someone sneak a touch and a feel of the hair down my back, where they thought I might not notice.

People would line up and receive their vaccinations and go on. Most often it was mothers bringing in babies, but men and older children came, too. The children would be frightened, and we'd have to do a lot of convincing. With some tribes, it was important for them to show that it hurt, because that would mean that it was really going to do some good. . . . Later, when we heard about the success of the smallpox campaign worldwide, we felt we'd been part of it.

■ **BILL:** Last year, Sue and I and our children went to visit the school in Kenya where we had taught, and we got to see some of our old pupils, who are now grown up and working. It gave us a great deal of satisfaction to see how well they had done. There's a newspaper editor, a banker, a librarian, and another who had a governmental post in telecommunications. One of our students has run for parliament, a number of them had jobs as business executives or were running their own independent businesses. Others had jobs in the civil service of the country—not senior jobs yet, of course, because they're still young, but they're on their way. It really made us feel very good.

Joseph Wiley

John A. Pietras/Trenton Times

*H*e now works as a senior administrator for the New Jersey Department of the Environment. In the Sixties, he joined the Peace Corps immediately upon graduating from Harvard. After two months of training, he and his new bride, also a Peace Corps volunteer, were sent to Peru.

We came in on the train to a little town in the highlands where we were going to be stationed. The railroad was a marvelous one built by the British for the Peruvian government in the 1880s or 1890s. It was sort of a corridor of Western civilization, going through a non-Western culture. Certain things along it represented the Western way: There was a telegraph, there were post offices, there were various other forms of communication, and there was a road paralleling the railroad.

When we arrived in the little town, it actually looked like a backdrop of a cowboy movie. It was a dusty little place, just adobe buildings. It looked like the only thing that ever happened was that a train went through once a day. It was the dry season and there was dust blowing all over the place. You didn't see any people, and everything was sort of earth-colored because of the adobe and the thatched roofs. I remember my wife thought it looked pretty desolate. I think she was a little bit shocked.

I had the feeling I was looking at a deserted village. Of course, it turned out there were people and things going on, but they were mostly behind closed doors, which is true in most Latin American countries. The people were all brown and reddish-brown, with American Indian–type features, but they were shorter and twice as wide, because they have tremendous chests. They're very, very powerfully built. They didn't pay any attention to us. They looked, but they weren't really curious.

Later on I saw a farmstead outside the town. If I'd seen it on the first day, I don't think I would have even noticed it, because a farmstead there blends totally into the landscape. It's just a tiny hut, a little shelter built into a hill away from the wind, so that if you look at it from a distance you won't notice it's there. It's just made out of stones and adobe and thatch. Of course, there'll usually be some activity, or animals will be around, and you'll see the stone walls of the corral. You'll see a little bit of smoke coming through the thatch, and then you'll see somebody by the door and you'll know that people are there. They really blend into the landscape, and that's the whole essence of the way they're living; they are part of the landscape.

Everything they have is made from scratch. They make their own clothes. They hunt and fish a lot. They're aware of all the plants around them, what their significance is. We're not aware of the changes in the weather. We don't have ten different names for different kinds of clouds or different kinds of rain. But they're aware of everything around them. If we didn't understand that, we would say they were just stupid or just brutes. They appear animal-like. They're dirty. They don't bathe. They have one set of clothes, and they live in conditions that we would never tolerate. But their physical endurance is unbelievable, just like an animal's. They're very, very poor. It's truly subsistence living. . . .

And here's something: We were wealthier in the Peace Corps than we've ever been since. Compared to the standard of living around us, we were the wealthiest class of people there. We could afford things that we could never afford here, unless we were in the upper one percent or five percent of the economic strata. If we wanted to have servants or if we wanted to buy the best food or eat in the best restaurants or have the best accommodations or whatever, we could do that there on our Peace Corps salaries. We went there to serve, and suddenly we realized we were better off than all the people we were serving. It was the differential; that's what we weren't used to. So we jokingly thought, Go into the Peace Corps if you want to get rich quick—relatively. . . .

From the very beginning I was assigned to the Agricultural Extension

Service. The Peace Corps was to work with them, and that was my assignment. We were to teach them how to progress and have a higher per capita income. The basic assumption was that everybody wanted to increase per capita income. I was to administer a loan program that involved giving out money to farmers to improve the quality of their cattle.

The idea was that the native cattle had bad genetic potential for the production of anything, whether it was meat or milk, and that was true. They were not as productive as any number of cattle breeds from Europe or the U.S. or anywhere, almost anywhere else where they'd been breeding selectively. These were a mixture, mongrels. And yet, they were tough, those cattle. They were just like the people. Anything could happen to them, but they wouldn't die. They might not produce much meat or milk, but they just wouldn't die. From the local point of view, these animals were doing fine.

After a lot of study, we introduced Brown Swiss cattle because they would do well in those high altitudes, and they would gain a lot of weight, and there would be more meat for the people to sell and to eat. They were nice, sleek cattle, but they had to have better food, a better quality of forage. They were used to eating nicely baled hay, not corn husks.

So, loans were made to farmers to buy the improved cattle, and the farmers bought them. They also got money to buy seed to raise crops to feed the cattle. But they'd never heard of raising crops to feed cattle. They thought cattle should find their own fodder. It seemed to the farmers that they were working for the cattle, planting the crops so that the cattle could eat, so they could be better cattle. That really didn't make sense to these subsistence farmers, whose whole concept was "Let the cattle go out and find their own food, and then once a year or so we might kill a cow for a special meal."

The fact was that if they did all these things to feed the cattle they would get fatter cattle, and they could go and sell the cattle for money so they could buy plastic shoes from Japan or synthetic-fiber clothing at a market. Actually it meant they had to do a lot of work to get something that they didn't need anyway. This never made sense to them, and they didn't do it.

So many of the poor cattle that were brought in with the money from outside started to sort of shrivel up. Instead of gaining weight, which they were supposed to do, they were shriveling up. And I was sent out to collect the interest on the loans to these farmers, who had cattle bought with American money. First of all, they didn't understand what a loan was, because they'd never had a loan and they hadn't needed any loans. They *had* signed the papers, but they were mostly illiterate. And I was the person who came to tell them the bad news: that they had to pay the interest and principal.

When I showed up, they didn't even know what I was talking about. In many cases they had lost the cattle, or they had sold the cattle because they couldn't feed them. And if they'd had the money, they had spent it by the time I got there. They'd had a big party and everyone got drunk for as long as the money lasted, and that was the end of it. So there was no interest, and in some cases there was no principal: no cattle left, no cows.

I think their understanding was that the money was a gift, and that's the way they acted. They knew that the United States was very rich. They'd heard about it, that it was a rich country, so they figured that if something involved money from the United States it must have been a gift. And in primitive societies, giving is an important part of life. If somebody is much wealthier than anybody else, they're expected to give wealth away. So I think many of them understood that the money was a gift, and that's the way they acted.

I concluded that the best thing to do would be to explain to them that it was a loan and they were expected to pay it back. And if they were having a problem feeding the cattle or something, to sell the cattle before they starved to death, and pay back the loan. I remember going out with two assistants with instructions to round up somebody's llamas, because they had sold the cattle. The people had sold the cows, so we said we'd take the llamas. Well, that didn't make sense to me.

I went back to the bank office, to the bank manager, and I said, "You can't put these people out of business. They didn't know what they were doing. They were poorly advised. They really don't know how to raise the crops to feed that kind of cattle. We can't get the money back. The cattle are sold or eaten. Write it off as a loss, write it off as a bad loan." That's how it ended up.

If I hadn't intervened, some of these small subsistence farmers would really have been ruined, because if their land had been taken—that was all that they had, and that would have been the end of them. I must admit there were a few, I would say ten or fifteen percent of the people, who actually benefited, but they were the better farmers, the more educated ones. They already owned land, they owned cattle, they owned vehicles, and in some cases they had tractors—they were commercial farmers. They were the only ones who benefited. . . .

My wife had a different experience. She started a group of artisans to make traditional handicrafts, woven things, knitted things, and leather goods made out of sheepskin. And the last year, I worked a lot with her group. It was a cooperative group to make and sell these things. Some of them are beautiful. They're all hand-dyed with natural dyes, each one made a different way. The tradition goes back to pre-Incan times, probably three or four thousand years. These people had remarkable skills in doing handicrafts, and great patience.

My wife designed things that had never been made there before, that you can make quickly, because we didn't want these people to take months to make something and then sell it for a pittance to tourists who wouldn't really appreciate it, which was what some of them were doing. We thought, Well, for the tourists let's make something that requires skilled labor or skilled handiwork, but that is not quite so time-consuming, or they'll never make any money at it. So we came up with some products which were much more Western-oriented, but which embodied some of their native skills and designs. And many of these were very successful.

We rented a building, which was next door to the house where we lived, and all the costs were paid by the cooperative. The Peace Corps put up, I think, fifty or a hundred dollars to start the cooperative. It was like a little factory. We figured out wages, a certain amount of money that went back into the cooperative to buy equipment and finance operations, and we were able to build up quite a lot of equipment in a year or two. After we got the cooperative going, we had a ten-thousand-dollar export order, which put a lot of people to work. And in those days, ten thousand dollars down there was a lot of money, especially for people who had no cash money before. When we left, they had a capital stock of a couple of thousand dollars, in addition to the wages that the people were earning.

But, you know, soon after we left, the group sort of folded. They went back to doing things on their own rather than as a group, which we had tried to get them to do. I think it was just that these people aren't into doing Western specialized labor. As long as we were there telling them this was a good thing to do, they would do it. But they didn't have a strong drive to want to continue doing it. Basically, they didn't need the cash money. They usually owned little pieces of land in the surrounding area, and they got along in their old subsistence way. For most of them it was a temporary boost. . . .

These people can survive and be very happy in conditions that would be just totally unthinkable to us. It's just that they're adapted to that kind of existence. There's starvation and disease, but they accept it. They're so fatalistic it almost seems insensitive, inhuman, to us. But I think they're more intense, in a way, in their enjoyment, because they don't have to worry about all kinds of things that we worry about. They don't pay taxes, they don't worry about college boards, they're not comparing themselves to their neighbors as much, because they're much the same in their aspirations.

I began to realize that their adaptation to their environment far surpassed our adaptation to our material world. Here, if one thing goes wrong, the whole society is in a confusion. If the roads to our town were cut for a week, people would be killing each other. But if there were a famine down there, there wouldn't be any rioting or looting or social upheaval; it would just be accepted. Everything here is very tenuous in its dependence on technology, yet they live in a very solid, simple world. Their world isn't going to disappear as rapidly as ours.

You know, the Peace Corps was sort of like a spaceship to them. It was just something that came in totally unexpected. They had to pay attention. They had to be willing to go along with it, because it was fate that these things would happen periodically, and then they would gradually sort of diminish and go away, and they wouldn't need to worry about it anymore. . . .

By Peace Corps standards we accomplished a lot, we were a success. But I gradually realized that those successes didn't last, and that's what made an impression on me, because I was used to seeing things keep progressing in a certain direction. Seeing something progress and *appear* to be working, and then just slide back to where it was, with no harm done, was a very sobering experience.

We changed some things temporarily, but we didn't change anything on a lasting basis. We kept the status quo. I don't think we hurt anybody, at least I don't know that we did. But I think we learned a lot. Of course, that wasn't the intention of the Peace Corps. I'm sure that Congress would be appalled if they thought that that's what they were getting out of spending all this money, that we came back and said, "Hey, you know, these people are all right down there!"

Hand in Hand Together

Mary Ward

*I*n the early Sixties, many idealistic young whites joined the civil rights movement and shared in its struggles and triumphs. Mary Ward was one of these. Once a State Department cryptographer, she is now a staff member of a nuclear-disarmament coalition.

In 1963 I joined the March on Washington when Martin Luther King gave his "I Have a Dream" speech. The most important thing that happened to me in those years, and probably one of the most important things that's ever happened to me in my life, was that 1963 gathering in Washington. I think if somebody said to me, "Are you happy to be a human being?" I would say yes, because I was there.

I remember sitting on the lawn with an older black woman. I can see her face. And there was a look on her face. . . . We started talking, and I remember her total disbelief that this would ever happen, that black and white would be there together. Her whole being, her whole body, was infused with wonder that this had happened, that black people had dared to come and that white people were backing them up. And I remember my disbelief at *her* disbelief at something that seemed so natural.

The day ended with King's speech, and, you know, I'm not a terribly emotional person in terms of stamping my feet or anything like that, but when he reached the end of the speech—"I see the mountain. I'm on the mountaintop"—when he reached that, there was a gospel kind of blackness in me. Inside, I knew why people in black churches were singing, and there was the same kind of feeling in me. I'd never be able to stamp my feet or shake my body or do any of that, but I understood it.

At that moment there was a kind of coming together of people with a man who in some way reached out to people. It was truly unbelievable. There'll never be another moment like that. I was privileged to have been there that day. I think that was one of the most, probably *the* most wonderful day of my life.

John Lewis

*B*orn into a poor black sharecropper's family in rural Alabama, he remembers the time when total segregation was the rule of law in the South and blacks were routinely denied the right to vote. He was the first chairman of the Student Nonviolent Coordinating Committee (SNCC) and an active participant in many of the early civil rights struggles of the Sixties. In 1966, he was ousted as chairman by Stokely Carmichael over the issue of whether whites should be allowed to remain in the organization, but he continued to be active in the civil rights movement. Recently a city councilman in Atlanta, Georgia, he is now a United States Representative from the Fifth Congressional District in Georgia.

When I was a boy, I would go downtown to the little town of Troy, and I'd see the signs saying "White" and "Colored" on the water fountains. There'd be a beautiful, shining water fountain in one corner of the store marked "White," and in another corner was just a little spigot marked "Colored." I saw the signs saying "White Men," "Colored Men," and "White Women," "Colored Women." And at the theater, we had to go upstairs to go to a movie. You bought your ticket at the same window that the white people did, but they could sit downstairs, and you had to go upstairs.

I wondered about that, because it was not in keeping with my religious faith, which taught me that we were all the same in the eyes of God. And I had been taught that all men are created equal.

It really hit me when I was fifteen years old, when I heard about Martin Luther King, Jr., and the Montgomery bus boycott. Black people were walking the streets for more than a year rather than riding segregated buses. To me it was like a great sense of hope, a light. Many of the teachers at the high school that I attended were from Montgomery, and they would tell us about what was happening there. That more than any other event was the turning point for me, I think. It gave me a way out.

When I graduated from high school, I enrolled at the American Baptist Theological Seminary in Nashville, because there was an opportunity there for me to work my way through the college as a kitchen helper and janitor. While I was there I began attending these workshops, studying the philosophy and discipline of nonviolence: the life and times of Gandhi, the works of Henry Thoreau, and the philosophy of civil disobedience. And we began to think about how we could apply these lessons to the problem of segregation.

In February 1960, we planned the first mass lunch-counter sit-in. About five hundred students, black and white, from various colleges showed up and participated in a nonviolent workshop the night before the sit-in. Some of them came from as far away as Pomona College in California and Beloit College in Wisconsin.

We made a list of what we called the "Rules of the Sit-in"—the do's and don't's—and we mimeographed it on an old machine and passed it out to all the students. I wish I had a copy of this list today. I remember it said things like, "Sit up straight. Don't talk back. Don't laugh. Don't strike back." And at the end it said, "Remember the teachings of Jesus, Gandhi, Thoreau, and Martin Luther King, Jr."

Then the next day it began. We wanted to make a good impression. The young men put on their coats and ties, and the young ladies their heels and stockings. We selected seven stores to go into, primarily the chain stores—Woolworth's, Kresge's, and the Walgreen drugstore—and we had these well-dressed young people with their books going to the lunch counters. They would sit down in a very orderly, peaceful, nonviolent fashion and wait to be served. They would be reading a book or doing their homework or whatever while they were waiting.

I was a spokesperson for one of these groups. I would ask to be served, and we would be told that we wouldn't be served. The lunch counter would be closed, and they would put up a sign saying "Closed—

not serving." Sometimes they would lock the door, leave us in there, and turn out all the lights, and we would continue to sit.

After we had been doing this for a month, it was beginning to bother the business community and other people in Nashville. We heard that the city had decided to allow the police officials to stand by and allow the hoodlum element to come in and attack us—and that the police would arrest us—to try to stop the sit-ins. We had a meeting after we heard that, to decide did we still want to go down on this particular day. And we said yes.

I was with the group that went into the Woolworth's there. The lunch counter was upstairs—just a long row of stools in front of a counter. My group went up to sit there, and after we had been there for half an hour or so, a group of young white men came in and began pulling people off the lunch-counter stools, putting lighted cigarettes out in our hair or faces or down our backs, pouring catsup and hot sauce all over us, pushing us down to the floor and beating us. Then the police came in and started arresting *us*. They didn't arrest a single person that beat us, but they arrested all of us and charged us with disorderly conduct.

That was the first mass arrest of students in the South for participating in a sit-in. Over one hundred of us were arrested that day. We were sentenced, all of us, to a fifty-dollar fine or thirty days in jail, and since we wouldn't pay the fine, we were put in jail.

After we were sent to jail, there was pressure coming from people around the country. Parents of arrested students were writing letters to the city. There were telegrams from people like Harry Belafonte, Eleanor Roosevelt, Ralph Bunche. All the big schools in the North were sending telegrams in support of the students. Somebody asked Senator John F. Kennedy, who was campaigning for the Democratic presidential nomination, "What do you think about these young people sitting in at lunch counters and getting arrested?" And Senator Kennedy said, "By sitting down, they are standing up for the very best in American tradition." All of this put pressure on the officials in the Nashville city administration, and they let us out before the thirty days were over.

After we got out of jail, we continued the sit-ins, and more and more people got involved. In April, unknown people bombed the house of our attorney. It shook the whole area, and it shook us. How could we respond to the bombing, and do something that would channel the frustration of the students in a nonviolent manner? We decided to have a march, and we sent the mayor a telegram letting him know that by noon we would march on city hall. And the next day, more than five thousand of us marched in twos in an orderly line to the city hall. One of the students walked up to the mayor and said, "Mr. Mayor, do you favor integration of the lunch counters?" And he answered her, saying, "Young lady, I cannot tell these merchants how to run their businesses, but, yes, I do favor integration of the lunch counters."

The next day the *Nashville Tennesseean* had a headline saying, "Mayor Says Yes to Integration of Lunch Counters." We began negotiating with the merchants, and in less than two weeks most of the lunch counters of downtown Nashville were desegregated. We'd have people go in, a black couple and a white couple, and wait to be served, and we'd do it over and over again, making it appear that it was normal. There wasn't any trouble, and the merchants began saying, "Why did it take all this time? We should have done it a long time ago." And so Nashville became the first major city in the South to desegregate its downtown lunch counters and restaurants. That was the power of nonviolence.

The next year, CORE [Congress of Racial Equality] decided to test the Supreme Court decision outlawing segregation in public transportation, and they settled on a "Freedom Ride" as the best way to test it. They were going to send groups of blacks and whites together to ride on buses in the South. I sent in an application to go along, and was accepted in the first group.

I'll never forget it as long as I live. I went up to Washington, and we got our orientation there, and I met the other people that were to go on the ride with us. There were two or three other college students, and some people from the American Friends Service Committee, a college professor and his wife, and a couple of others—altogether seven whites and six blacks. We stayed in Washington for two or three days getting our training and preparing ourselves. On the last night we went to a Chinese restaurant, and some of the people were joking, saying, "Eat well. This may be our last supper." We knew that we would be facing trouble as the ride went on.

We went south from Washington, testing the facilities. My seat mate was Arthur Bigelow, a tall, handsome white man from Connecticut, and we sat in the front of the Trailways bus when we left Washington, side by side. As we went through Virginia, we both used the so-called white waiting room and the toilets marked "White Men," and sat in restaurants in the so-called white areas without any problem. People would stare, but there was no outbreak of violence in that state.

When we got to South Carolina, the bus arrived in a little town called Rock Hill, and Arthur and I, walking together, tried to enter the white waiting room. Several young white men met us at the door, and when we tried to open it, they knocked us down in the street and began beating us with their fists. We both shed a little blood. The next day I had to leave the ride temporarily to be interviewed for a program I had applied for with the American Friends Service Committee, so I wasn't on the bus when it got to Anniston, Alabama. It was bombed and set on fire. One of the men had his skull opened up, and it took fifty-seven stitches to patch him up. At that point, Robert Kennedy, who was attorney general, suggested there be a cooling-off period, and CORE dropped the ride. I flew back that night, and a group of us— three young women and seven young men—made a decision that we wanted the ride to continue. . . .

We got to Montgomery on a Saturday morning. Just seconds after the bus stopped, a white mob came out of nowhere that grew to more than two thousand people. It was very angry and hostile—mostly young people. They had baseball bats, lead pipes, chains, bricks, sticks—every conceivable weapon or instrument that could be used as a weapon. I thought it was my last demonstration, really. I'd never seen anything like that. They were looking for blood.

First they jumped on the press. If you had a pencil and a pad, or a camera, you were in real trouble. Then, after they had beaten the press people, they turned on us as we descended from the bus. I was hit on the head with a soda crate and left unconscious on the street.

While I was lying there, according to the Montgomery paper later, the attorney general of the State of Alabama stood over me and read an injunction prohibiting white and black groups to travel together through the state of Alabama on public transportation. The mob was going around beating everybody at that point.

What saved the day was that the public safety director of the city showed up and fired a shot straight up, and said, "There will be no killing here today. There will be no killing." And the mob dispersed. Some white postal officials opened the basement door of the post office, which was right near the bus station, and allowed some of the Freedom Riders to come in there, and several white citizens in Montgomery assisted us in getting to the doctors' offices or hospitals.

During the night, we made the decision to continue the ride into Mississippi. I had some reservations, because Mississippi is supposed to be worse than Alabama. I didn't know what we were getting into, but I had a feeling that we had to go on, in spite of the fears, in spite of the beating. We had to continue the ride. We couldn't let a mob defeat us.

When we got to Mississippi, we got off the bus and walked into the white waiting room of the bus station. The police captain was standing there, and he said, "You're under arrest." One of the white men with us was arrested for trying to use the colored men's restroom, and one of the black men was arrested for trying to use the white restroom, and others were arrested for drinking out of the fountain marked with one race or another. We were all charged with disorderly conduct or failing to move on.

That summer we filled the Jackson city jail with people testing the segregation laws. Hundreds of people from all over the country came to Mississippi to go to jail. They poured into the state and got arrested at the airport, at the train station, and at the bus station.

Finally the ICC [Interstate Commerce Commission] issued a ruling banning segregation in all places of public transportation, and said that train stations and airports must place signs saying that "seating on this vehicle or in this station must be regardless of race, creed, color, religion, or national origin." They just banned it. [*Snaps fingers*.] And it was wrapped up.

I felt very good about that, because I thought I'd had a part to play in keeping the ride going. If we hadn't continued the ride that summer, I'm not so sure we would have received that ruling from the ICC. It was a real triumph of nonviolence.

Late that summer there was the March on Washington. In the beginning, President Kennedy had been doubtful about the march. He had told us he was afraid that some acts of violence or disruptive behavior might set the civil rights movement back. But when the day came, it all went well, and he had us back to the White House after the march was over, about eight of us, to have refreshments with him in his private quarters, and he was glowing. He said it was the right thing to do, and it had gone right. It seemed like the beginning of a new era for America. And then, not long afterward, President Kennedy was killed. It was shattering. . . .

After President Johnson became president, we began to focus on a voter registration bill, because black people were being denied the right to vote or even register to vote in many places in the South, and we had a number of demonstrations in various places. A young black man, who was leading a demonstration near Selma, Alabama, was shot and killed by a state trooper while he was leading a peaceful, orderly, nonviolent march. And we made a decision—Dr. King, Reverend Ralph Abernathy, Andrew Young, and myself—that we should march to Montgomery from Selma to dramatize the need for a voter rights act, and to dramatize the violent climate that existed in Alabama.

A day or so before the march was to begin, Governor George Wallace made a statement that it would not be allowed. SNCC debated all night over it. Some were saying that the days of marching were over—someone might get hurt, someone might get killed. But people were coming from all over to join the march, and I felt that if people wanted to march, we should be there with them. Finally, the committee said to me, "You can march as an individual, but not as a chairman of SNCC." And I decided to do that.

We met outside the church to participate in the march. We lined up in twos, and Hosea Williams and I were the first two. I don't know what we expected. I think maybe we thought we'd be arrested and jailed, or maybe they wouldn't do anything to us. I had a little knapsack on my shoulder with an apple, a toothbrush, toothpaste, and two books in it: a history of America and a book by Thomas Merton.

It was a sunny afternoon. When we got to the top of the bridge crossing the Alabama River, we looked down and we saw this *sea* of blue. It was Alabama state troopers. The night before, Sheriff Clark had asked all white men over the age of 21 to come to the Dallas County Courthouse and be deputized to be part of his posse. So they'd all become state troopers. When we looked down we saw all these men with guns, and we thought, "Well, they're probably going to stop us or arrest us," so we kept on walking.

There was total silence. You could hear only a soft *stomp-stomp-stomp* of people walking. When we got in hearing distance of the state troopers, a major identified himself and shouted on a bullhorn and said, "This is an unlawful march. It will not be allowed to continue. I give you three minutes to disperse and go back to your church." We kept on walking, and in a very few minutes, less than half a minute maybe, he said, "Troopers advance."

We stopped then. The only thing moving in our line was my trench-coat flapping back and forth in the wind. I think I said to Hosea something like "Shall we stand here in a proper manner or should we kneel?"

But before we could do anything, they came to us—men on horses, men on foot. The horses were trampling over the people, and the state troopers that were not on horses were hitting us with clubs and beating people down with bullwhips. We couldn't go forward, because if you tried to go forward, you were going into the heat of the action. You couldn't go to either side, because you would have been jumping over the bridge into the Alabama River. They came to us as if they were mowing a big field, and they left a path of people lying down on the ground behind them, hollering and screaming.

I was hit in the head, and apparently I blanked out, because I don't know what happened after that. The doctor later said I had a concussion. Someone must have got me back to the church, and I remember saying, "I don't understand how President Johnson can send troops to Vietnam, to the Congo, to Central America, and he can't send troops to protect black people who want the right to register to vote."

The next morning, Dr. King came over to the hospital where I was, and he said something like, "John, don't worry. We're going to make it to Montgomery. I've issued a call for ministers and priests, rabbis and nuns, the religious community of America to come. We're going to make it."

The next day they tried another march, which I couldn't participate in, and several hundred religious leaders got as far as the line of state troopers on the bridge and were turned back. That night the Reverend James Reeb, one of the young white ministers who'd come down, was beaten by a group of white men in Selma. He died a few hours later in a hospital in Birmingham.

Afterward President Johnson went on nationwide television and made, to me, what was the greatest speech ever on the whole question of civil rights. He spoke from the soul about the point in history when fate and time come to a meeting of the ways. He said, "So it was at Lexington and Concord. So it was a century ago at Appomattox. So it was last week in Selma, Alabama." Then he went on to say that the most powerful nation in the world has heard the moan, the groan, the cry of an oppressed people, and we are responding. He said one good man, a man of God, was killed. Two or three times he said there was a need for a strong voting rights bill. At the end he said, "We shall overcome." I saw Dr. King cry that night. Tears came down his cheek, and I knew then that it was just a matter of time till we would have a voting rights act.

Then came the second phase of the march, and it was one of the most meaningful efforts of any demonstration that I participated in. It was black people, it was white people, it was Protestant, it was Jewish, it was Catholic. There were young people, old people, some very poor people, some very rich people, a senator's wife, a cousin of Governor Rockefeller, a former attorney general. People came from all over. They blended together, and we all marched together.

I was still recovering from the concussion, but I marched, too. We had roadside tents along the way for people to stay in, and it took us four or five days to get to Montgomery. We had someone responsible for the preparation of the food, we had trucks to carry the food, and we carried toilets along the way.

President Johnson called out the United States military to protect us, and at night they would shine these huge lights and light up the fields where we were staying. We would see the soldiers on the roadside inspecting the bridges, looking under bridges before we walked across them. It was as if we saw the government of America saying, "These people have a right to exercise their constitutional rights, a right to peaceful protest, to assemble." And President Johnson used the military to make it possible.

Along the way, people made up little songs, marching songs, you know: "Pick 'em up, lay 'em down, all the way from Selma town." There was such a sense of family and sense of community that you sort of wanted to keep on going. There was a sense that we'll get there, we'll make it, because the cause we were involved in was right. It reminded me of Gandhi leading his march to the sea.

The last night we made it to outside Montgomery and gathered together on a grassy field on the campus of Saint Jude's School and Church. There was a huge rally, and people like Harry Belafonte and Joan Baez, Pete Seeger, Peter, Paul and Mary, and others came and sang with us out in the open, to support our effort.

In the morning, we marched down the streets of Montgomery, up to the steps of the capitol. People kept joining us and by the time we got there we had over thirty thousand people. . . . In October of that year the Voting Rights bill was passed and we all felt we'd had a part in it.

In the spring of '66, there was a movement in SNCC to get the whites out of it, and in the struggle over that my chairmanship came to an end. I understand the feelings of some of the blacks who didn't want to work with the whites, but if you're really going to be true to the discipline of nonviolence, you have to accept it as a way of living. It can't become a tactic that you turn on and off like a faucet. If we're struggling to bring about an open society, a beloved community, your tactics must be those of love. I think some of my colleagues in SNCC and some of the other organizations missed the boat during those days. Because if you turn on the reservoir of nonviolence, where do you turn it off? Do you apply it only to your own ethnic group or people of the same color or class? No, you have to cut the chains of hatred and say, "No more."

I worked on civil rights for the Ford Foundation for a couple of years, and then in 1968 I campaigned for Robert Kennedy. I felt he was serious in his commitment to civil rights—you felt it was coming out of his gut, really—so I wanted to be involved in his campaign.

I was in downtown Indianapolis with him at the time we heard that Martin Luther King had been assassinated. He was to speak at a rally in a transitional neighborhood, and I guess his guards, the FBI agents, or somebody who was with him, were insisting that he not speak because it would be too dangerous. But Kennedy made the decision to speak, and he stood on the back of a car and gave one of the most moving speeches I'd ever heard. He announced to the crowd, who hadn't heard the news yet, that Dr. King had been shot, and the crowd just went sort of "Oooohh." And then he said something about his own brother being shot, and that we don't know who killed Dr. King, but let's be peaceful and pray for his family. The crowd was calm, and we were all crying. . . . I went home for a while after that and helped Mrs. King and her family in the funeral, and I sort of dropped out of the campaign for a week or so.

When I went back, I felt so terrible and sad, because I had lost Martin Luther King, who'd been sort of a hero to me, and I felt a tremendous sense of loss. Then I said to myself, "Well, you still have Bobby Kennedy," and so I worked for him in Portland, Oregon, and then in the California primary. Campaigned all over Los Angeles and Los Angeles County.

I'll never forget the last day of the primary. On the evening of the election, a group of us were up in Bobby Kennedy's room on the fifth floor of the Ambassador Hotel before he went down to make his victory speech. Then he told us, "You can come down or stay up here with my sister and the other people." So we saw him on television making his statement, and then we heard that he had been shot, and we all just fell to the floor and started crying. To me that was like the darkest, saddest moment.

The Kennedy family invited me to come to New York to the Mass, and to stand as an honor guard there. I stood with Reverend Abernathy for an hour or so in Saint Patrick's, and the next morning I went to the service. And after the service, we all boarded the train from New York to Washington to Arlington Cemetery. On the train you had the body of Senator Kennedy, the family, a lot of friends, and the people who had been involved in the campaigns and in the Kennedy administration. All along the way, you saw people coming up to the train crying and these handmade signs saying, "We love you, Bobby," "Goodbye, Bobby," "God bless you, Bobby," and so forth. In a way, you didn't want the train ride to stop. You wanted it to go on and on, because in a sense it was like marching, and when you stopped at the train station, and then at the cemetery, it was so final, you know. . . .

There are people today who are afraid, in a sense, to hope or to have hope again, because of what happened in 1963, and particularly what happened in 1968. Something was taken from us. The type of leadership that we had in a sense invested in, that we had helped to make and to nourish, was taken from us when these three men, all very young, were killed. Something died in all of us with those assassinations. . . .

In 1970 I became head of the Voter Education Project. I helped register hundreds and thousands of black voters and low income white voters and Hispanic voters. I didn't have any desire to run for public office, but I encouraged other people to run.

Then, in 1980, several friends and supporters said, "You should run for city council in Atlanta," and I ran and carried all of the districts except two. I got more than sixty-nine percent of the vote, and I was reelected in 1985 with eighty-five percent of the vote. I like being in politics. I've always said the ballot is probably one of the best nonviolent weapons that we have. . . .

The civil rights movement that I was a part of has, in a short time, changed this region. There are still problems, no question about it, but when you go around this area, you see people working together in a way that is simply amazing. It's a different climate.

You go back to some of these same communities where we had marches, and you see some of the same people. I was in Selma not long ago, and the mayor who was mayor then gave me the key to the city. You go to lunch or dinner with some of the people who were in power then, and the guy will say, "John, I was wrong. I was on the wrong side. I tried to keep you all from marching. I had you arrested. We thought you were an agitator. We were wrong. We made a mistake." In recent years, I've met with Governor Wallace and with other officials. I met with the son of the major who gave the orders for the troopers to advance at Selma, and this young man said to me, "We're sorry about what happened, and about what my father did."

I'm telling you, they are entirely different people now, and I think one thing the movement did for all of us in the South, black and white alike, was to have a cleansing effect on our psyche. I think it brought up a great deal of the dirt and a great deal of the guilt from under the rug to the top, so that we could deal with it, so that we could see it in the light. And I think that in a real sense, we are a different people. We are better people. It freed even those of us who didn't participate—black people, white people alike—to be a little more human.

Clark Olsen

© *Barbara Beirne*

fter a civil rights march beginning in Selma, Alabama, met with a brutal attack by Alabama state troopers, Dr. Martin Luther King, Jr., issued a call for white ministers to come from all over the country to join a second march. It was hoped that the participation of many whites would prevent further violence. Clark Olsen was a young Unitarian minister in California when he heard the call and responded. He is now a vice president of the Unitarian Universalist Association in Boston.

The plane that I was to fly to Selma on had engine trouble, and so I was delayed. I missed the training on protective tactics: how to bend down and cover the back of your neck and assume a sort of fetal position if you're attacked by people with a club. The crowd was just pouring out of the church where the meeting had been when I got there. Martin Luther King was speaking on the steps of the church saying, "Tomorrow we march again." I was a little scared, but excited, too.

I saw two young Unitarian ministers who had been at the theological school with me the year before, James Reeb and Oloff Miller, and we decided to go out to get something to eat together. They'd been down there for a couple of days already, and they had lots to tell me. We walked over to a place in the black section of town, Walker's Cafe, and had our supper there.

When we came out we were a little confused as to how to get back to the place where we were to stay, and by accident, we walked through a white section. It was dark by then, just the street lights on, a typical Southern town—wide sidewalks, trees, sort of pretty in a way—and we were walking along, and all of a sudden these three fellows loomed up out of a side street. As they came across the street at us, they were shouting, "Hey, niggers." They were calling us niggers, in effect nigger lovers, because they had seen us as whites coming out of a black cafe, and it was clear to them that we were among the demonstrators.

James Reeb was walking on the outside nearest the curb, and I was walking on the inside nearest the buildings. These white guys came after us, and we kept up our pace and sort of quietly spoke to each other. "Just keep on walking," Oloff said to me.

The white guys came up behind us. One of them carried something heavy and long and narrow: a club or a bat or a lead pipe. He swung it at Jim Reeb's head and hit him just above the ear on the side of his skull. I remember the noise it made as it connected, and I saw his face as it hit. Jim fell to the ground.

Oloff had gone down as he'd been instructed to, on his knees with his hands at the back of his head—the nonviolent posture. But because I hadn't learned it, I was just standing there staring at everything.

I ran a step or two away from the incident, and one of the guys chased me and beat me on the back of the head and my glasses fell off. Other than that, I was not bruised. He stopped hitting me after a short while. Oloff had been kicked a few times, but he wasn't badly hurt either.

When the white guys went away, Oloff and I went back and helped Jim Reeb to his feet. He stood leaning against a building and babbled for a while. It was clear that he had been hurt terribly. We were afraid to stay there. There was nobody around. We put Jim's arms around our shoulders and stood him sideways, and then just helped him walk back to a black insurance agency office that we had passed on our way to the restaurant. We went in there, and they offered a cot to Jim.

It turned out there was a black funeral home right next door, and they had a big car available that was used for funerals. Really, it was a hearse. They took us to a black clinic in town, and a very kind, caring doctor looked at Jim for a while. Finally, he shook his head. He realized it was beyond his ability or the clinic's equipment to deal with it. Jim was unconscious by this time.

Finally the hearse came again, and the doctor put Jim Reeb on a cot in the back. Oloff sat on one side and I sat on the other, holding the cot. We had to hold on tight, because the cot was thrown from side to side as we went around corners. We didn't call the police, because with the officers of the law acting the way they had been, there was no way to tell that anybody was going to be on our side. It was frightening not to know what was going to happen or who would attack us or who we could go to for protection.

Anyhow, we started out in this hearse, and suddenly, just on the outskirts after we'd passed the last house, we had a flat tire. We were scared and we wondered, "What should we do? Should we change it out here, or should we turn around and drive back on the rim of the wheel into town and change it?"

The other people, except for us, were blacks. They tried to call on the radio telephone, and it didn't work. We began to think, "Oh, my God, is this some conspiracy of some kind?" Then a car full of white people drove up behind us. They parked and just sat there. We didn't know who they were. All we knew was they were white men. The radio was gone, the tire was flat, and these people were parked behind us. I remember very strongly having the image of Schwerner and Goodman and Chaney, the three young people who'd been murdered and found in a ditch down in Mississippi not long before that. And I remember feeling that I wanted to get out and run. I was just so frightened.

Somehow we turned the car around, went back to the parking lot of a radio station, and the driver went to make a telephone call to ask for another ambulance. The car full of whites turned around and followed us back and just drove around in the parking lot—round and round, while we waited there. We were really frightened.

Finally the ambulance came, and we had to get out, which was in itself frightening. One of the whites came up close to me and said, "What's going on there?" And I remember saying to him simply, "Please don't," with such enormous feeling: *"Please don't, please don't."* The "please" was sort of an entreaty, and the "don't" was sort of an ordering of them. I was simply terrified after seeing what happened to Jim.

But there was no way I could run. I couldn't leave Jim. There was nothing else to do but just to go ahead and hope they weren't going to do anything, that it wasn't part of a conspiracy or something.

A policeman came by after what seemed to be an interminable length of time, and we asked him for an escort out of town to Birmingham. He said, "You won't need it." Again we thought, "Is *that* part of a conspiracy?" But he said, "I'll escort you out of town and get you on your way," which he did. He sped ahead and there was a turning in the road, and at that point he sort of stopped and waved us in the right direction. And we went on from there in the ambulance.

We got to the hospital about midnight or so, and I remember they were well prepared for us. The medical staff was ready, and there were FBI agents there, too. They had got the news and they were waiting. There were all kinds of reporters there, too.

As soon as Oloff and I knew that Jim had been taken care of, we went off to an upstairs room, and the FBI questioned us for the next two hours—got statements from us about what had happened.

We stayed there most of the next day. President Johnson sent his own plane, Air Force One, to bring Jim Reeb's wife and his father to the hospital. They were in the room next to the one that the hospital provided for us. Mrs. Johnson sent yellow roses.

We never saw Jim again. He died about thirty-six hours later.

President Johnson used the incident in Selma to trigger the call for an immediate session of Congress. He spoke to both houses, and urged the passage of the Voting Rights Act. It got passed soon after that, and he said later that he thought that incident was what put it over— the final trigger.

forms, and their majorettes had uniforms, too. Every time we were going to be in a city parade, we had to conjure up something different for our majorettes to wear.

Anyhow, there was one parade, and we had just got this new band-leader. He was very young, just out of college, and he didn't like that. "We're not going to be in a parade if we can't have uniforms," he said. You know, in the winter when we had white shirts on and that was all, it was cold, it was freezing. So I guess he went and talked to somebody and finally we got our new uniforms. The band was so excited. The uniforms were burgundy and gold and they read, stamped on the back, "Martinsville High School." Our colors were burgundy and white, and Martinsville High School's colors were burgundy and gold. These were their old uniforms. But still, we had uniforms. We were very happy that we had gotten them. I didn't think that things should be any different, and neither did anybody else.

When I went to Hampton Institute for college, and they started talking about civil rights and all, I sort of thought back to the way things were, and I realized there was discrimination, but I hadn't known about it, because people didn't talk about it when I was growing up.

That was when the sit-ins were starting and I thought it was right to do them, but I was scared, too. A lot of us were very frightened because of the dogs and the fire hoses and all of that. My feeling was, "Are we really going to do this?"

At that time, in Hampton, if you went downtown and you wanted a drink, a soda or anything, there was just one drugstore and they had a carry-out place. Blacks had to stand at the edge of the counter near the door and order a soda. Of course, the white people could sit down and have theirs in the store.

Finally we started to do the sit-ins there. I'd go in, and they'd say, "We don't serve you. Leave." Well, I was never the type of person to say anything back. I would just get up and leave, because I was afraid of being put in jail. I'm glad that the people who did go to jail didn't have the same mentality that I did.

There was one time we went into Newport News, Virginia. We all went on the bus together, and we went into this particular department store there where they have a tea room upstairs, and I said, "I want to integrate that place." So we went upstairs, and they said they couldn't serve us, and we stayed. We didn't leave. We stayed there quite a while. That was one of the biggest do's in that town. Finally

Jackie Bolden

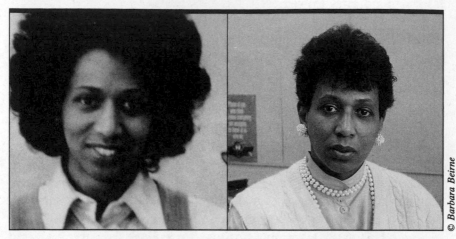

*S*he teaches business education in a large high school in the Northeast. *Her husband is a senior scientist for a pharmaceutical company. Together with their three teenage children, they live in a comfortable, modern, split-level house in an attractively landscaped suburban development.*

I grew up in Martinsville, Virginia, a small town in the Shenandoah Valley. My only contact with white people while I was growing up was with the people in Globeman's Department Store there. My dream was to be like one of those ladies behind the counter. They were always so immaculate, so put together, so neat. I used to admire that. I wanted to be like them. But of course they were white; they didn't have any black girls as salesgirls then.

Our high school was the Albert Harris High School, and the white high school was the Martinsville High School. Our books, I noticed, always read "Martinsville High School." I suppose they were hand-me-downs, but I wasn't aware of that at the time. It didn't bother me, because I didn't know any better.

In high school we had a band, and we wore our own white shirts and black pants. We'd be in parades that involved the whole city, you know, Thanksgiving or some other big parade, and we'd say, "Why don't we have uniforms like Martinsville High School?" They had fabulous uni-

they brought out the dogs and we left. When they got us outside, they turned fire hoses on us. That was the most devastating experience. It made me very angry. Why was this happening?

You know, you'd stop to think you might have a brother or a cousin or an uncle who was in the service and serving his country, and yet you didn't have equal rights. Why have them fighting for the country, if we couldn't have equal rights? The dogs and the fire hoses were all so motivating. I think that's what changed my head around, and I think it did for a lot of people my age. So we went on doing the sit-ins all through my college years. One lunch counter after another, and a lot of fire hoses and a lot of dogs.

After I graduated, I went to Washington and got a job as, well, they call it administrative assistant now, but it was really a secretary, for the Air Force. Six of the girls I graduated with came down and got jobs, and we all got apartments in the same apartment building. The people in the Air Force that I had to work with were the first white people in large numbers that I'd ever had much contact with, but they were very welcoming to me, and it really was a very good experience. I was the youngest person in the office at that time, and I think they acted sort of like parents and big sisters to me. I didn't find anything negative about them. Maybe it was the spirit of the times. This was the early Sixties, you know.

I remember the March on Washington in 1963. My husband and I took a bus down to the Mall that day, and a white couple that worked with him at the National Institutes of Health came with us. We got down where all the people were. There was an enormous crowd. Everybody was friendly, everybody was warm. It was the right thing to do, it was the right timing, and everybody was willing to talk. I remember Peter, Paul and Mary singing. I could hear them very well. And I could hear Martin Luther King's speech. His was just so brilliant. You felt that those white people who were there really came to help you with the cause. It was just togetherness, no matter black, white, whatever. It was a camaraderie. That was a great day.

On the day John F. Kennedy was killed, I was working in my office at the Air Force, and we had a radio on, and we heard the news. It was just devastating. I tried to call my husband at the National Institutes of Health, but those were government lines, and you'd pick up a phone and all you'd get was *bzzz-bzzz-bzzz*.

We left the office and it seemed like everybody wanted to gather around the White House. It was so crowded, all the way from the Capitol building down to the Lincoln Memorial. People were crying. I was crying, everybody was crying.

When I finally got home, I made the decision to go down to the Rotunda and be with everybody—just to be there and to say this was a shame, how sorry I am, how sad for the family. And I was worrying, too, of course, about who was going to carry through for us. Who will be a white spokesman for us? It was really bad. And then when Johnson got started and carried it all through, that was just great. . . .

Later on I began teaching high school in Washington, and I was there the day Martin Luther King was killed. The principal made an announcement on the PA, but he didn't say that Martin Luther King was shot, he just said we were going to get out of school early. There was quite a bit of noise on the street already, but we were sheltered in the school, so we didn't know anything. And I remember right after he made the announcement, I looked out the window and across the street from the school was a Jaguar model salesroom full of all those fancy European cars, and as I looked out the window, I saw the place just exploding. The windows were broken, and people were running all over the street.

I got very concerned, because I was pregnant then with Artie, my oldest son. I went downstairs and thought about getting home. By that time we had moved to Maryland, and another teacher, a white girl, and I were driving in together. She'd drive one week and I'd drive the other. She lived near me in Maryland, but she worked in another school. It was my turn to drive. I didn't want to drive over to her school because it looked like that's where the trouble was, but somehow she got a ride to the school where I was, and we started driving out on Florida Avenue. I had to go along a corridor of storefronts, and that's where the riots were. We were driving along and I was really gripping the wheel tight. There were people running all over the streets, fires burning, young people breaking into stores.

When we got to the light at North Capitol Street and Florida, there was a Volkswagen in front of me. I was driving a Plymouth, and I was up there and I could see everything. In the Volkswagen there were a white man and woman, maybe a husband and wife. The light turned red for them to stop, and they stopped right in front of me. Mine was the car behind them. Some kids walked off the corner and grabbed the Volkswagen and turned it upside down.

I gripped the wheel and I was saying to myself, Oh, my God, I'm sitting in here with Jean, and what are they going to do? "Quick," I said, "Jean, lay down, lay down, lay down!" I felt bad about that, because she was somebody I really liked, I could really talk to, but I didn't want anyone to get hurt. I didn't think they were going to hurt me, but then I didn't know what they would do with me when they saw that I had somebody white with me.

Jean scrunched down on the floor so far that she might still have a red spot on her bottom from it. Right after that, the light turned green, and I went around as quick as I could. I don't remember us saying anything to each other on that ride home. The thing was just to get out of there, you know.

Washington looked like a war zone. They had the National Guard out and they were saying on the car radio, "Don't drive into the city if you don't have to." After that they suspended school, and we just stayed home and watched everything on television. People just didn't know what to say. With Martin Luther King killed, we were sort of stunned. It was just low, as if everybody had a family member killed that day.

I know during the latter part of Martin Luther King's life some black people were saying, "Oh, I'm so tired of him talking about the non-violence thing, 'cause no changes will be made by nonviolence." But you know, we got the bills passed.

. . . Almost every day I think about the changes that were made in the laws. You can go to a restaurant if you want to; you can drink out of a water fountain if you want to. And a lot of black people have jobs they wouldn't have had before. All that marching did accomplish something.

We went down South to visit my husband's mother in South Carolina a few weeks ago, and we went out to the tennis court that my husband would not have been able to play on as a child. He called another black guy he knew, and they were going to play tennis together, and I went along with them. We got to the tennis court, and there were three young white people there, two boys and a girl. I didn't have any tennis racket, and the girl came over to me and she said, "You want to hit with mine?" And I said, "No, my knee hurts." So her boyfriend and the other white man played with my husband and his friend. While they were playing, the girl and I sat down and talked.

Finally when my husband and the others got off the tennis court and we were back in the car driving home, he said, "Guess whose son that was?" He was talking about one of the young white guys. I said, "How would I know?" He said, "That's Mr. W——'s son." It didn't mean anything to me. He said, "Mr. W—— was the biggest redneck in town. He was in the Klan, and I saw him march in it. And you know, the son isn't prejudiced at all. He didn't seem to have any of the mental outlooks or qualities of his father."

My husband used to be really afraid of that man. When he delivered papers, he'd have to carry that paper up to the porch in case it was raining. He used to tiptoe, he was so scared. And this was his son! My husband was just amazed. He said to that young man, "You mean you're the son of Mr. W——!?!" He couldn't believe it. Isn't it funny how things change?

We moved up North in 1970. We went to a real estate agent, and we asked where black people lived in the different towns, and where the black neighborhoods were. And the real estate agent said, "We don't have any special areas." He took us around to look at houses. We wanted a nice backyard. Finally we bought this place. We were the fifth house in this development, you know. Most of the people are friendly, and I do have some "good white friends," and I feel comfortable with them. But there are only about five black families in this area. It still doesn't attract black people.

I've been concerned about my kids growing up here, because I want them to know who they are. There are only a few black kids in their school and none in our neighborhood. I see to it that they meet black kids from other towns, and we've talked to them about going to a black college. Hampton, where my daughter will be going next fall, is where I went, and it's primarily a black college still. My husband and I are both very happy that that's where she's chosen to go.

Bob Zellner

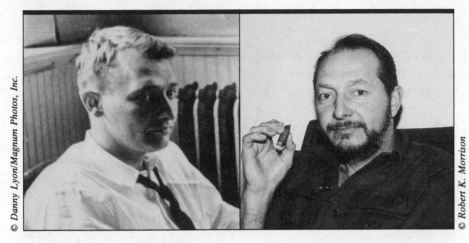

*H*e grew up in Alabama, the son of a Methodist minister, and attended Huntington College in Montgomery, Alabama. During his senior year, while doing research on a term paper on "the racial question," he began going to meetings with local black civil rights organizations. As a result of his activity, the Ku Klux Klan burned crosses on campus, and he was pressured to resign from college. He refused, and upon graduating in 1961, he became one of SNCC's first white staff members—and eventually one of the last. He now works as a building renovator and carpenter based in New York City.

I grew up in Alabama. Many people don't realize that twenty-five years ago, apartheid was the system in the South. Everything was segregated. It was just the way things were. You didn't think about it. Sometimes when you're inside a system, you can't see it very well. But children are not born racists. They are taught to have racial attitudes.

I remember I worked in a little country corner store, and one day the owner said, "You can't do that," after a black couple had left the store.

I said, "What do you mean?"

He said, "Well, you didn't treat those people right."

"Well, wasn't I polite and courteous and everything?"

"Yeah, that was the problem. It's okay with me, and it's all right if it's just you and I here. But if there are other white people here, you can't say 'yes ma'am' and 'no ma'am' and 'yes sir' and 'no sir' to a colored person."

"Well, why is that? They're older, and I was always taught to be respectful to my elders."

"Well, I know, but you can't. You're not supposed to say 'sir' or 'ma'am' to the black people."

I remember being very puzzled about that: "Why are black people different? Why should I do that?" And he said, "Well, I don't agree with it, and you don't have to agree with it either, but it's just something that you have to do, because people expect it." I remembered that later as a very poignant kind of a lesson. Here was a man who probably was not an unusually racist person, yet still having to pass on these racial lessons to a young kid.

For the first few months working with SNCC I was in jail every other month. The first time was in McComb, Mississippi. What happened in McComb was that Herbert Lee, the local person helping in a SNCC voter-registration campaign, was murdered. A Mississippi state legislator shot Lee to death, right in the middle of town, because he'd gone to the city hall and asked to register to vote. There were two black witnesses, who gave the whole story to the FBI, and the sheriff immediately confronted them with their testimony and broke one's jaw with a flashlight or a billy club. One of them left town immediately and the other witness was shotgunned to death in his front yard. So this was the situation in McComb.

We went there for a staff meeting, and about 125 black students walked out of the high school and said they were going to march to the county courthouse to protest the murder of Lee. I remember hearing in the far distance the soft strains of "We Shall Overcome," and it got louder and louder as the students came up to this SNCC meeting. And their question was: "We're going to the county courthouse. Who's going with us?"

My immediate response was, No, I can't possibly go, because I'm white and I'd be the only white person in the demonstration, and that would cause more violence. Plus, my parents would get in deep trouble. My mother would lose her teaching job, my father wouldn't be able to get a church, and so forth and so on. And the more reasons I gave myself for not going, the more I realized that these students were going to participate in the first march in Mississippi history since the Reconstruction. They were going to march in the open countryside and protest the murder of one of their fellow workers. And I said, What *they* have to lose is so much greater than anything I have to lose. Of course I have to go.

There were big mobs, the line of march was attacked, and it was stopped at the city hall. The mob surrounded me, and some of the SNCC people tried to protect me, but the cops came over and beat them with billy sticks and dragged them off and just left the white mob to get me. And then the mob did their best to kill me. At first they were beating me tentatively and watching the reaction of the police. They were actually saying, "Is it okay for us to get this guy?" And the cops were saying, "Absolutely."

We were up near the steps of the city hall, and then this huge mob out in the street just started screaming like banshees, just hysterically, "Bring him to us. We'll kill him. Bring him here." So they picked me up bodily and were carrying me out like a tide into the street, and I realized that if I didn't do something I was going to die. Earlier somebody had given me a Bible, so I had been holding this Bible, and I remember thinking, rather ironically, God helps those who help themselves. So I put the Bible down as I passed down the steps of the city hall, and grabbed ahold of the rail with both hands. Now this was resistance. I wasn't fighting back or anything, I was just resisting being carried out to the street, where I thought I would die.

So there became a whole contest about getting me loose from the bannister. They started hitting my fingers with baseball bats and prying them loose. They got ahold of my belt and five or six guys got ahold of my legs, and they'd pull. They ripped practically all my clothes off. One guy started gouging deep into my eyes with his fingers. He pulled my eyeball out onto my cheek and tried to get it between his finger and his thumb, to pull my eye out. Because I was holding on to the rail, I couldn't protect my eye very well.

My brain was functioning extremely well the whole time. Along with moving my hands to keep the baseball bats from crushing them, I was moving my head in such a way that just as he would get a grip on my eye, my eye would pop back into my head. I remember it would just *thunk* right back into my eye socket. And I also remember being amazed at the hardness and the toughness of my eyeball. I never had understood what eye gouging meant, but that's what it means, reaching into your head and getting ahold of your eyeball and pulling it out. This was raw, downright raw, violence.

Anyway, I worked my way up to the top of this rail, and then they all just clambered on top of me and pressed me down, and I fell loose from the rail. The last thing I remember was somebody kicking me in the head repeatedly with a big boot.

Then I woke up inside the city hall, and the police chief was saying, "I ought to let 'em have you. I ought to let 'em have you." I immediately said, "I want to make a telephone call," and he laughed, and everybody else laughed. The mob was inside city hall by this time, so he just said, "You're free to go." I said, "I don't choose to go. I want to remain here and make a telephone call." He said, "You got no choice," and he pushed me out, and the mob just took me away. Loaded up in cars and away we went.

They said that they were taking me to the county seat, which was Magnolia, about ten miles away or so. But at the edge of town the sign said Magnolia to the left, and they continued straight. We went out into the woods, and they threatened me with a lynching. They had a rope and everything, and I really thought that I was going to die.

At this point, the men started arguing among themselves. They said everybody saw them leave town with me, and then they were saying, "Well, we'll turn him over to those guys down at Liberty, and they'll do it." So then I started accusing them of being cowards. By this time I was so convinced that they were going to kill me, I just wanted them to remember me as a brave person.

Anyway, they lost courage or lost interest, and eventually they did take me to Magnolia and turned me over to the police. That was the first time I was ever in jail. I remember when that jail door finally slammed closed, it was the sweetest sound that I've ever heard.

Then the FBI came. Three or four guys in nice suits and ties. I remember them being clean and crisp. They took me outside the jail and started taking pictures of my eye and all. I must have been a wreck. My clothes were all ripped up, and my face was all bashed. And I remember one of them sort of sidling up, and he said, "It was really rough out there on the city hall steps, wasn't it?" And I said, "Yeah, it was nip and tuck there for a while." He said, "Well, we didn't want you to think you were alone. We were out there, and we wrote it all down. We've got it all down." This was my first experience with the FBI, and I realized they were a bunch of gutless automatons. I never had any illusions about the FBI from that point on. This guy thought that it would *comfort* me to let me know that he was out there recording my death.

Anyway, that was my first demonstration. After that, I thought everything else was *lagniappe*. That's a French word popular in New Orleans. It means "extra." Everything else was extra. That was the baptism of fire. And I never worried about anything else that I had to do, because nothing was ever as terrifying or as close to death as that was for me.

That was news all over the South, especially since I was a Southerner. My parents supported me, but it was very alarming to my mother. She was always pleading with me to be careful. Once, when we took up a freedom march, my mother sent me a telegram, and she said, "Bob, in the unlikely event that you're allowed to march through Alabama, please, for God's sake, drop out of the march if it goes through Birmingham, because your grandfather and your uncle have threatened to kill you." I took that rather seriously; they were members of the Ku Klux Klan. But, in any case, we weren't allowed to even get near Birmingham. We were arrested when we reached the Alabama line.

In those days, people were giants. Ordinary people did heroic things—people who were totally unknown and totally unsung. There was a little-known but very bloody campaign in Danville, Virginia, in the summer of '63. There were sit-ins at segregated restaurants, theaters, and so forth, mass meetings and marches, demands for more hiring of black workers in stores and in the mills.

One of the most brutal attacks on any march that I ever saw occurred there—a demonstration by one hundred twenty people, ninety-nine percent of whom were hospitalized. It was a march from the church to the jail to demand the release of some civil rights people. The marchers were trapped in an alley by fire trucks, and then the white sanitation workers—the garbage men—armed with table legs from a furniture factory, went in and beat the goddamn hell out of everybody. Dorothy Miller, whom I married later that summer, was one of the people who was beaten and washed under a car with a fire hose.

I was staying out of the march, because at this time they were arresting me for whatever I did. I was with the press, with my camera, taking pictures, when the fire trucks came. I realized what was happening because I saw the garbage men behind the fire trucks with these big clubs. They were opening up with the fire hoses, and these garbage men were converging, and nobody was moving, nobody was taking a picture. I said to the press, "You've got to take pictures of this. This is the only protection anybody's got." And they said, "No, they said we can't. They're going to kill us if we do. They'll bust all our equipment and everything."

So I stepped right up with my camera, and I said, "This is the way you do it. You aim your camera, and you say, 'snap,' like that." I had a flash and everything. The chief of police spun around, grabbed my camera, swung it down, and beat it on the pavement. He looked back at the rest of them and he said, "Anybody else takes a goddamn picture of this, they get the same treatment." Then the police rushed me and bundled me into jail, under arrest. I said, "What for?" And he said, "For assault on the police chief."

They arrested the minister who was leading the march, and then they had me out of the way and the minister out of the way. Then they started beating the people. We were under arrest, but they deliberately set us right inside the door, where we had to watch this carnage that was going on. Two cops stood right in front of us with their guns on their hips, and one of them said, "Your girlfriend's out there, isn't she? They're washing her under a car right now and beating her in the head. Don't you want to go help her?" That was the kind of taunting that you got. They were offering to kill you if you moved.

It went on for ten or fifteen minutes. They literally hospitalized practically everybody in the demonstration. There were split noses, skull fractures, many, many broken limbs, women with their breasts lacerated—absolute mayhem. And who knows about Danville, Virginia, 1963?

I don't know how in the hell I ever survived that summer. They must have shot at me on at least a half-dozen occasions. One night we were having a party. We didn't do this very often, but we just sort of let our guard down a little bit, and we had a party out behind somebody's house in the black community—there was a little record player, and we had some beer and some wine. We felt safe right in the middle of the black community. Everybody was dancing and just having a totally wonderful time relaxing.

Well, in the middle of all this, the cops surrounded the place and just out of the blue started shooting at this party. I mean fire erupted from everywhere. I don't know how in the world there weren't tremendous casualties. Everybody scattered, and I ran into the house next door, along with a couple of black guys.

I tried to hide in a closet, but the woman of the house said, "Oh, my God, you gotta get out of here. If they find you in here, I'm done for." I had run in the back door, and I said, "Well, they're after me. If I go out there, I'm afraid they're going to kill me." She said, "Well, I'm sorry, but you have to go. I'll put you out the front door." So she took me to the front door, and out I went.

The minute I got outside, a big spotlight hit me, and they said, "There he is!" And shooting just erupted. The fire was spitting out of the guns, leveled at me, and the wood was splattering all around the house. I couldn't believe they weren't getting me. I turned and ran down the porch and jumped off the end. It was on a big hill, probably ten feet in the air, and I remember just jumping and wondering where in the hell the ground was. Eventually I hit the ground, and I rolled over two or three times, but it gave me enough time. The house was between me and where the cops were, and I ran to the back. And as I ran, the cops rounded the corner and were shooting at me again.

You know, the sound of a bullet that's next to your head is the most horrendous sound in the world, because eventually there's going to be one you don't hear, which is the one that's going to kill you. But in these situations something takes over, and you just think extremely clearly. At least I always did.

There was an outbuilding behind this house, and behind the building was a huge pile of brambles and brush, and I said, There's my one chance. I knew that behind this house was a lot of woods. So I said, Okay, if I can make it around this building before they hit me, I've got a chance. So I zipped around that building and leaped just as high and as far as I could into that bunch of brambles, and as I did, I just turned a flip on my back. I didn't even know what was in there. I didn't know whether there were wrecked cars or nails or glass or anything, but it looked solid enough for it to sort of hold me. I remember crashing down through this stuff not knowing what I was going to land on, but it sort of cushioned my fall, and I just totally relaxed when I hit the bottom.

The bushes and everything kept crackling, and I said, Oh, my God, they're going to know I'm in here. But they were shouting so much and shooting when they rounded the corner of that outbuilding that they didn't hear all this going on. They literally ran by about four or five feet away, convinced that I had gone into the woods. And they searched.

I heard them going all through the woods. I just stayed there like a possum, and pretty soon I couldn't hear anything, but I still stayed there for what seemed like hours. I said, Well, I'm safe here. I'm not going to move.

Pretty soon I heard a little voice saying, "Bob, Bob," and I realized that it was a friendly voice. I said, "Yeah." He said, "I know you're in there. I saw you jump in there. They're all gone. Come on, I'll show you how to get out of here." So this little black kid, about ten or twelve years old, pulled me out of the brambles and walked me through the woods.

Then there was the beginning of the whole Black Power movement. A lot of that came out of the summer of '64 and the huge influx of white volunteers who came down to Mississippi. One of the things that happened was that young white students had skills—typing, mimeographing, and all that stuff—and a lot of the local young black people were still learning the skills. Everybody would say, "Well, of course, let Mary do it. She types sixty-eight words a minute, and you can barely get a thing done all day." So there were a lot of hard feelings.

There were exceptions made in my case. The blacks would say, "Bob's not like that. Bob is a Southerner. He's just one of the niggers." But eventually it was decided that white people wouldn't be on the SNCC staff. I thought it was a mistake. It was playing into the hands of the enemy to have a formal policy of exclusion of whites from SNCC. I didn't think it was necessary. SNCC was always a black-controlled, black-led organization. Whites never seriously threatened the leadership.

They didn't want to say outright, "Bob Zellner, you can't be on the SNCC staff anymore." I was a charter member of the staff, and I had paid my dues, as they say. That was very important in the Movement. If you had paid your dues, you were one of the band of brothers and sisters, part of the circle of trust. To say that that no longer existed was a tremendous thing to say. So they wanted to compromise.

It was sort of like union negotiating: I was in one room, and the ruling body in SNCC was in another part, and people were shuttling back and forth. They said, "You can remain on the staff, but you can't come to meetings as a staff person, and you can't vote." And I said, "I won't accept that. SNCC has never required second-class citizenship of anyone yet, and now is not a good time to start, so I won't do that." Then later they came back: "Well, you can come to meetings, but you can't vote." And I said, "I can't accept that either, unless everybody can't vote. I'm not going to accept any special conditions. I'm either going to be on the SNCC staff as a full staffer, with all the rights and privileges and responsibilities of anybody else, or not at all." And the final vote was that white people would no longer be on the staff of SNCC.

I have a lot of difficulty talking about that. . . . It hurt. SNCC was the most important thing in my life. But I decided a long time ago, after the first year or two in the Movement, that it was going to be a long-term commitment, that I was not going to burn out. I was not going to get bitter.

. . . Anyway, those were heady days to me, to have the effect we had. I mean, we made a difference in history. The civil rights movement destroyed segregation in the South. I go down now to visit my family and friends, and I think about it a lot. When I see the waiting room at the bus station in Mobile, Alabama, I say, "I integrated this bus station." When I see blacks and whites bowling together and going to movies and not thinking a thing about it, I say, "You know, I had something to do with this. I integrated this theater. I integrated this bowling alley."

The
Distant
Drummer

Jim Hoagland

© Robert K. Morrison

*H*e is now a high-school teacher in Brooklyn, where he grew up in
a blue-collar family. In 1964, he was just a couple of years out of
high school himself when he became restless with his menial book-
keeping job.

I went down to the recruiter, signed up. The Marine Corps. That's
what my father did, so that's what I did. It was the normal thing for
me to do. It was the way kids in my situation got out of where they
were if they wanted to go somewhere.

This was August 1965. I knew I was going overseas, and we were
told in boot camp that half of us would be dead. We landed on this
peninsula in Vietnam, and cutting the peninsula in half is a river. The
village on one side is friendly, the village on the other side is all VC.
I didn't understand how two villages this close together, one could be
good and the other could be bad. You know, they got cousins in both,
extended family. They're a stone's throw away. How does everybody
not know everybody else? But anyway, this is what we were told.

We were also told that all the Vietcong wore black pajamas. They
give you the silhouette with the round hat and black pajamas, so that
if you see anything with black pajamas, you are geared up, you are
psyched up that you are going to blow it away.

This artillery battery was attacked and one of the guns was hit, so they called us out. We get out on the side of the peninsula and see there's black smoke coming up. "Let's go." So you're riding along and you've got the rifle slung over your shoulder, you're feeling like Marlon Brando or John Wayne or somebody like that. You're ready to blow 'em away.

So we're coming along this beach, and just as we're coming around a curve, we swing out onto the edge of the peninsula. We turn a corner and there's a whole crew—maybe sixty, seventy—women and kids. Black pajamas, right?

I remember this so vividly. I saw the black pajamas. Gun went *click*. I'm just ready to pop, you know. And then one of the guys is yelling at the top of his lungs, "Don't shoot!" I say, "What?" He says, "Don't shoot!"

I'm just so close, there's no measurement. Guys are grabbing other guys' rifles and pulling them up in the air and putting them on safe and all this total confusion. "But they're wearing black pajamas." "They *all* wear black pajamas." "Then how do we know who to shoot?" "We *don't*."

Dave Baker

*H*e owns and runs a stamp and coin collector's shop near the county courthouse in his hometown. All day long old Army buddies, former high-school classmates, policeman friends, and hunting companions stop in to pass the time of day with him.

All my life I have hunted. I go deer hunting and I get maybe five or six a year. When I was little, it was squirrels. I think I was twelve years old when my father gave me my first gun. We had about six acres, and behind that there was land that you could hunt and I really enjoyed it. My father always told me, "If you kill it, you eat it. If you don't want to eat it, don't kill it." Nothing was just shot and dropped on the ground.

When the Vietnam War was going on I thought there was a real need for us, and I wanted to sign up. A bunch of friends of mine, five of us who all went to high school together, were going to join the Marines. We were going to go in at the same time, but by the time I got done with my chores at home, some lawn work and stuff like that, I didn't get down until after they were there. They'd already signed up in the Marines, and the Marine Corps recruiter took them out to lunch.

I started to walk out of the Marine recruiting office, because there was no one there, and this Army sergeant said, "Who you looking for?" I explained to him what it was, and he said, "Well, why do you want to go in the Marines? Let me show you what the Army has." Then I took this test, and it turned out I had high enough marks that I could do anything I wanted to. He said, "Well, you get your choice." I remembered a guy I'd met who'd been a dog handler in the Army, and I said, "Can I get to be a dog handler?" And he arranged it, and that's what I got into. You had to be a volunteer for dog handler, and you knew that if you went in, you were going to Vietnam. But that's what I wanted to do.

I'd had dogs at home, but this was totally different. You had to be a hundred percent responsible for taking care of your dog: cleaning his teeth, giving him a shot, grooming him every day, and training with him. You had to be very careful when you were grooming him, because those dogs are vicious. One of the fellows training with me had his thumb bitten off just cleaning his dog's teeth.

The dogs are trained to be hateful against human beings, really aggressive. I think if the ASPCA ever found out what you did, they'd be at the government's door so fast. . . . Those dogs are hung by the tail, beaten with barbed wires, their ears are sliced with razor blades. Of course, you don't do it to your own dog, okay? Because then they'll hate you. When you go through the course, there's twenty people altogether. Ten people will tie the dogs up, and they'll be agitators for the ten that are holding their dogs. I'll be hitting someone else's dog with barbed wire, and he'll be hitting mine.

Instructors come by and zip the dogs' ears with razor blades. They know just what to do not to go too far. And they switch them and beat them. You want to stop them, but you don't, because you know that the meaner your dog gets, the better the chance of you staying alive when you get over to Vietnam. So you let it happen, because you want to come out of there with the best poodle to keep you alive and do your job. It's like a weapon. Do you want a piece of junk that jams, or do you want something that really works good? My dog was a really good dog—a very, very aggressive dog.

The village I was sent to in Vietnam had been built earlier by the French and had a few cement buildings, but the majority of it was just sticks with tin roofs. When people went to the bathroom, they just came out and did it in the street. It stunk, it stunk. And on a hot day it *really* stunk. But you got so used to it that it was, after a while, you know, like being home. I mean, you know, it was just a normal thing.

Walking down the street any day you'd see two or three kids with elephantiasis—like a pretty little girl with a leg blown up using two sticks to walk with, and she's pulling the worms out of her. And there's nothing you can do to fix her, either. You think to yourself, Oh my God, what should I do? Shoot her and put an end to all her misery or what? If you felt sorry for everybody you saw in that village there, you'd be a blabbering slob by the time you got to the end.

The dog handler's job was to patrol the bush outside the village at night to make sure none of the VC could sneak up on us. There were tunnels around our unit, and the VC would use them to get close to the fence. Then they'd come up and get through the fence and get to our main communications center. Tried to blow it up a number of times. One night I was out with my dog on guard duty, and someone from the tower yelled that there was a guy in a tunnel who kept coming up to the fence and trying to get through. So off my dog and I go. We're going to get this VC.

As soon as he sees us, back down in the tunnel he goes. So I brought my dog to the fence line and unleashed him. The fellow doesn't see that the dog's back here. Well, by the time I get to the other end of the tunnel, the guy's back here at the fence line, trying to come out of the hole. As soon as he stuck his head up, my dog saw him, grabbed him by the throat, ripped him right up. When I got to them, the dog had taken his head off, torn his arms off, taken his intestines out, and was eating him. I never saw anything like that before in my life, you know.

I went to get the dog off, and I reached behind him and grabbed him, and he bit my knee. Right here. [*Pointing.*] Just four puncture holes. Let go. Went back to the VC. I backed up. Sat down on the ground, wrapped my leg all up, and waited until he was done. You know, when the dogs are taught to be killers, they're so sick, it's as if they're nuts. If they get someone, they consider it their reward. They worked for it and they deserve it. So I had to let him finish. I couldn't go near him, because he'd kill me. His eyes were wild and he was foaming. There was no way I could stop him.

In the village I was in and in the villages around, there were just local VC. They'd have maybe two or three bullets allotted to them to shoot for the night, and they'd come out with their single-shot rifles and go *blinkety-blink*. About every two weeks or so, they'd put on a mortar attack, but primarily it was just snipers. You always had to watch your back, because there was no front line there, and you had women and kids as warriors, too, and you really didn't know who was trustworthy and who wasn't. It was all a battlefield.

There'd be accidents, bad accidents. In one village that I had to go through, the kids would play a game: They would try to touch the killer dogs. If they could touch a killer dog, they were big heroes. But this wasn't known to me when I first got there. A lot of the old-timers don't tell you all the tricks of the trade, you know. So I knew nothing of this game of the kids. One night I was working, cutting through the side of the village, and I'm looking into a shack over there and I see a bunch of eyes. I didn't know whose they were. I just figured to myself, Jesus, somebody in there is going to shoot me just when I get to the right spot.

I had my gun on my side with my hand on it, and my dog was pulling ahead real hard, but I wasn't paying too much attention to him. I was looking at those eyes as I walked. And I was on the ready, because if I saw anything that looked wrong, I was going to start shooting. What I didn't know was that those eyes were all little kids watching their buddy, who had dug a ditch and hidden himself under some weeds right by the path. When I came by, he was going to jump up, touch my dog, and then take off, and he would be a hero. And they were watching for him to do it. So as I went by, he jumped up, touched my dog, and my dog took his head off instantly. [*Sharp snap of fingers.*] Just popped it like that. You know, some of these Vietnam people are very, very thin, especially the young kids. The neck was like a dog bone to him.

I didn't know what to do. I mean, I'm standing there—the head's sitting over there, spitting and gurgling. Oooooh. . . . I get goose bumps now just thinking about it. It was a real ripper for me. I pulled the dog back quick, and I looked this way and that way, and the kid's mother was coming after me. She had something in her hand, and I thought, "It's a grenade. It's cocked. I'm in real trouble now." So I had to pack her down. I shot her. We can't take a gamble, you know. I just blasted her, and I kept shooting as I backed out.

When I got back to my base, they sent an alert out to see what went on, and it turned out she just had a rock in her hand, but I didn't know that. I just thought, She's going to get me, and I'm going to blast her. . . . That was a rough one.

And, you know, it stays with you. When you're that close to them, and you see it happen—it's not like when you're in the dark, and you're shooting, and the next day you hear that somebody fell down dead. Here, you're with them, and you see it, and it stays with you. I imagine a lot of guys who were there don't mention things like that to anybody. They keep it in, because it's hurting them, and it hurts them to keep it in, too.

Another time we were sent to the wrong end of a village, just me and another kid. The dogs weren't with us that time. We were supposed to get out some VCs who were in this house, and we had been told that they were armed. So we went in there figuring everybody there was armed and bad guys.

We broke into the hut, and the rule is, one guy shoots to the left and the other guy shoots to the right. That way you don't wind up shooting each other. You know, when you're shooting like that, you don't stop until everything stops moving. You get a little smacked out, sort of high. You get a rush when you go in, and then when you settle down off that rush, you see what you did. And I shot *three ladies and two kids*, and he shot *one lady and a pig*.

It turned out we'd been sent to the wrong damned place. The lieutenant had his little map turned around, and he'd sent us a hundred and eighty degrees in the wrong direction. After everybody was dead, we called up the lieutenant on the phone and said, "Hey, you jerk, there's nobody in there, just women and kids." "You go to the right place?" "Yeah, right up here in the northeast corner, red shack." And he goes, "Oh, jeez, I sent you to the wrong place." And I said to him, "Well, you go to the right place then, because we ain't going to the right place. You come up here and see this mess, and you're not going to go anywhere else either, I bet."

I never forgave that officer for doing that, you know. Two of the ladies were nursing their babies, and these babies couldn't have been more than two, three months old, maybe. That stays with me all the time, all the time.

Were there any repercussions from this?

No, nothing. It was like it never took place, like nothing ever happened. But that was typical. . . .

There were a couple of fragging incidents while I was there. My lieutenant got it the first week I arrived. A black guy blew him up with two grenades, because he'd been harrassing him, giving him all the jerk jobs and abusing him and so on. So he just blew him away. Killed him, you know. Got put in the stockade. And when he came back here, he got life. Another lieutenant got his arm blown off in another incident. It went on all the time. . . .

I got friendly with some of the people in the village where we were stationed, and they'd come up, if there was going to be a VC attack, and tell me, "Look, be careful tonight." I wouldn't ask them why, I'd just say, "Okay, thank you," and maybe the next day I'd go to the PX and bring back some soap for them or something that they needed.

There were some little boys in the village I sort of adopted. When I met them at first they had sores all over them, because of the humidity and the filth. They were top-to-bottom nothing but sores. The sores were open and pussy, and the kids were in misery. I started bringing soap to them, and I'd take them down to the river and pass out the soap and make sure they washed. I had some liniment that I used on my dog, a sulfa-based ointment, and I brought them a big jug of that, and some hydrogen peroxide. When I came in the morning, the kids would be waiting at the edge of the village for me and after they washed, I'd pour on this hydrogen peroxide and rub this yellow cream on. And slowly the sores got better. It took maybe three months, working on these kids with the hydrogen peroxide and the dog ointment, to clear it up.

These kids were really grateful to me. They would practice their English on me, and sometimes I'd buy little bowls of soup for them in the market. It was only a nickel for a bowl; expensive for them, but cheap for me. One time we were down in the market, and there were three guys there buying supplies from the hardware stall. One of the kids tells me, "Wait here. VC there." And I looked at the guys, and they looked at me, and I stayed right where I was, and they went on with their business and walked away. As one of them left, he just nodded his head to me, because I stayed still, and then he turned and walked away. And when they were out of sight, I continued walking my way, you know. That's the way you stay out of trouble, live and let live. There's a time for the shooting, you know, and a time for just taking it easy. Tomorrow's tomorrow.

One night I went out on patrol with the dog and some riflemen. I was on point, about three or four hundred yards in front of the rest of the group. The VC had a mortar out there and they hit me good. I was blood all over. It was coming out of my mouth, my nose, my ears, and I couldn't stand up. The rest of the patrol backed out, and I was left there in the jungle alone with the dog. It was three days before anybody could come and get me. During that time I ate a lot of dirt, because, you know, you can get protein if you eat ants, but they're in the dirt, and so I ate a lot of dirt along with the ants. I had only one canteen with me, and I had to share that with the dog. He stayed right beside me for the whole three days. Didn't bark, didn't growl, didn't do anything. He was there to protect me.

During those three days, I memorized the faces of all the girls that I went out with in high school, and I had dates all over again. Anything to keep your mind busy. I played checkers, maybe ten games a day in my head, and at night I dreamt over and over again about a spaceship coming down and getting me, getting me the hell out of there. Finally, the third day, they came back for me when they felt the area was cool.

When Tet started, we were overrun. There were seven or eight hundred people pouring in on us—human wave attacks. I was sleeping when the shit hit the fan. Everything lit up. Rockets, mortars, you name it, it was coming in. They blew up the ammunition dump, and then it was just all hell. They were coming in by the hundreds and shooting. We ran out in our underpants. All we had was rifles and a case of ammo. It was terrible. There were foxholes, but the foxholes were full of scorpions big as a fist, so you don't want to jump into them. When the fighting let up, we put up sandbags to protect ourselves. Finally, Puff the Magic Dragon* came and bailed us out. If it weren't for that, we'd have been overrun completely. The place was really torn up.

After Tet, the whole village I'd been stationed in was wiped out. Our planes hit it with the big bombs—five-hundred-pounders. They just wiped out the whole place. I was due to leave Vietnam three weeks later, and I was picked up in a tank. We drove through the village at sunset, after the jets had hit it, and I don't think there was anything standing higher than this. [*Indicates knee height with his hand.*] Everything was burning. No trees left, no huts, no nothing. I don't think any of the kids that I'd been helping made it. The whole village was just wiped out, pulverized, you know.

I got back to the United States in '68 and there was a lot of antiwar movement going on. It hadn't been like that when I left, so I wasn't expecting it. I got off at Kennedy Airport, and I didn't have any money in my pocket because I'd spent it all on my airplane ticket. So I thought,

---

* helicopter gunship

"Oh, well, I'll go out and hitchhike." I thought that in the uniform, you know, they'd pick me up right away. But no one would touch me. You were the kiss of death in a uniform. So I walked and walked. It took me from early in the morning until late at night to get home. I got a few rides, but most of the time I was walking. One time a fellow I knew came by. I'd been to school with him, and he'd been in one of my classes. He came up and slowed his car and looked at me, called me by name and everything, but when he saw the uniform, he just said, "Oh, shit!" and drove away and left me there. And I thought to myself, Boy, some howdy-do this is.

When I got into my hometown, they were burning the American flag at the monument in front of the police station. One of the cops saw me and saw the medals on my uniform and ran down the street and grabbed me and brought me away. He said, "Dave, you don't want to see what's going on here. You don't want to see it." He told me, "The kids don't really know what's going on. It's not aimed directly at you." And, of course, I understood it wasn't, okay? So I went on my way.

When I was about a mile away from home, my next-door neighbor drove by. She slowed down and looked at me, and then *zoom*, she took off. I was tired as hell, you know, walking all this way and carrying a big duffel bag, but she took right off and left me. And this was a lady I'd shoveled the driveway for when it snowed. I was really pissed. Everybody had this stereotype of a Vietnam veteran coming home either a murderer or a cuckoo.

Why did they shun me? I went to do what they wanted to be done, and now, all of a sudden, they change their mind, and they don't want what is being done to be done, and it's my fault. . . .

I didn't feel like getting a job right away when I came back, so I went out to the California, rented a house on the beach, and drank all night and slept all day. I wasn't ready for anything else yet. People back home bothered me. You'd hear them complain about the silliest little thing, like "It's too hot," if it's ninety-two degrees and a little humid. Think about 130 degrees for three or four months at a time, and ninety-eight in the shade. That's tough.

They would complain about everything. There was a water shortage on, and they were complaining about maybe only taking a bath every two days, or a shower just once a day. Shit, over there we were lucky if we got to take a shower every two weeks or a month. And during the monsoon season, we would go through a month wearing the same clothes, until they rotted off. You couldn't wash, you couldn't change your clothes, it was pouring rain, everything was wet and mucky. And here people complain, "Oooh, it's raining out." Tough. Get an umbrella. Live with it. I just hated people in general. I don't know why. I just hated everybody.

My mother said a different person came back than what went over to Vietnam, different as night and day, and it changed me, no question about it. When my father died, it seemed I could care less, you know. I was standing right there, my mother was crying, and my brother and everybody else was crying, and I could only see that he was dead. Big deal, you know. I've seen that before. What's next?

I have a very thick wall around me now. I don't let anyone come too close. They know a little bit about me, but nobody knows the inside me. I have a girlfriend living with me now. She's been with me for four years, but I don't even let her come that close. I think being over there made me very cold to people.

And yet, you know, I'd go back today to Vietnam if the people wanted help, and we could help them. Because that's what I thought we were going for in the beginning. I would like to give them a good staple food. So much of the inland water has been ruined there, because of the bombing and defoliation, and a lot of the areas where they were raising fish before are history. I'd like to do that, give something to the people. That was supposed to be the reason we were there anyway. I felt cheated after the war, that what the government said we were going over for we weren't doing.

There are some Vietnamese families living in this town and the next town, and I guarantee that if you went into their houses, you'd be afraid to sit down. I mean the couch has got holes in it, and the springs are sticking out. Not like your house or my house, with nice furniture around. They've just picked up what people have thrown out, but it's like gold to them, you know. I go in and visit them and sit down, and I make believe that what they have is absolutely beautiful, because you don't want them to think it's not nice or a good enough place for you. This is their castle, their home.

You know, my sport is to kill. And when I go hunting or fishing now, I can't eat all the stuff I get, so I put it in plastic baggies, and I give it away to my Vietnamese friends here. I might get five or six deer a year, and they can't afford to go hunting, so I give them the meat. I stop off at their houses, and I give it to them. And if I go fishing for bluefish,

I'll come back with maybe thirty bluefish, and I'll give it to them. Not for thanks, or to make my head swell, you know, but just to see a smile on their faces.

Am I doing it because of what I did over there? Making up for it in my own noodle? It's nothing that I think about. Maybe subconsciously there is something in there telling me to do it, because of what I did over there. Who the hell knows?

Doug Simon

Judi Benvenuti

He joined ROTC in college, and after his graduation in 1963, he was assigned to Air Force intelligence in Vietnam. He now teaches history at Drew University in New Jersey.

My job was to brief pilots on what to expect when they flew into North Vietnam, to keep track of air defenses in North Vietnam, and to help plan bomb routes in and out—trying, of course, to keep our losses down as much as we could. As planes got shot down, we had to analyze why they were shot down, what got them, what the patterns were of defense, and that sort of thing.

It was a little uncomfortable because I had to talk to pilots who were actually going in and being shot down. I remember once I had to face a squadron that had gone out the day before. A third of the squadron had been shot down, including the commander and the vice commander, and I had to face the remnants of this group—the pilots who had survived—and brief them about capabilities in terms of statistics and altitudes and so on. These guys had just lost a third of their buddies. I must say they treated me very well and asked me over to the officers' club for a drink afterward, but it was doom and gloom on that base that day, I can tell you. It was awful.

One thing that stands out in my mind from the whole experience over there was the extraordinary losses that we were taking in Vietnam, in terms of our aircraft being shot down. You know, we had these modern superjet fighter bombers, the F-105s and the F-4 Phantom jets. And what we found out rather quickly was that a traditional, poorly equipped army, with a little ingenuity, could bring one of those aircraft down relatively easily. Ordinary peasants shooting sidearms and rifles on top of the buildings could bring these aircraft down.

They would do things like block barrage. Of course, a single rifle aiming at an aircraft couldn't hit it. But if they could get enough rifles and small machine guns and so on, and assign them block by block, street by street, and tell them to elevate the first rifles to approximately so many degrees, and the next rifles a little higher, and the next rifles a little bit higher, they could put a lot of lead in the air.

Our airplanes would go in low to drop their bombs, and when they went through that stuff, it didn't take much to bring them down, because they were such sophisticated airplanes. They were so complicated that they were vulnerable—all that electronic gear, all that navigation gear, if one thing went wrong, they'd go down. The F-105 had a major fuel line and the fuel backup line right next to each other. That didn't make a lot of sense. And these were jet airplanes: One piece of lead getting into the air intake of a jet plane would just tear the blades up. I think it was very difficult for a lot of Air Force people to accept that. Here you have modern, twentieth-century supersonic technology, and yet the enemy was bringing these airplanes down one after another with rifles.

I had a map of North Vietnam that I kept for briefing high-ranking military officers and congressmen and senators and so on who would come through. Mike Mansfield was one. John Tower was another that I had to brief. Part of my briefing was to talk about our losses in the North—why they would happen and so on. I had the Navy aircraft losses and the Air Force losses color-coded: little red airplanes for the Air Force and little green airplanes for the Navy. I'd stick them on the map, and by the time I added them together, North Vietnam was almost obliterated with little airplanes.

After one of these briefings, my brigadier general came up to me and said, "Boy, I wish you'd tone that briefing down. You're just scaring hell out of those guys."

You never really get away from that war if you've been through it. I remember sitting in front of the television set in 1975 when the first word came that the Vietnamese armies were sweeping south into the outskirts of Saigon. The American correspondents were gone, but there were some Italians and Swiss who were sending pictures back. They were rushing the videotape back as fast as they could. I sat in front of the television set for about eleven straight hours without getting up.

I was absolutely glued to it. My wife never bothered me. She knew what was going on. It was an intense emotional experience. It wasn't good or bad or positive or negative. It was almost like being at the point of exhaustion. I didn't cry, but I felt intensely emotional. The whole chapter was over. A commercial would come on, and I'd switch the station so that the coverage would continue. I couldn't get enough of it, the fact that this was finally done. The last chapter was written. It was over, finally.

Peter Mahoney

*H*e was nineteen years old when he went to Vietnam as a second lieutenant in 1968. After he returned, he was active in Vietnam Veterans Against the War and recently served on the commission responsible for planning and building New York City's monument to Vietnam veterans. The monument, located in lower Manhattan, is a translucent green glass wall etched with passages from letters American soldiers sent home and received while serving in Vietnam. Peter Mahoney is now an investment banking associate in a brokerage firm.

I served as a senior adviser on a mobile advisory team, training South Vietnamese troops and also what we called People's Self-Defense Forces, which were local civilians that the South Vietnamese would give sort of outdated weapons to. They were supposed to protect their hamlets from VC infiltration.

I had trained this group of twenty-nine People's Self-Defense Forces. They were mostly kids, pre-draft age, because they were just about the only ones left in the hamlets. My advisory team put them through a six-week training course, and then there was a big graduation ceremony, and the province chief came down and gave everybody little neckerchiefs. It seemed like a job well done.

Well, about a month after the training period was over, all twenty-nine of those kids walked off and joined the NLF [National Liberation

Front], taking their weapons and their training with them. I had worked closely with these kids, and my feeling was that these kids had to know the ability of the American army, what our firepower was, what our potential was for destruction, and yet, despite knowing that, they still decided to join the NLF.

That really got me to thinking, If these kids feel that way, then who am I, as an American, to tell them that they're wrong?

Clarence Fitch

N *ow a postal clerk in Jersey City, New Jersey, he is active in the antiapartheid movement. He was still in high school when he attended the 1963 March on Washington and heard Dr. Martin Luther King's "I Have a Dream" speech. In 1966, he joined the Marine Corps for a four-year hitch, and after training in radio communications, he received orders for Vietnam.*

We weren't living in no vacuum in Vietnam. There was a certain growing black consciousness that was happening in the States, and also over there in Vietnam. People was aware of what was going on. One of the characteristics of this war was that people didn't come over there together. People just had tours of duty, and so every day somebody was going home and you had somebody coming from home, bringing information. And guys that would leave Vietnam would send stuff back. You know, "Okay, send us all the *Ebony*s and *Jet*s and black publications you can get your hands on." Like I sent stuff when I got back to guys I left over there.

The militancy really grew after Martin Luther King got killed in '68. It made black people really angry. You remember the riots after Dr. King's death was some of the fiercest, and the brothers took that up in Vietnam. People changed after that. People were saying it doesn't pay to be nonviolent and benevolent. There were a lot of staff NCOs, the type of so-called Negro that would be telling you to be patient, just do your job, pull yourself up by the bootstraps. So we called them Uncle Toms and that was that. People were saying, "I'm black and I'm proud. I'm not going to be no Uncle Tom."

There was a whole Black Power thing. There was Black Power salutes and handshakes and Afros and beads. It was a whole atmosphere. All that was a way of showing our camaraderie, like brothers really hanging together. When a new brother came into the unit, we used to really reach out for the guy, show him the ropes and tell him what's happening. It was like a togetherness that I ain't never seen since.

I think people really listened to Martin Luther King. We didn't hear his speech about Vietnam until much later, but somehow or another we got a copy of the speech, and we was really impressed. He talked about how blacks were dying in Vietnam at a greater rate, and he was the first person we really ever heard say that, even though it was something we knew.

We saw what was going on. I was there for the Tet Offensive of '68, and I was at this aid station. The place was always getting hit, and I got wounded there. It was like ten miles from the DMZ. I saw a lot of blood and a lot of death, and we would be humping stretchers for all the casualties from all the units operating in the area.

It would still be more Caucasian bodies coming back than black bodies, but what Dr. King said was that blacks was at the time ten percent of the population and thirty percent of the KIAs. It was like more white guys was in the rear with the easy jobs. They were driving trucks and working in the PX and shit like this, and we're out there in the bush, and that's why we was dying. A lot of the line companies over there were mostly black. There were white grunts, too, assigned to infantry units, but there was a *lot* of black grunts.

And then, as jobs became available in the rear, they would pull people back for jobs like company driver, stuff like that. You know, after so much time in the field, they pull you back to rear-area jobs. And we wasn't getting pulled that easy to the rear. Black guys were staying their whole tour in the field. You just looked around you and said, "Well, they're just using us as cannon fodder."

We saw it for what it was, and we didn't want to participate in it no more. People just didn't feel like it was their war. There wasn't no real ideological theory we had. It was very basic. We were just getting screwed.

A lot of blacks fought valiantly at points, but a lot of them didn't see the sense in dying in this war. It was more honorable to go to jail. People were refusing to go to the field anymore, just refusing and getting locked up. This was a hell of a thing to do, because brig time didn't count on your tour in Vietnam. They called it "bad time." You did your six months in jail, and then you still had to serve your time in the field. But guys did it. Guys were sitting in the Marine brig for long periods of time. I guess they were hoping the war would just end while they're sitting in jail.

The form the militancy took most often was brothers just saying, "We're not going back in the bush." And we'd come up with all sorts of ways to avoid going back in the bush. It would be, like, instead of going out two klicks* on a patrol, you'd say, "Hey, I'm going to stay back. It's dark. We're squatting right here, and we don't want no contact."

There were people that would go so far as to hurt themselves enough to get out of going into the bush. I seen people shoot themselves in the arm or the foot or the legs to get one of those Stateside wounds. I seen people fake injuries. I had this friend of mine, a brother from Birmingham, Alabama, he broke his ankle three different times to stay in the rear. Every time they took the cast off, he would get a hammer and whack it again, and it would swell up, and they'd put another cast on it. He'd be in the rear playing cards for another month or two, and then they would take the cast off, and he couldn't walk. He would play it right out to the max.

The powers that be knew it, but they couldn't prove it. He caught a lot of flak. They would call him a traitor and all this crap. And he said, "Well, fuck it. I'm not going out there." And that's the way it went down until his rotation date. It wasn't like World War II, where you stayed for the duration. You did have a date, and the thing was to survive until that date and that's what people did. The other brothers supported him. We didn't put him down or ridicule him. We respected him. We knew we was dying at a higher rate, so we felt very much justified not to add to this fucking figure.

There were fragging incidents for the same reason. It didn't happen every day, but after a while it got to be an unwritten rule. A lot of times you get these boot-camp second lieutenants, just out of Quantico, the officer training school, no field experience, and they just give them a platoon. The smart ones would come over and take suggestions, use

* kilometers

their NCOs and squad leaders—guys that have been in the bush six, seven, eight months and really know what's going on—to show them until they get the ropes. But you get these guys that want to come over with schoolbook tactics, and they might want to do something that's detrimental to the company. Then you're talking about people's lives. Well, hey, the first firefight you get in, somebody takes him out. "Killed in action."

I seen one fragging incident up close: a new lieutenant, fresh out of Quantico. He was an asshole, very gung-ho. He would run patrols and set up ambushes, and he wasn't very careful. He took a lot of chances, and people didn't like it. They were trying to take him out, but they didn't get in the right kind of firefight that they could fire on him.

One night we were stationed on this bridge to keep Charlie from blowing the bridge up, and I was on radio, monitoring communications. About four or five in the morning, just before dawn, I seen this brother come out with this hand grenade, and he said, "Hey, Fitch, don't say nothing, man." The lieutenant's bunker was maybe ten yards from the bridge, and this guy went over, pulled the pin on the grenade, held it for a couple of seconds, and rolled it into the bunker. I said, "Oh, shit. I don't want to see this."

Then I heard *boom*, and the lieutenant came staggering out of the bunker. They got a medevac helicopter and medevacked him out of there. He was hurt pretty bad, but he survived it. Went back to the States, I guess.

One guy that was murdered in my unit was an NCO. This guy was one of those uneducated rednecks, been in the Marine Corps for fifteen years. When we were in the rear area, he would always be in charge of the shit-burning detail. They have these outhouses with fifty-five-gallon drums of kerosene underneath the toilet seat, and then every couple days, they pull the drums out, put them on a cart or truck, take them outside the compound, and throw a match to them. The drums would really stink, because all this shit is burning. It's a nasty fucking job, and every time, this sergeant would assign blacks. He used to say, "You, you, and you pull the shit-burning detail." He always chose blacks. He's dead now for that shit. He got drunk, somebody beat him up, and he died two days later. It wasn't no life-threatening situation, but people dealt with it.

I saw a lot of craziness there. In retrospect, the reason I think so much of it happened was that everyone was just living a violent way of life. It was a world where everyone carried a gun and had access to all the ammunition they wanted. There would be fights between GIs that might begin over a card game, and one guy would just pull out a rifle and slap in a magazine and say, "I'm going to lock and load on you." I think this must be the way it was in the Wild West when everyone carried a gun.

I left Vietnam in January '69, came home, and got stationed in Camp Lejeune, North Carolina. It was all Vietnam vets there, and people just wasn't into that Stateside regimentation no more. People were tired of the whole military scene. There was a lot of discipline problems. It was pretty hard to keep up haircut regulations in Vietnam, and some brothers hadn't had haircuts in a year. When we returned, they wanted you to get a military haircut. I think Marine Corps regulations said your hair can't be longer than three inches. For a white guy, if his hair is longer than three inches, it looks like a lot of hair. Very seldom does an Afro go higher than three inches, but they still wanted to make us get a haircut. So it was a lot of struggle around the Afros.

After going through Vietnam, people just weren't taking the same old bullshit. There were a lot of racial incidents out in town, Marines on liberty, and then there were incidents on the base. There was a whole struggle around music on the jukeboxes. There'd be all the country-and-western songs and white pop songs and maybe one black song, and these guys weren't going to take it. So they'd turn out the club.

It was a pretty nasty time between blacks and whites. Blacks tended to stick together in groups, and there were whites going the other extreme. There were Ku Klux Klan chapters. I was glad I was getting out, because things really got bad. Any small disagreements would be blown out of proportion. I remember these rednecks started a fight because a black guy was dancing with a white girl. Then other guys jumped in, and somebody got stabbed and killed. There were riots.

The media got ahold of it, and I remember the Commandant of the Marine Corps getting on television and making this big announcement that Marines would be able to wear Afro haircuts, that there would be more black music on the jukebox in the enlisted clubs.

But they were still disciplining the shit out of people, and a lot of black people got really hurt. People got in a lot of trouble, trouble that they're probably going to have to live with the rest of their lives. The facts show that blacks got bad discharges—dishonorable or bad conduct or undesirable—that are proportionately higher than white GIs. Guys were getting kicked out of the service left and right and not really caring, because when you're young you tend to live for the day. Since then all that bad paper is coming back to haunt people, because now, if the employer knows, it can hurt you.

I got busted for marijuana, and they recommended me for undesirable discharge. They endorsed it as undesirable at every command level, except when it got to Marine Corps headquarters in Washington, they upgraded me to a general discharge under honorable conditions for reasons of unfitness.

It could have been a lot worse, but it really pissed me off. I was short—I only had about six months to do. I had never been busted before. I was an E-5 sergeant. I had two Purple Hearts. I had jump wings. I had a Good Conduct Medal for three years of good conduct. Why fucking do this?

They gave me ten days to check out. They cleaned out my locker, took my dress uniforms. I had two MPs escort me to the gate and hand me my papers, and I left. I got the certificate, and I said, "I will never tell anybody that I got a general discharge." I tore up the discharge paper in little pieces of paper on the bus, and stuck it down the side of the seat, and I said, "That's the end of that." It was like they fucked me for the last time.

Steve Wilson[*]

*H*e served with the Army in Vietnam in 1967 and 1968.

A lot of people were killed in accidents and by fragging while I was over there, and some were deliberately killed. There was one guy, and I guarantee you he's on the MIA list, but it wasn't in action that he was killed. Here's how it happened: There was a new kid in the company, just been in the country three days, and he was sitting down on the bunk writing a letter to his parents, and there was another guy who had been around for maybe six or seven months, getting his rifle ready for guard duty. It was an M-14.

He got it cleaned, and was trying to check it out, to see if it operated okay. He takes a magazine with twenty rounds in it, and sticks the clip in, and—this is a real no-no—he takes the safety off. It's on fully automatic, and he holds the trigger, and he's beating the back of the receiver to get the thing to go through, not thinking that the son-of-a-bitch is going to go off, and *boom-rap* off it goes and blows the new kid's arms off—the one who was writing the letter home. His arms have just blown off into the the lap of another kid in a bunk on the other side. We got one kid over here in shock, and another kid over there with both of his arms off.

Well, I'm in the club next door, playing the slot machine and listening to some music, and the lieutenant comes in with this guy, got him by the back of the neck, holding his .45 in his hand. He walks into the club and yells to me, "Turn the music off." So I unplug the thing. "Yes sir." And he tells the story of this kid getting his arms blown off, and this is the fellow that did it. And he says, "Now, I want you to hear what this man's words were to me when I asked him how he felt about blowing this kid's arms off." So he looked at the guy, and he said to him, "Now tell them what you told me." And the guy said, "Well, he'll go back home and he'll get artificial arms that'll be stronger than

* Not his real name.

what he's got, and he won't have to put up with this hell over here for a whole year. At least he's going home alive."

Well, the lieutenant looks out at everybody in the club, and he says, "You make the decision. What do we do with him?" And everybody yells out, "Kill him." So he sticks his gun right up to the guy's head, and *boom* shot him right in the head, right there. The guy flopped to the floor, and the lieutenant points to a bunch of kids standing around in the club, and says, "Now you bury him." And he walked out.

I'm just standing there looking at it. Then I went back to my slot machines and the music, and these guys dragged that guy out and buried him, and I guarantee he's an MIA. Guarantee it. There was no paperwork. There was no nothing. Zero.

Danny Friedman

© Robert K. Morrison

*D*uring the Sixties college students received draft deferments as long
as they were in good standing. In 1967 and 1968, when American
involvement in Vietnam was growing rapidly, it didn't take long for
a student who lost his deferment to find himself in the Army—as Danny
Friedman found out. He is now on the staff of the New York State Veterans
Council.

I went to high school from 1962 to 1965. I guess I knew there was a
Vietnam. I was on the football team, and when I was in my junior year,
some of the seniors on the team joined the Marines. But I was very
apolitical; I mean, I didn't know what politics was. I knew about football, I knew about girls, and occasionally I even did some homework.
Very occasionally. So I went on to college very lighthearted. It caught
up with me eventually. After three semesters, I was on probation and
I dropped out.

I got a 1-A rating, and literally the next week I got my draft notice.
Okay. I did, like, a month of heavy-duty partying, and I was in the
Army. I'd never left New York in my life, except upstate to the moun-
tains a couple times. I'd never been away to camp. And then there I
was in Fort Jackson, South Carolina, getting my head shaved and waking up at five o'clock in the morning and put through all this ridiculous

training. I never freaked out, never reacted one way or another. I think back now, and I'm totally amazed at how I just adapted to it.

You know, you're weaned on John Wayne movies and *Combat*—Sergeant Saunders, Vic Morrow, right? And war was just another game. As a kid, you had wars with carpet guns—you take a two-by-four and stick a nail in one end with a big rubber band and nail a clothespin on the other end, stretch the rubber band out and hold it with the clothespin. I don't know why they call them carpet guns, but they call them carpet guns. You just take a square of linoleum or something like that, stick it in there, and flip the clothespin, and it shoots the square of linoleum or tarpaper or whatever you have. You know, it'll make it across the street.

In the wintertime, the snowplows would make these huge piles of snow, every third corner or so, and that pile of snow became your fort, which you hollowed out, and you made snowballs, and you warred with the kids two blocks down, who had their fort. Ring-a-Leevio, that was a sort of war. And dodgeball was sort of war. You know, you start early and you just go on and on and on, and the Army was another game. And then I went to Vietnam.

I remember the pilot saying, "We're now over Vietnam. There's some incoming on the field right now, so we're gonna be making a very direct approach." The plane just dropped like five thousand feet straight down—none of this circling-and-gradually-coming-in approach—and landed. And I said, "I really don't think I want to get off this plane." I looked at the stewardess and I said, "You gonna let these guys take me away? How can you let them do this to us?" Still got my fingernail marks on the side of the plane as they dragged me off it. That was my first political statement: "If there are things dropping out there that explode, I really don't want to go out there." But I went out there.

That year in Vietnam was like a million nightmares. I was a combat soldier, out in the field most of the time. After the Tet Offensive, all hell broke loose. People were getting killed all over the place, out in the jungle, in the rice paddies. We were getting hit from every which way. We couldn't go through any type of village or anything without receiving fire. I got wounded twice. One time it was just shrapnel. I was treated in the field. The other time I caught a bullet in the neck that put me out of action for about a month, but I finished up my last couple of months back at my unit.

And this was deep into the southern part of South Vietnam, the delta area, not like up north with North Vietnamese coming over the border.

For the most part we were fighting with South Vietnamese, reinforced by some North Vietnamese regiments. I got to learn just how determined the people we were fighting were. It was like a general understanding among everybody there that nobody wanted us there, except maybe the government. It got to be a game of survival, a realization that we weren't there to save anybody but ourselves.

They had these news crews come over to interview us: "What do you think about the demonstrators?" and stuff like that. I remember one of my sergeants—he was just a draftee like me—saying, "Shit, if I was back home, I'd be with them." So I was aware of the demonstrations, aware of what was going on, but still not political.

I was home on convalescence leave after I had my last operation—the bullet—and a whole group of my friends I grew up with were in Hunter College. I guess they were seniors, class of '69, right? I went down to Hunter College and I was hanging out with them in the cafeteria, and in the hallway just outside the cafeteria was this couple of women at a table, an antiwar table. I was in uniform, and I remember sashaying over there and trying to be a tough GI, you know, and intimidate these hippie Commie women. They started giving me their rap, and I responded with my rap.

I found myself giving a verbatim recital of everything that we were told prior to going to Vietnam about why we were supposed to be in Vietnam. And about halfway through my rap, something clicked. It was an incredible feeling, like an awareness: "Whoa! This is what you were told *before* you went to Vietnam. This isn't what you know to be true from your experiences in Vietnam." Like people talk about having religious experiences? I guess this was as close to a religious experience I ever had. I just stopped and walked away. I just sort of filed it away as "Hey, Jack, check yourself out. You're telling about what you were told, not what you've seen and experienced." And I didn't really talk about it anymore with anybody.

So I got out of the Army and got a job on Wall Street. I was right there when they had the Wall Street riots with the construction workers. I was on my lunch hour, and I found myself in the middle of all this mayhem, some construction worker beating up on a fourteen-year-old girl, if she was that old. It just blew me away. I couldn't believe that these kids were getting beat up because they were trying to stop a war. They were against people dying, and they were getting their asses kicked for it by these animals. I got very polarized. You know, you gotta take a side.

I got into an argument with some construction worker who called me a draft-card-burning, welfare-collecting hippie. I freaked out and got into this whole mess with him. He knocked me down, and I bounced up, and there were some police standing around laughing, and I went at them. I was able to get away because I had my I.D. pass to the stock exchange, so I zipped across the street to the stock exchange and got my ass out of there fast.

I started volunteering to collect petitions to withdraw the troops from Vietnam. I believe it was called the Cooper-Church amendment. The first petition I ever signed. Not only did I sign it, but on my lunch hour on Wall Street I was collecting signatures. It was, like, a heavy thing. They started giving me trouble at work, and I started wearing my hair longer, and I got laid off of my job.

I hooked up with Vietnam Veterans Against the War, and it was a nonstop, full-time thing for me up until '74. All sorts of things were going on. Demonstrations, marches throughout New Jersey, Pennsylvania, Connecticut, Long Island; live guerrilla theater; speaking engagements; distributing films and buttons. We started Vietnam veteran rap groups; we were the first people to recognize post-traumatic stress syndrome and start dealing with it. Back then it had a lot of people laughing at us, but now it's recognized as a major problem of Vietnam veterans. We had a lot of support. We were getting letters from guys in Vietnam, whole units signing up as members while they were in Vietnam. *Playboy* ran this full-page ad for us free, and we got a huge response, especially from Vietnam.

The vets became the security of the peace movement. Many times at a demonstration, VVAW would be assigned security, and we always did a good job. We took CD, civil disobedience, and added some military tactics in pulling off demonstrations. We never initiated any type of violence, but we weren't pacifists. We felt strongly about things, and we were willing to fight for those things.

Once, in Miami, the Nazis* had taken over the stage. This was the Republican convention, and there were thousands and thousands of people in Flamingo Park, all different kinds of peace movements, and they're all being intimidated by fucking Nazis. When our convoy pulled in, it took us about a half hour to bounce their asses out of there. We literally carried them all out. There were injuries on both sides, but they got the worst of it.

---

* American Nazi Party members

When we pulled off operations, they always went off. Like when we threw balloons full of blood at a dinner honoring George Bush, who was U.S. ambassador to the U.N. It was at a high school in the Bronx. The place was ringed by police. There was a demonstration outside that we coordinated to be a diversion, and meanwhile we had already gotten in through the cooperation of the students. Some guys threw blood at the dais, getting these guys in their tuxes and ladies in their minks. We said something about "the blood of the Vietnamese people is on your hands." And then we were able to extricate ourselves without being caught. Rolled down the hill on the other side, where we had a car, and we were gone. It was just good military tactics.

Since September 1982 I've been working full-time on the New York State Veterans Council. Basically, we are veterans' advocates. We help veterans with claims, write letters, and make waves on an individual, case-by-case basis. I work with traditional veterans' groups like the American Legion and the VFW, although I'm very uncomfortable with their national and international politics. But the nature of my job is to incorporate organizations that are strong veterans' advocates. I'm also involved with the Vietnam Veterans of America. Some of their local chapters are right-wing, but generally in any organization that's all Vietnam veterans, you get the feeling that their heart's in the right place. Every guy was in Vietnam, learning the lessons of Vietnam, and not about to see those situations repeated.

Every high school has military literature in it now. The military is getting involved in sending military personnel, in uniform, into the schools to teach clubs like the electronics club and this and that, to try to convey the esprit de corps of the uniform to the student. So the student sees the uniform around the school and can't wait to get into one. And every time you watch a sporting event or anything, you see "Army, Navy, Air Force, Marines, The Great Way to Be." You know, if I were a seventeen-year-old kid, that would look good to me, too.

Recently, a lot of the guys that were involved in VVAW have gotten together again, and we started going to schools and speaking out as Vietnam veterans to educate people about our experiences and try to keep the kids that are following in our footsteps from following in our footsteps.

Kids going to school today don't know what Vietnam was. You tell them about it, and you get blank faces. You know, they got a couple paragraphs in a history book. You show a film, and they say, "Wow, what kinda planes are those, man? Do we get to fly a plane like that?"

Irma and Harold Moore

A *small house on a small street in a small town. A maple tree shades the two garden chairs on the neatly trimmed lawn. The name of the street is Fairview. Inside, Irma and Harold Moore have assembled the mementos of their son Robert's short life. He died on April 6, 1968, in Ap Nam Phu, South Vietnam, six weeks after his paratroop unit arrived there. It was the spring of Tet.*

■ **MR. MOORE:** Bob was born at All Souls' Hospital, and he went to Hillcrest School, and then on to the high school. About a week after he graduated from high school, he told me he was going to enlist. He thought it was the right thing to do. He felt very strongly about it. He thought everybody should serve and do their part, and he just went and done it.

■ **MRS. MOORE:** He didn't tell me about it until it was time for him to go, because he knew how I felt about it. His dad come in when I was in bed, and he says to me, "You know Bobby's going in the service, don't you?" And I said, "No, I didn't." I was shocked. . . . The next day he left. They left from the American Legion building uptown.

You know, he wanted to go to college. He wanted to be a history teacher. But he wanted to get his service over before he went on to college. Even while he was in service, he kept sending reports back to his history teachers on what was going on. He really loved history.

He had a teacher in the high school that had been in the Eighty-first Airborne, a paratrooper, and he used to talk about it. He used to tell the boys that they'd never make it, you know, and that must have inspired Bob to try. And then when he went in the service, he got into the Airborne, and he became a paratrooper. He was excited about it. That's when President Johnson sent them all over for that big offensive. You know, Tet. The minute they got him over there, he was headed right into combat.

■ **MR. MOORE:** Well, that's why they sent them over. They needed them.

■ **MRS. MOORE:** You know, when we went down to Fort Dix for his graduation, his commander said some of them would be going over and wouldn't be coming back, and I just felt he would be one of the ones that wouldn't come back. Maybe my faith wasn't strong enough. . . .

One Sunday we'd gone out and been out most of the day, so they missed us the first time they came. But a little while after we got back— I was already getting ready for bed—there was a knock at the door.

As soon as we saw them, we knew what it was. I mean when you see a major with a policeman with him, it couldn't be anything else. The major asked us if we had a son, Robert, and he regretted to inform us that he had died on Thursday in Ap Nam Phu.

They were very good. They stayed with us and made telephone calls for us and answered all the questions they could. They said it was very quick. It was an airborne assault, and there was sniper fire. He never knew what hit him. Of course, they couldn't give us many of the details.

My two daughters were home then, and my little boy, Tom, was only about five. I don't think he understood at first. Finally when the body was going to be coming back, and we were to have the funeral, we sat down with him one night and explained to him that his brother Bob wouldn't be coming back. I think he already knew, in a way. But after we told him, he wanted to go in the bedroom to be alone. He didn't want anyone to be with him. You know, there'd always been a bond between the brothers. They'd play ball and they'd talk. Bob was sort of his star.

We're a close family, and he was everyone's hero. He had a lot of friends, and he smiled for everyone. He was just a happy-go-lucky guy that nothing could ever happen to, you know. He was very lucky. He was the kind who would have a hole-in-one at the golf course, a perfect game at the bowling alley. He was always very lucky until . . . [*Covers her face and weeps quietly.*]

The War
at Home

Julie O'Connor

*S*he is a photographer now living in New York City.

There were people all over the Washington Monument. It was very exciting to be with that many people. And you really had that sense that you could change the world. Especially when there were so many people doing the same thing and thinking the same thing. We felt the president was watching us on television and he was going to pull out of Vietnam because there were just *so many* of us out there that day. We found out later that we really couldn't change the world. But right then we never would have believed it.

Michael Carlebach

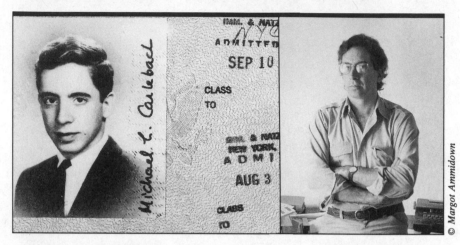

*N*ow a photojournalist, he was a student at Colgate University in the mid-Sixties.

I can remember sitting in the fraternity house and watching Walter Cronkite every night with the rest of the fellows. The media provided a very important link for us with the outside world, because we were really stuck out in the middle of nowhere.

There was one program I remember that gave us a look at a war that wasn't really the war we'd been told it was up to that point. I think Morley Safer was the correspondent, and he showed a platoon of soldiers going into a supposedly hostile village that had, the Army said, been a base of support for an indigenous Vietcong population. The village was to be destroyed, and it was burned. The only people in the shot were women and children, as I recall—some very old people too—and they clearly weren't the enemy. And you had soldiers out burning their houses. I can remember being stunned. You know the sound that the Zippo lighter makes when it opens? I can still remember seeing that Zippo lighting those houses on fire. It was an image that simply ran counter to traditional notions of fair play and everything. It was a scary thing.

You know, my field is photojournalism, and my feeling is that photographs act as symbols. If you really think about the war in Vietnam, there were about five still images that eventually persuaded everybody that what we were doing was wrong. The monk burning himself in Saigon. The police chief in Saigon shooting the Vietcong suspect. The children running down a dirt road having been napalmed and their clothes burned off, and the little girl up front yelling in pain. Her mouth was like a black hole. The photograph of a protest at the Pentagon of a lovely little flower child putting a flower in the muzzle of a soldier's gun. And, of course, the photograph of the student at Kent State, lying dead on the ground, and the girl with her arms up in anguish over the body, crying out. That was a symbol, too.

Those pictures made a difference. Millions of people would hold the same image in their minds at the same time. Those things, for millions of Americans, *became* the war. And if there was anything that turned America against the war, it was those images, because symbols are powerful things. Symbols can affect reality.

William Sloane Coffin

© Barbara Beirne

*D*uring the war in Vietnam he was chaplain at Yale, one of the first universities to become involved in the antiwar movement. Today he is senior minister at Riverside Church in New York City and a leader of the nuclear disarmament movement. His church maintains a feeding program for the poor and has been providing sanctuary for refugees from Central America.

At the end of World War II, I was a twenty-one-year-old Army officer on the Austrian-Czechoslovak border; and thanks to a quick course in the Army, I was moderately fluent in Russian, so I was put in charge of liaison with a large camp of Russian prisoners of war. These were Russians who had either defected to the Germans as the German army advanced through Russia, and then later joined the German armies as a Russian unit, fighting on the side of the Germans, or had been impressed into the German army directly. Some of them were prisoners of war who had been captured by the Germans. Whatever they were, they were looked upon by the Russians as traitors. At Yalta, the Allies had agreed that these prisoners should be repatriated to Russia, and it was the American Army that had to effect this.

Since I was the liaison officer, I had a great deal to do with the day-to-day running of the camp. The prisoners were treated only nominally as prisoners of war. They were lightly guarded, and they ran their own organization within the camp. I had become quite friendly with the commandant of the Russian camp, and we'd had many pleasant evenings together, discussing literature and art and other things, as well as my liaison duties. These Russians were extremely fearful of going back to Russia, and they frequently told me how they thought they would be treated. Many of them feared death.

One evening, the American Army officers, including me, were informed that trains would be arriving the next day to take the Russian prisoners back home. We were told not to say anything to anyone. That evening I was invited to a big party put on by the Russians in the camp. I sat with the Russian commandant at the head table and we shared a bottle and exchanged pleasantries, as usual. It would have been very easy for me to slip the word to him, and if I had, the word would have passed very rapidly to all the prisoners. They could have easily slipped through the fences and melted into the countryside. Europe was full of displaced persons then, and there wouldn't have been any question of recapturing them. I certainly felt the urge to tip off the Russians, tell them what was coming down on them. But I was in the Army and I'd been ordered to keep silent, and I did.

The next day when the trains came, there were horrendous scenes. Some of the prisoners tried to throw themselves onto the tracks under the train. They tried to get away. Many of them had to be put forcibly aboard the train by American soldiers. Two of them committed suicide. One of them thrust his head through a window and cut his throat in front of me. It was a very shocking and very educational experience. I certainly learned at that time that orders are not orders when it comes to life and death. A person who executes the orders has to consider himself or herself as responsible as the person giving those orders. Otherwise, we're back with the Nazis all over again. I'm certain that incident played an important role in my decision to commit civil disobedience later in opposition to the war in Vietnam.

I remember exactly when I became aware of Vietnam. A Yale graduate student, a harpsichordist and recorder player, came to see me and asked me when I was going to speak out against the war in Vietnam. I said, "What do you want me to say?" And he said, "I'll bring in my file." So he disappeared and came back an hour later with a very thick file of articles, mostly in English, but a few in French, from *Le Monde* and other French publications, and I sat down to read it about ten o'clock that night. And about three in the morning, when I got finished with it, I was persuaded that there was a lot more to this than I realized. That was kind of the conversion moment, I think, for me.

You know, you have this vague feeling something's wrong, but you're not quite sure what it is, and then suddenly you begin to do your homework and it pushes you over the line. It was clear to me that it was a civil war, and I was against American intervention. What right did the United States have to decide who lives, dies, and rules in this small Third World country eight thousand miles away?

In the fall I began to be involved in a campus movement for the reappraisal of our Far Eastern policy. And then after Johnson's election and the beginning of the bombing, I went to a conference in New York of Clergy and Laity Concerned About Vietnam, and we set up a committee on a national scale.

The first days were pretty heady. The teach-ins started and they were just wonderful. We had faculty and students together as we've never had them before or since. The Yale Law School auditorium, which seats eight hundred fifty or something like that, was absolutely jam packed—with English professors, political scientists, scientists, a lot of people from Yale's Far Eastern studies, a lot of experts. They had real expertise, and we all listened to them with rapt attention. After one of the experts had spoken, out would come some English professor, you know, who just said how outraged he was by the inhumanity of this, and then you heard from the sciences, you heard from the historians and the humanities people. It was a wonderful time together.

Then, of course, came the demonstrations, the demonstrations in New Haven. Yale was one of the early campuses to be aroused about the war in Vietnam. And then there were demonstrations in New York and demonstrations in Washington, and always petitions being signed, letters being sent off to Congress and the president.

Things began to get more agitated and tense when all these resorts had been exhausted and we didn't seem to have had any effect. As a kind of last resort, we began to think about civil disobedience, and that's when the draft card turn-ins began. This was in the spring of '67, and I was spending an awful lot of time with students who were in considerable agony as to whether or not to turn in their draft cards, and what it would do to jeopardize their futures. These were very real dilemmas, you know. If someone wanted to be a doctor, for example, he would jeopardize the chance of getting any federal funding for his studies. Without that you can't become a doctor, unless you're exceedingly rich.

I remember there was one young law student who was going to turn in a draft card, and I said, "No," because I was thinking of his future, and he said, "Forget it, Reverend. I'm not going to be a lawyer, after all."

Those kinds of problems were very real, and I spent many, many hours on them. By turning in draft cards as a protest against the war, students and resisters were opening themselves up for a total of five years or ten thousand dollars in fines. It was a very courageous act. And for students, it was coming out from behind exemptions, because students were exempt, and they were saying, "We don't want your exemption. We're going to turn in our draft cards and challenge the war."

I never counseled people to protest the draft or to resist it. I aided and abetted those who decided to, but in my pastoral role, I felt it wasn't up to me to counsel anybody. It was just simply to be a good listener and reflect back the conflicts that I heard, and to help people reach their own decisions. If I'd been more of a political leader, I wouldn't have had these scruples, I guess; I would have just said, "Now, look, we need troops," and tried to recruit people. Well, I never tried to recruit anybody to protest the draft or to resist the draft. Now, I grant you, it's a fine line between aiding and abetting and counseling, but I tried to at least keep that line pretty clear.

About this time, in '67, a group brought out the "Call to Resist Illegitimate Authority." It had been written by Marcus Raskin. There were about four hundred fifty people, I think, who signed it: professors, clergy, one college president—where else but Antioch?—and some writers like Norman Mailer and so forth. They'd signed it and published it, but there was no practical thing for them to do, and that was very much on my mind. We had to find something practical for all these people to do who say they're going to resist illegitimate authority.

I remember Mitch Goodman was sitting in my back garden in September in 1967, and we came up with the idea of collecting all the draft cards that were going to be turned in all over the country in October, and taking them down to Washington and delivering them to the Justice Department and saying, "We support these young men in their hour of conscience. If they are arrested, we must be, too, because we are now turning in their draft cards." It seemed like a pretty good idea to us. It was simple enough when you're sitting in a garden.

Then things got really interesting. We went down to the Justice Department with the cards in October to turn them in. We'd picked names from our group that we thought would add respectability to our movement. Dr. Benjamin Spock, Professor Seymour Melman of Columbia, Professor R.W.B. Lewis of Yale's English Department, Arthur Waskow, Marcus Raskin, and then there were Mitch and myself. We walked along from the church where we'd met, with all the draft cards in a briefcase. In addition, there were three representatives of the war resisters from all over the country, who had brought collections of draft cards for us to turn in.

Spock carried the briefcase with the draft cards in it. When we got to the Justice Department, we were led down a long hall, secretaries peeking out their doors at us as if we were wild animals. We went to Attorney General Ramsey Clark's office, but Ramsey Clark didn't meet us. It was his number three guy, name of McDonough. He gave us some coffee. Spock put the briefcase with all these draft cards on the table, and I tried to hand it to McDonough. He pulled back, and I said, "Well, let's try this again."

McDonough didn't want to handle it, and Waskow got up and said, "Ever since I was a kid I was brought up to respect the law of the United States, and here you accuse us of breaking a law for which we offer you concrete proof, and you, number three officer in the Justice Department, refuse to accept the evidence. Where, man, is your oath of office?" I remember he was screaming that. I thought he was just terrific. But McDonough wasn't about to conspire in our little conspiracy. We had to leave the briefcase on the table, and as soon as we went out, the FBI were in there collecting the evidence. And that was the beginning of arrests for quite a few of us.

I guess I began to realize how serious it was going to be the very next week. FBI men were all over the Yale campus, asking questions, looking at people that turned in their draft cards. That did have a kind of chilling effect on everybody. We gathered in the chapel that evening, and it was packed with all these guys who had turned in their draft cards, and their friends and their girlfriends. A few teachers and several law school professors spoke.

The first one was Charlie Reich of *Greening of America* fame. He said, "Now, undoubtedly, there are FBI here in the chapel with us. I just want to warn you to be a little careful about what you say. Make sure it's exactly what you mean to say." Well, jeez, you know, everybody started looking around, and there was one guy standing next to me who said, "There he is, that one in the trench coat over there, he must be FBI." And I looked over, and there was a big burly fellow, and I said, "Oh, no, no, no, he's an older man who is just starting the divinity school. He's not FBI." "Oh," he said, "then that little one, the baldheaded one." And I said, "No, no, that's the Lutheran chaplain at Yale." [*Laughs.*]

You can't tell them by their trench coats or bald heads.

That's right. . . . By that time, I was beginning to think, Well, this is pretty serious. This is a pretty serious brush with reality, and probably more. One time I got a call saying, "If you preach on Sunday, Reverend, we'll kill you." I answered briefly, "See you in church," and hung up. That Sunday, two campus cops showed up in church. The only way they could have known of the call was because my phone was tapped. The FBI must have kindly passed the warning on to them.

I remember the moment when I felt, "This is it." I came into my office and my secretary told me there were two FBI guys in the office waiting to see me. I thought, Oh, it's just another routine check, you know. Yale students who'd applied for federal jobs often put my name in as a recommendation. So I went in and said jocularly, "Well, what's the suspected danger? Is it drink? Is it homosexuality? What is it this time?"

They looked very embarrassed and said, "No, as a matter of fact, Reverend, it's *you* we want to talk to." And I remember thinking, Uh-oh, now it's really coming. But I tried not to show my sinking feelings. My feelings were mixed, you know. I didn't want to go to jail. After all, I had better things to do, and I was a married man with three small children. But on the other hand, we were forcing the issue pretty hard, and it wasn't surprising that the government would strike back in some form or other.

So I said, "Well, come on now, men, you know that I know the law well enough that I'm not going to say anything, so why don't I just ask you what your feelings are about the war?" And the FBI men said, "That's not our job." And I said, "No, I know it's not your job, but as human beings you must have some feelings about the war. Are you for it or against it?" And they said, "We don't know." And I said, "You know, at this point, I'm very happy I'm in my shoes and not in your shoes, because I do know, and you ought to know. So, bye-bye, gentlemen. I hope we won't be seeing each other again real soon."

They left, and I said to my secretary, "Well, I think it's coming soon." And about a couple months later, down came the indictments. They weren't served for quite a while, actually. It was announced in the press when they were put in the mail. Spock was standing up in the subway, and he read the headlines: "Spock Arrested." That was the first he'd heard about it. And I was in Washington and a newspaper man came running up as I was going through some swinging doors, and he said, "Hey, hey!" And I came around through the swinging doors again, and he told me I'd been indicted. All I remember is going through that revolving door, and then revolving back again and going in and finding out that we'd been indicted. It was kind of a sinking feeling, but then it was pretty combative, too, you know. "Okay, we can handle this one. This is what we've been asking for, so we're getting it. That's all right."

When I found out who the other five were in the conspiracy trial, I realized that Ramsey Clark had clearly decided to arrest five older people who could take care of themselves, rather than hundreds of students. And I thought, That's pretty good. I asked him about that later—we are very good friends now—and he said, "Yes, that was my decision. You were pushing the law pretty hard, and with civil disobedience the law has to hold at some point. I was as set against the war as you were, but either I had to resign or have you arrested, as I saw it, and I preferred to stay in, because I had a lot of unfinished civil rights business to do."

Yes, he was dead set against the war already at that point. He and one other in the cabinet were, and he said, "When Johnson found out we were against the war, well, that was the last time we ever had a chance to say anything to him about that or almost any other subject."

After we were indicted, my first instinct was to plead guilty and go to jail. I thought that would be the most effective way to carry on the "witness." But a group of law professors came to see me, and when I suggested going to jail, they were over me like the front line of the New York Jets. "How dare you, Bill, not fight a charge of conspiracy!"

"You owe it to the country. You have a duty as an American citizen to fight this charge of conspiracy, which is a kind of vacuum-cleaner charge, you know."

"The government has no right to slap that kind of conspiracy charge on you."

They were very impressive people, and I didn't know anything about the law. I didn't know the history of conspiracy charges and why they had to be fought, et cetera. They told me there were all kinds of constitutional issues that could be raised—the constitutionality of the war and the question of war crimes—so that this might be a way of putting the war on trial, instead of just doctors and clergy and graduate students.

I succumbed to that reasoning, finally. I say succumbed, because in hindsight I don't think it was such a hot idea. Because we weren't able to argue any of those points. Perhaps with another judge we might have been able to, but judges and prosecutors, of course, prefer to conduct trials along the most narrow legal lines possible. Every time we tried to raise an issue like war crimes, every time we tried to raise an issue about an undeclared war, the prosecutor jumped up and said, "Objection, your Honor," and this eighty-four-year-old judge would say, "Objection sustained." So the whole trial was demeaning in the sense that whatever made an important case important was not heard. The issue was not joined.

In the trial all they wanted to know was where I was sitting in the garden with Mitchell when we thought up the idea, was I in the same hall as Raskin when they issued the Call to Resist Illegitimate Authority, and so forth. So if they could show that if we were together here and together there, then that was the only kind of case they were interested in making. The fact that we knew something about the war, about war crimes that had been committed, and that we knew what the laws were all about and that the war was undeclared, they didn't want to hear about that. None of the things that motivated us were admissable as evidence.

Wasn't there a question as to whether you had conspired together? Had you all been together at any time?

The first time we met was after we had been indicted, and I was the only one who knew everybody, so I had to introduce all the conspirators—a strange conspiracy. And what makes it even stranger is that everything we tried to do was shouted from the rooftops. There was nothing conspiratorial about anything we did: We made it as public as we possibly could. Common sense revolted against this definition of conspiracy.

All of us except Raskin were [found] guilty in the first trial. There was a split verdict on the appeal, and eventually the government quietly dropped all the charges.

Still the case made a certain point: that if people of the stature of Dr. Benjamin Spock or the Chaplain of Yale University are getting arrested, then there must be something wrong with the country. I mean, that's not a normal state of affairs. In that sense, I think it served the cause. On the evening news, John Chancellor said, "If people like this are doing things like this, I guess we'd better pay attention." So I think we achieved something.

. . . When I opposed the government, it was in the name of my country—in the name of American ideals. It was always a lovers' quarrel, not a grudge fight. My patriotic fervor has always been at a very high pitch, second only to, I hope, my very deep Christian convictions. I was never tempted, for instance, to go to Canada or leave the country, but I was sympathetic to the feelings of those who did.

I remember once after addressing the Yale alumni in Buffalo during the Vietnam War, a doctor who had me in tow asked me what I wanted to do, and I said, "I'd love to see Niagara Falls at night." So we went over there, and you know it's better from the Canadian side, so we went across the border, and suddenly I said to him, "Stop. Let me out." And he did. And I just burst into tears out of this overwhelming sense of relief at being outside of America for fifteen minutes. I hadn't realized what a burden it was during the war in Vietnam to be an American.

David Miller

*I*n August 1965, Congress passed a law prohibiting the destruction of *draft cards. Two months later, a young man stood in front of the induction center in lower Manhattan and deliberately burned his draft card. He was interviewed on television and became the subject of extensive press coverage. Later he served two years in federal prison for his offense. Today David Miller works in the San Francisco office of the Central Committee for Conscientious Objectors. He has recently completed law school, and is awaiting a law association decision on his fitness to be admitted to the bar.*

We were a poor, white family in Syracuse, New York. I was an altar boy, and I went to Catholic schools: Christian Brothers High School and then a Jesuit college. While I was in college it became clear to me that I was opposed to the Vietnam War, morally and politically. It wasn't a just war. It clearly couldn't be right to defend the interests of imperialists within Indochina. Actually, I concluded that under modern conditions there couldn't be any just wars, that modern weapons made them impossible. The methods were just too indiscriminate.

About this time, I read *The Other America* by Michael Harrington, which introduced me to Dorothy Day and the Catholic Worker group,* and I wrote to her and said I wanted to go to work with her. It was the combination of living the Sermon on the Mount—feeding the hungry and clothing the naked—along with involvement with antiwar stuff. I felt that I'd like to have my feet in both camps, serving the poor and being politically active at the same time.

My family wasn't too happy with the decision to go and serve the poor instead of staying home and getting a job and serving the poor in my family. [*Chuckles.*] They thought it was about time I started contributing. But I told them what I'd be doing, that I'd be noncooperating with the draft, because I thought in conscience I couldn't cooperate with preparation for a war. I just couldn't acquiesce in that. And my mother said, "Well, if you're going to do that, maybe it's better for you to go down to New York to do it." I think she didn't want the fuss that might be caused by it in our hometown. Little did she know, of course, that later on a much greater fuss would be caused by my going to New York.

Anyhow, I went to the *Catholic Worker* within a couple of weeks after graduation from college, in June of 1965, and lived in a little apartment there with several other Catholic workers. It was just off Mott Street, not much heat, toilet in the hall. We served breakfast, we served in the soup line, we passed out clothing, and we sold *Catholic Worker*s on the corner in Greenwich Village at Sixth Avenue and West Eighth Street. We sold it for a penny a copy. It was mostly down-and-out transients and alcoholics in the Bowery that we were serving, and no one was really taking care of them but us. I found the work very satisfying. It's good to know you're doing something that's needed.

At about this time, my relations with the draft board were hotting up. My student deferment was over, and I'd sent back my draft cards, and they sent me another set. I had written and told them that I wasn't going to cooperate, but I wouldn't hide. I'd tell them where I was, which I did do.

And then a law was passed specifically prohibiting the destruction of draft cards. Up until that time it had been required only that you have it in your possession, although precisely what that means has never been tested, because it's impossible to enforce. If they tried to enforce that, it would be an internal passport. When the law was passed, a lot

---

* A group of lay Catholics in New York City, who were committed to pacifism and serving the poor.

of people regarded it as a challenge, but no one did anything about it right away.

On October fifteenth of that year, I was to be one of the speakers at the first International Day of Protest Against the War in Vietnam. The night before, I discussed with some of the other Catholic Workers that I'd probably eventually go to jail for resisting the draft, and that burning a draft card at this demonstration would be just one more element. I decided that tomorrow was the opportunity, and I would do it.

It was a Friday afternoon, and there was quite a crowd outside—an unruly crowd, as they were in those days. Some Why-don't-you-go-back-to-Russia? types on one side of the street, and a friendly crowd on the other side of the street. There were a few newsmen around, but I didn't know whether they would pick it up or not. It wasn't for that reason. To me, burning the card was just another act of noncooperation—you know, a good way to use my five minutes on the platform, so that I didn't have to stumble over words, because I was a shy young man. It was going to be a symbolic speech, action instead of words.

When it came my turn, I went up and took the podium. For some reason, that day I decided to wear my suit, the one suit I had—my college suit. Later I was described in the news as being nattily attired, and a friend said to me, "You really have to have more than one suit to be labeled 'nattily attired.' " I'd had my hair trimmed, so I looked like a very clean-cut, just-out-of-college athletic type.

When I got up, I said that I was opposed to the war in Vietnam and to conscription, and I remember saying, "I'm letting this action speak for itself," and then I tried to burn the draft card with some matches that I had. The wind kept blowing it out, and somebody below gave me a lighter, and that worked. But I was holding on to the corner of the card with my finger. It's kind of hard to burn an entire card, when you're holding onto it. Later people got more sophisticated and had little cauldrons for the burning, you know. But I was the first. Anyhow, what remained of the card dropped to the ground, and an FBI agent snatched it up pretty quickly. I didn't know it at the time, but it was later introduced as evidence in my trial. It still had part of my signature on it.

When I started burning the card, the crowd sort of quieted down. There was a sense of something important happening. Right afterward, Gabe Pressman came over and interviewed me live on television. It was one of those early live interviews on the street during the six o'clock news, with a big sound truck and everything. I'm sure they carry the equipment now in a backpack, but at that time they needed a big truck, and I remember him saying that he was trying to get everything together. He said, "I seem more nervous than you are." And, you know, I just smiled.

I was feeling calm then, really calm. I knew it was a decisive act, but it was among other decisive acts. I didn't attach any special magnitude to it, although it did have its own magnitude, well beyond anything that I felt at that time. It sort of took on its own life.

A few days after the draft-card burning, the FBI came and arrested me. They showed me a picture that was me, a picture from the newspapers. I said, "It looks like me," and they gave me the Miranda warning. But there was never any argument about the facts. I didn't deny them. My defense was a question of constitutional law.

The case dragged on in the courts until it was eventually decided against me in 1968. Basically, my defense was that the act was symbolic free speech. The argument was that when you combined speech and action, there has to be an overriding purpose of the government that is furthered by denying that free speech. But, unfortunately, that wasn't bought by the Supreme Court. They just said, "Well, there's an important purpose here. People have to carry their draft cards; it helps them to make contact with the local draft board."

That was really sort of nonsense. The merest rational justification possible for the law. There's no reason why anybody had to carry a draft card. The real crunch comes with whether they know where you are, and whether you respond. It has nothing to do with whether you have a draft card on you or not, absolutely nothing. But from the time that I burned the draft card, I realized that I would go to jail sooner or later, that it was just a matter of time.

I eventually did go into federal prison. There were a lot of other draft resisters there, and we had sort of a little community within the walls. But, you know, I was young, and prison was a difficult experience.

It really took two years to get myself together after I got out. Prison had been about that long, and there's sort of a rule of thumb, you know, that it takes you as long to get back to real life as you have served in prison. At the end of two years, I went up to New York and began living with a woman named Irene, whom I eventually married and with whom I'm still living.

By 1977, my wife and I both wanted to go to law school. Irene was admitted to law school in New York, but I kept applying and being turned down. I'm sure my record was why I was refused. But eventually I got into Golden Gate Law School, and we moved out to San Francisco. I was working full time and going to law school at night. My wife was going to law school full time, and we had two kids under five by that time, but we managed to make it.

We've both finished law school now, and I'm working full time now for the Central Committee for Conscientious Objectors. We have a panel of military lawyers throughout the country that we can refer people to. There's not much money, but it's an ideal combination for me. It's a job and a cause.

Now I'm waiting to see whether I'll be admitted to the bar on the moral fitness question. They may delve into my past, or they may just accept that it was a long time ago. You know, it was twenty years ago, and I was only twenty-two. After all, it wasn't a crime involving moral turpitude. I'll just have to wait and see what happens.

Peter Matusewitch

*B*rought up in a left-wing household in New York City, he calls
himself a "pink-diaper baby." He is proud of the fact that both his
grandfathers deserted the Russian Army during World War I and
that his father was an antiwar activist in the 1930s. During high school and
his freshman year in college, he became involved in the antiwar movement
and worked as a draft counselor. Then his own eighteenth birthday approached.

I had my birthday party at the office of my local draft board. There
were about thirty of us. My parents came, and my friends from high
school, and I had a birthday cake, you know, the real traditional one.
All the napkins said "Happy Birthday" and the whole bit.

We went to the office of my local draft board in midtown Manhattan.
We just showed up, walked in, and had a birthday party. I handed in
the letter explaining who I was and why I wasn't going to register. The
letter was filled with the rhetoric of the period, and when I look back
on it, I think nowadays I could say it better or differently, but I said it
and it was clear. I ain't registering, you know? This is who I am and
this is why I won't.

They were all surprised to see us. They called the cops and by the
time the cops got there, they had pretty well realized that we weren't
going to trash the place. We were a bunch of people having a birthday

party! We negotiated with the cops a little. They allowed us to stay a few minutes longer, and we cut up the cake and asked if we could leave it on the counter for incoming registrants and for the workers, if they wanted, so they could take it back into the offices. People liked the cake.

Then we held hands in a circle and worshipped silently for a few minutes, and then we left. It had not been my intention to have a great confrontation or anything like that, you know. I did what I wanted to do. This was something to get it off the ground.

When I was a draft counselor, working with all these people facing the same kind of personal choice, I got to see what it did to people— even the COs and the people who beat it. Their lives were just so ruled by this fight over the draft and beating it, staying out. It's incredible how it infected young people during the Vietnam era. People were just getting ground up *every* day, it was so numbing. And it was clear that it was just going to keep right on going. There was just such an urgency to *force* this war to end. I opted for what seemed to be the personally most powerful decision, to choose not to be part of it. It was also the simplest. There was no convoluted politics, there was no balancing this against that; just *no*.

I also wanted just a little bit to keep it light, not be too serious about it. I mean, you can really get into this gray, grim, moral righteousness stuff. Because it's a frightening thing to do, the thought of going to jail and all the rest of that, and I was consciously looking for ways to shake that up. I guess that's why I had the birthday party at the draft board.

About six months later the FBI showed up and arrested me, four of them, straight as razors and serious about what they're doing. They took me in the elevator and put the cuffs on me, two in the front and one on either side of me in the back. I was an eighteen-year-old hippie, right? Long hair, sideburns, and dirty work clothing—the whole image, you know. What was I going to do, who in the world would ever be scared of me?

Anyway, they did it by the numbers, and I was arraigned pretty quickly. I stood in front of the magistrate, was given personal recognizance, and that was it. By that time, it was some sort of automatic routine in New York, because there had been so many thousands of resisters. And then I proceeded with two years of trials and appeals. I certainly wasn't going to offer them my ass to just put away. I was going to fight it.

The judge was seventy-four years old, a senior judge because he was over the retirement age. He was very paternalistic. I reminded him of his grandson; he loved to tell me that. His grandson was somewhat rambunctious and gave him all kinds of difficulty, but he loved him.

The trial was a joke. The transcripts of the trial are so funny to read when I look back over them. Oh, Lord! The things that judge did in that case—some of the questions . . . I had witnesses, people who'd been there, and I was handling the direct examination of them. The judge would just intervene and start asking questions. My mother was there. I figured, "Hey, she's a good lady, I'll put her on the stand. She's a good witness." He takes over. He wants to know all the details about the birthday cake. "What kind of birthday cake was it?"

I couldn't believe it. This is my direct examination of a witness in federal court, and he wants to know about the birthday cake! Oh, Lord! I couldn't believe it was real. I was just dumbfounded. I knew I was in trouble. All of the witnesses kind of went like that. I mean, he was just busy teaching me a lesson here. As my older brother is fond of telling me, the law is whatever the judges tell us it is.

The whole thing was only a couple of hours. I presented all my witnesses, rested, and then prepared for the final arguments. He told me to stand up. He told me I'm convicted. Just like that. I stood there with my mouth open and I finally said, "I was under the impression that I had the right to make oral argument." He said, "Oh, you can now, if you want to." *After* I'm convicted!

I just never had a chance. He sentenced me to three years, suspended, five years' probation, two special conditions: one, that I register, and two, that I do work in the national interest for the entire five years of the probation. I told him I would not register. I would not have gone through all this if I was going to. We went to appeals, but the judges just did not want to hear another draft case. Period. As for the judge's conduct, they didn't say anything. Basically what they said was, "You didn't intend to register, right?" They found no error.

First they dumped me in the hole on West Street, and that was a funny story. West Street was the old federal detention headquarters. It was a converted eighteenth-century/nineteenth-century warehouse, and there were what they call tanks. Each floor had these very large cages, about seven-and-a-half feet high, bars all around, and twenty to forty bunks and two lockers. Each would have a toilet and a sink, and shower and larger bathroom facilities outside the tanks. Everybody there was waiting for trial, waiting for sentencing, waiting to be shipped out, doing a very short sentence, waiting to testify or something else, whatever.

By now I had a lawyer, who was a good draft attorney but didn't know anything about jail. He called up the associate warden and, without consulting with me, just thinking he was doing me a favor, said, "Listen, he's a young kid, he's a draft case, he's never done this before, you know. Separate him from the rest of the population for a while. Give him a chance to work in. I'm afraid something will happen to him." You know the image of what could happen.

So my first evening there, I've just gotten settled in where everybody starts out in the joint, and I went to bed. They came by at ten-thirty P.M., woke me up, and said, "You're moving." "Where?" I said. "Across the hall." "What's across the hall?" So I went across the hall and was in a segregation cell.

Segregation on West Street was not individual cells, it wasn't solitary. There were three other people in a very small cell, with double bunks, toilet, and a sink. But it was twenty-four-hour deadlock. You know, maximum-security-house stuff, and they dumped me in there. What the fuck am I doing in the hole? I mean, scared out of my gourd. Why did they put me in here? Every story I'd ever heard, about the atrocities that happened in the joint, could happen to me now. I was not frightened in the population out there, where everybody else was. *This* scared me! So I started making my bed, and I was looking at these three guys, and they were looking at me. They finally said, "Well, what did they throw you in here for?" I said, "I don't know."

They didn't like that answer. You go to the hole because you did something that's considered prestigious by the prisoners: You were in a fight, you attempted an escape. *Or* you're a stool pigeon, and someone knows that you were, and you're put there for your own protection. They're getting you away from the population for that kind of reason. If I was saying I didn't know, clearly I wasn't in for fighting or some such as that. What's the other possibility?

So I got in the bed, you know, it was late, I was tired, and I just wanted to close my eyes and obliviate the world, right? And the last thing I heard, my first night in the joint, was this one dude looking at me and saying, "You'd better not let us find out you're a stool pigeon." So this was where my lawyer wanted me put for my protection, right? It was a bad night, a *bad* first night.

I woke up in the morning, got to know these guys a little, tried to find out why I was in there. They made some tentative judgments that maybe I was all right. I was a nice guy, you know, I made good conversation. It was kind of a strained day, but they weren't hearing anything through the grapevine, and I seemed like I really didn't know what was going on.

We found out the next day what had happened, that my lawyer had asked for that. It broke them up. They thought that it was so funny that they put me in there with *them* for my protection! They thought it was the funniest thing they'd heard in months. These guys were facing a thousand years between them—murder, bank robbery, you know. These folks were hard-core folks, right? They thought this was the funniest thing they'd ever seen.

We became fast friends after that. They took a real liking to me. It made their day, you know! We got along great. There was perfect harmony in that cell. I've never gotten along with three people in close quarters that well in my life. Well, part of it is these folks had done a lot of time, and they *knew* how to get along. And I just followed their lead. We had mutual interests in this or that, and I'd get lots of books, and they were delighted to have new books to read and such like. We were still just chuckling over it.

Then they found out what I was in jail for, and they thought it was kind of strange. One of them in particular—the guy who'd said, "You'd better not let us find out you're a stool pigeon"—thought it was kind of neat in a way. He had never met somebody who'd go to jail for a cause as opposed to money. It made perfect sense in his mind to do things that might get you sent to jail for money, but for politics, this was not something he was used to. I didn't convert them, but there was some human connection that got made.

After being detained at West Street, I was taken over to Allenwood, which is a minimum-security prison camp in Pennsylvania, to do my time. Patty, the woman I was in love with at the time, was waiting to visit me when I got there. I am probably the only inmate in the history of that joint who had a visitor *waiting* for him. I was well known in the camp my second day. Everybody had heard about the guy who had a visitor waiting for him when he got there.

That's a good way to start—with a funny reputation. You're just avoiding the heaviness, the seriousness, the really distressed stuff from which the problems evolve. It's a great position to be in. Patty unwittingly did the single best thing that happened to me in terms of preparing my reputation in the joint.

I had prepared real well for doing the time. I'd talked to every resister on the East Coast I could find, and I had a very good sense of what a prison was like and how you handle it. You don't want to be a loner—that makes you a target. So it's how you set up your friendships. I immediately met all the resisters in the camp. There were fourteen of them. I got to know them real fast.

I did a lot of things like that. I had met a guy in West Street who had done time several times before, and he knew I was going to Allenwood. He met another guy in West Street a couple weeks later, who also got sent to Allenwood, and he sent a message for me with him. This was a guy who'd also done time, and he knew people there. Through the network that existed, I got a message from somebody who's also in that network, and it was a real nice message. It was somebody saying "Hi" to somebody.

All these things are what establish you. From having had no contact with this culture before, I had found all these ways to become an accepted part of it.

Allenwood was a forty-six-hundred-acre farm or something like that, and they raise a thousand head of cattle. They feed them there and everything. They raise a lot of acres of food for the cattle: corn and hay and various grains, alfalfa, and long-grain grass. Some friends who had done time had recommended it as the way to do the time, so I was a farmer. I drove tractors. I fed hay for a while, and then two people were assigned to the silage feeding, which was mechanized. The wagon drove along troughs and spit out the silage, and you went and got another load into the wagon and spit it out in other troughs. You just drive around all day feeding cattle.

I was a New York kid. I'd never driven anything, and they didn't even teach me how to drive a tractor. The first day on the job, I was bringing a hay wagon into this barn and there was a big ditch in front of it. I didn't know how much respect you were supposed to have for a ditch. I bounced into that ditch and bounced out, lost control, and *b-o-o-m*, just hit the side of a barn with a tractor. The other guys thought it was funny as hell. I was a little embarrassed. Well, what could I say? I did it. I did it. I took the general position of, you know, make use of the embarrassment.

I truly tried to deal with this whole thing on that level: Just don't take it too seriously. Just try to keep your head above the shit. You gotta remember it's a jailhouse. You can't go home. They got complete control over you. But you keep it light.

I'm in engineering school now, an old interest that got sidetracked by my political activism. A lot of times I think about draft resistance and the role of personal action in the larger picture. Why had I done this? Has it been worth it? Of course, we didn't end the war in the long run. The combination of it becoming impossible to hold on at home and impossible to keep it up over there just ground it to a halt.

Basically what happened was the Vietnamese people simply persisted long enough. That's how the war was won. The Soviets didn't win it for them, the Chinese didn't, you know. The American people didn't defeat the American army or any of that crap. The Vietnamese people simply persisted long enough, which is an *incredible* achievement of human endurance. Now, I don't want to belittle what we did as a movement, but in the end, the Vietnamese just simply persisted. I think without the movement they would have had to persist a bit longer. And I'm glad we gave them some time off. I mean it was at least *something* we did for them.

Lorraine Brill

LORRAINE SUE BRILL
Lori . . . "Surprise quizzes" . . . Mr. Solomon's 5th period Art class . . . To try everything once.
ACTIVITIES: Honor Society 3,4; Future Teachers of America 3,4; Nightingales 4; Intramural Sports 2,3,4; Congress 2,3, Alternate 4; Usher Squad 3,4, Vice-President; French Club 2,3; Spanish Club 3, Class Show 3.

In 1967 she was an eighteen-year-old freshman at New York University when she went to her first antiwar demonstration with her boyfriend.

We went down to the March on the Pentagon. There were buses, and we were with a bunch of other college students. I was a little scared, but at first it was kind of peaceful. We were out on the grass, chanting, "Peace now. Peace now." This went on for quite a long time, and then all of a sudden there was a sort of signal, and people were being hit by soldiers or MPs. I was never touched, even though I was close. I remember people falling on me, and I remember seeing blood. It was all kind of chaos. One minute was peaceful and fun, and then all of a sudden they're hitting.

I got separated from Steve at that time, but somehow we found each other, and he was limping because his leg was hit and it was bleeding, and he needed to have it taken care of. So we tried to get to the hospital. It was starting to get dark. The two of us were trying to find the hospital, and I remember asking directions of a number of Washington people. They knew who we were. I mean, it was obvious from looking at us that we came from the march. And they wouldn't even tell us where the hospital was.

We were in a pretty nice neighborhood, and the street was kind of dark. All of a sudden, the door of one of the houses—really, it was almost like a mansion—opened and out came a young man and a girl about our age. They stopped at the top of the steps for a minute, and we looked right up at them. It was as if they were on the stage, because the streetlight was shining on them, and they were in evening clothes. The man had a tux, and the girl had a strapless gown, and she looked just beautiful. And we just stared. We stopped and just stared at them. We couldn't say anything. They were like creatures from another world. They were *our age* and they were going to a *prom*. We had thought the whole world was with us, and here were these two people living in a movie. I'll never forget that.

Steve sort of shouted at them, "Don't you know there's a war on?" But they ignored us. I guess they thought we were just a couple of hippies, and probably they couldn't really see us. We were in the dark, and they were in the light.

Dee Knight

© Barbara Beirne

*D*uring the Sixties, thousands of young men left the United States to avoid the draft. Dee Knight was one of these. An early opponent of the Vietnam War, he applied unsuccessfully for conscientious objector status and worked on the McCarthy campaign until the Democratic convention of 1968. But when Hubert Humphrey won the nomination, it seemed there was no end to the war in sight.

It was a time of decision for all of us, and for me it was crucial. I had gradually concluded during May and June of '68 that if McCarthy didn't win, or if Kennedy didn't win—and that was out, once Kennedy had been shot—I would have to leave the country.

It was the least troublesome among the set of clearly definable alternatives I saw: one, accept the draft and go to Vietnam and commit a crime; two, accept the judgment of the government that I was a criminal, despite the fact that I wasn't, and go to jail, subjecting myself to unknown dangers; three, go underground in this country, again subjecting myself to those dangers; and four, go to Canada. In my opinion, going to Canada was by far the best and simplest and cleanest approach. Given its momentous character, it was an amazingly easy decision.

That weekend in Chicago, after the convention, I made the arrangements. A friend of mine had a job waiting for him as a teacher at the

University of Rochester, and he was going to drive through Canada. He agreed to drop me in Hamilton, which is near Toronto. From there I could take the bus to Toronto. We left the very next day. All I had with me were a couple of suitcases, something in the neighborhood of thirty dollars, my driver's license, and a Social Security card. No books or papers. I was traveling very light. I was exhausted, and I slept in the car from Chicago to Detroit.

When we got to the border, the process of passing through was amazingly simple. We were both U.S. citizens in good standing, and he was en route to Rochester, New York. Americans and Canadians go back and forth at that border crossing by the thousands on a daily basis. Our stated intent was that we were just going to go through Canada on our way to Rochester. The only border officials we saw were the Customs and Immigration officials on the Canadian side. It went very fast.

I was still dazed when we went through the Detroit-Windsor tunnel, which was kind of a frightening experience for me. I suppose it was good from a symbolic point of view that it was a tunnel we had to go through to get to the other side. I was still waking up as we went through the tunnel, but after that the adrenaline and nervous energy kept me wide awake until we got to Hamilton. The Canadian countryside in that area is relatively barren and uninteresting. It's sparsely populated, very flat, and there's a law against highway poster advertising. Everything seemed to be very empty. My emotions were very mixed up.

After my friend dropped me in Hamilton, I took the bus to Toronto, and arrived at the bus depot there on the first or second day of September 1968. I hadn't planned what to do next, but I figured there must be a draft counseling organization around somewhere. I wondered if it would be underground. I looked in the telephone book under "Alice," because there was a song called "Alice's Restaurant" that was being sung about that time. [*Chuckles.*] I don't know what made me do that. Later I realized it was totally nonsensical. Of course, I knew in a minute it wasn't going to help, so I looked under "Draft," and there it was: "Draft Resistance Counseling." Right there in the phone book!

I called them up, and they made an appointment for me for the next day and sent me to a hostel a few blocks from the bus depot, where I could sleep overnight.

You know, the experience of going to Canada had different effects on different people. Some people were really traumatized by the experience. The separation from everything they knew as a support structure, together with the sense that they were criminals, tended to freeze them in a certain sense, to incapacitate them. They just weren't able to do any of the survival things that are so necessary for a person on his or her own. But it did just the opposite for me. It released tremendous energy. I felt a great deal of excitement at the challenge. I was filled with curiosity about this new place. I got someone at the hostel to show me where there was an open-air market, and I bought some food, came back and made dinner, and then got a good night's sleep.

The next morning I went to the counseling office, just a short ride on the Toronto subway. I told them I thought it would be better if I didn't stay at the hostel, because it seemed to me a dismal place.

They had a list of supporters who were willing to take in war resisters, and they sent me to one, a professor at the University of Toronto. His wife was a British immigrant to Canada, and they had two or three children and a nice house in a pleasant neighborhood. They talked to me about my experience and also about what Canada was like.

The counseling center provided me with a very well-published manual for immigrants that explained the Canadian immigration laws in detail, and gave me advice on how to get myself set up. I had to obtain a job offer, return to the American side of the border, and come back into the country. Then I could apply for immigrant status. The official policy was that a person's military obligations and background were not to be considered a factor in the application for immigrant status.

The first thing to do, then, was to get a job. You know, my parents had done me a tremendously good service, because they had encouraged me to work every year of my life from the time that I was eight years old. That was a big plus for me, and helped me survive. I had experience working in a grocery store in high school, and when I looked in the newspapers in Toronto that first day, I saw an ad for just such a job. It was a store in the suburbs of Toronto, a real hike from where I was going to be living. But I applied for the job and was accepted for it.

I had no idea what to expect in terms of people's attitudes. After the guy had hired me, I said, sort of nervously, "If it is your policy not to hire draft resisters, then I do not qualify." [*Laughs.*] I had made the decision that it would be better if we got that cleared up right at the outset. It sort of took him aback. I think he had an immigrant background himself. He looked at me and said, "Oh, no, that's not an issue with me." So I said, "Good, because I have to go down to the border and get my immigrant status taken care of, and they may call you." I didn't feel I could get a written job offer for that kind of job, but at least I had an offer that could be confirmed, so I could get in.

Then I had to get my Social Insurance card, which is like a U.S. Social Security card, which you can get without any reference to your other status. I just filled out a form, and I got it. I was ready to go down to the border by the end of the week. That was the worst, but it turned out to be just routine. It went very fast. They didn't even call the fellow in the grocery store. And then I was *in*.

After I got the job and had my legal status straightened out, I went out and found a room of my own. I was very grateful to the family who had taken me in, but they were going to be taking in others who were needy as time went on. You know, it was a major thing that American war resisters were well supported by these progressive Canadians. I know my survival and personal well-being were enhanced tremendously by their kindness. If circumstances had been more difficult, I would say I owe them my life. I certainly owe them a very deep debt of gratitude, and have warm feelings for them.

After I was settled, I wrote to my parents to inform them where I was, and to explain to some degree why I had done it and what my prospects seemed to be. They were horrified—horrified and shocked. I had really given them no warning, but it would have done me no good to do so. They were not in a position to contend effectively with my decision. At least, that's my opinion.

They were deeply concerned that I had committed a crime, and that I was in deep trouble with the government. My father had served in World War II and was not a pacifist, but he certainly had no great enthusiasm for the war effort either. I think there was just a feeling that I'd gotten into big trouble, and done it impetuously. But I hadn't asked their permission and I didn't need their approval. I was an adult, and I had to do what I thought was right for me.

It was a brutally cold winter in Canada that year, with lots of snow—a very wet cold that goes through you. I think my reaction was tinged slightly with fear. There are many places in the United States that are colder and more miserable in the winter than Toronto: Chicago, virtually all of the Midwest, Buffalo. I think it was psychologically, as well as physically, intimidating, and the added pressure did cause me to feel the cold . . . and it was lonely the first few months.

There was an organization called the Union of American Exiles that became a very important support group for me. We had Christmas dinner together and picked the turkeys clean. I've never seen a drier turkey carcass in my life!

After a few months working in the grocery store, I got a white-collar job as a clerk, and then later a job with a division of Oxfam. The skills I'd gained in the McCarthy presidential campaign were suited to the kind of work being done there. I found a few Canadian friends through this job, and I got an old Volkswagen to help me get around and learn the city. But my main support was being with other people who were going through what I was at the time. It gave us a way of defining ourselves and overcoming the feeling of helplessness that can seep in from isolation. My parents were not exceptional in the fact that they were horrified and upset and embarrassed. So this thrust us out on our own, and we needed each other, the exiles.

People faced a lot of problems adjusting, especially military deserters from the U.S. who came to Canada by the tens of thousands in 1969 and '70, only to find that despite the fact that their military background was not a legal obstacle to immigration, their class background was. Many couldn't stay in Canada, and there were a number of war-resister suicides that year. A lot of my time and energy was spent dealing with their problems.

Later I began going to college at York University, driving a taxi at night to support myself. My concerns were really elsewhere, although I had been a very good student before. I remember getting a D in international relations, and that was my favorite subject. The professor was a retired foreign-service officer from Ceylon and very much a right-winger. I probably would have done better if I had kept quiet in class.

The Union of American Exiles had a newsletter, and I became a member of its editorial staff, on a voluntary basis, of course. It was called *AMEX Canada*. There were many debates in its pages about whether we were exiles or expatriates. I tended to vacillate on the issue. Later the amnesty debate became a big issue, and I remember writing an editorial in *AMEX* denouncing the idea of amnesty, saying that we couldn't expect it anyhow, and it would be an appeal coming from weakness rather than strength. Underlying my feeling, I think, was a mood of "Who'd want to go back anyhow to that terrible place?" It was a feeling of bitterness that I, as well as many others, felt about what had happened. My position on amnesty changed drastically later on.

I felt very ambivalent about staying in Canada permanently. I thought it was necessary to look on it as a possibility, rather than torture myself with thoughts of return. But I didn't want to become a Canadian citizen, because I didn't want to give up American citizenship. I wanted to be able to return, to be a part of what the country was going through.

After I had been in Canada for a while, my parents came up to see me. They'd come around to supporting me, but they didn't want to be involved. Another of my brothers had gone into the military, and is a lifer to this day. When my parents visited it was a difficult time. During that period, we felt absolute and total alienation from the U.S. government, and we were in no mood to discuss whether we were wrong and the government was right, or whether we were bad and they were good, or anything like that. We were just taking care of ourselves on our own terms.

I was living then in what you might call a commune. We were trying to run a good household, very clean, but it didn't feel right to my parents. They didn't quite know what to expect or how to deal with it. There were five of us, myself and two couples. And there were a lot of political posters on the wall—antiwar posters. After all, there was an antiwar movement going on. [Laughs.] Maybe there was a poster of Che Guevara on the wall. I wouldn't be at all surprised—he was a great hero of ours. And maybe a picture of Ho Chi Minh. My parents seemed a little shaken by it all. It was sort of what they'd hoped I wouldn't get into, I think.

My draft board tried four times to draft me while I was in Canada. They just kept sending notices to me. I had applied for conscientious objector status very early, and when it was turned down, I had written a new application, based on a study of Bertrand Russell and so on, not on religious grounds. That was also rejected, and I received 1-A status. My papers were sent to the U.S. attorney for prosecution in the western part of Oregon. He realized that since I had made a timely request for appeal and it hadn't been taken up, the indictment against me would have to be dismissed. And so in the spring of 1972, just as the amnesty campaign was heating up, my legal status was cleared on that technicality. I could come back to the United States.

I had changed my position on amnesty with the help of Jack Colhoun, a military deserter who had also gone to Canada, and was then a Ph.D. candidate in U.S. history at York University in Toronto. Since amnesty was becoming an issue in the 1972 election campaign, he convinced me that we should try to shape the debate to get real justice for all war resisters—not just for draft resisters, but also deserters and veterans with less than honorable discharges and antiwar activists with criminal records. Jack joined *AMEX*, which then became the leading voice of all exiled war resisters. I was the spokesperson at a press conference in January 1972 in Toronto where we laid out our position.

Now that I could return to the States, the first thing I did was let my parents know that I was free to come and see them, if they would like me to. They encouraged me to do so, and it happened that the McGovern campaign was taking a turn through California at the time. So I used my trip both to see my parents and to contact the McGovern campaign and push them on amnesty. I was happy to be able to set foot on American soil again—California is a beautiful place—and I was on a mission. I was not traveling solely as an individual, but as a representative of a highly charged cause. Amnesty became a vibrant issue in the campaign, and it ended up a tremendous liability to McGovern, along with acid and abortion—the three A's.

We wanted to show that the majority of those who needed amnesty were military deserters and veterans, and that leaving them out would be unfair. The way of proposing amnesty was a subject of division among liberal sectors in this country. Some wanted to negotiate for various chunks of the loaf rather than the whole loaf, but we felt *AMEX* had to go right out front with the demand for universal, unconditional amnesty.

During this time, we were frequent guests on radio and TV talk shows. Talk show hosts would call us up and put us on the air because the issue was so hot in the election campaign. Sometimes they organized debates between us and American military people on TV. I once debated an Army general on a TV show in Philadelphia during a speaking tour organizing support for amnesty! It was exciting, and I felt we were doing good work—making amnesty a reality by fighting for it.

There was usually some sort of social activity after these meetings and talk shows. I met quite a few Vietnam veterans at these times. I remember once in St. Louis after a talk show, a guy came up to me and said, "You know, I just wanted to tell you that when I was in Vietnam, the first few months I was in some pretty fierce firefights, and I lost a couple of friends. We used to read articles sometimes about the Vietnam draft resisters, and I figured that I'd kill the first one I ever met. But after I was there for another six months, I figured I'd like to shake the hand of the next one I met. And I'd like to shake your hand now." That was very moving to me.

Unlike the stereotype of war resisters and veterans not getting along, in my personal experience our relationship with Vietnam veterans is special, because we have gone through the same process of disillusionment and bitterness, as well as the struggle to get our lives back together, having been subject to a life-destroying machine that we had made the fateful error of believing in, even for a few brief years in our youth.

I came back to this country for good, ironically, to help publicize and coordinate support for the boycott of Ford's clemency program in 1974. I was to continue my work in the amnesty movement in this country, since my legal status was clear, and we needed more presence here. We called Ford's program "alternative punishment," and protested the fact that it applied only to draft resisters and not deserters, veterans, or antiwar protesters. We knew the clemency was proclaimed just to offset the Nixon pardon, which was an insult. We weren't criminals, and Nixon was, but Ford proposed to pardon Nixon unconditionally while offering "alternative punishment" to us—and not even to all of us!

Two of my closest friends and coworkers in exile, Steve Grossman and Gerry Condon, volunteered to actively challenge the punitive terms of the clemency program by returning defiantly and publicly to demand true amnesty instead. Steve faced a prison term as a draft resister, and Gerry, an ex–Green Beret, had already been convicted in absentia by a court-martial for refusing to go to Vietnam and for leaving the U.S. My job, along with other supporters, was to manage their reentry and help with travel arrangements and the media.

Steve and Gerry spoke all over the country without being arrested, because they were "too hot to handle." The tours were a big success, and I was delighted to be part of it. The experience was hair-raising for all of us. This kept me busy right through the spring of 1975. After that, we entered a tough period, because the attention of the media shifted politically from dealing with the amnesty issue to the election campaigns that were coming up in 1976.

Every step of the way up to the election we kept up the pressure for an amnesty that would include deserters, as well as bad-paper vets and antiwar activists. It was a question of justice and human rights, and we fought from high ground since the war was clearly immoral. And we finally got a lot with the amnesty that Carter declared. We didn't get everything, but we got enough that most of the people who desperately needed either to return home from exile or come up from underground could do so without violating their self-respect.

After that, we knew that this phase of the battle was over for us. I realized that I had to get a genuine, ordinary job. It was a time of personal crisis for me, because I had essentially been a "professional war resister" and organizer for many years. It was like getting out of college, you know, and having to look for a job. Except that by then I was almost twenty-nine years old. It was hard to adjust. The intensity of my work had really changed my self-concept completely. You know, this sort of thing gets into your blood. It was hard to figure out what to do with myself. I went from job to job for a year. Finally I got a job as a typesetter and I've been doing that kind of work pretty much ever since.

My personal life has been affected by all this, of course. The constant high pitch and stress interferes ridiculously with the process of anything resembling family life. I know that like other veterans of the Vietnam experience I carry deep wells of rage and fury at having been placed in a position of being called a criminal, forced into exile, and made an outcast in my own country. This has caused some painful adjustments at times.

My life is undoubtedly different from what it might have been. If it hadn't been for the war I probably would have followed a more or less straight course. I might have gone to graduate school and made a career as a teacher or professor. I might have carved out a home and a family somewhere in a medium-sized city in northern California and had several children by now. But I feel that what happened shaped me into a person I would far rather be than what I might otherwise have been. My life has been an adventure and an education to me and to some others.

I was fortunate to have been raised by strong parents, who gave me a clear sense of goodness and self-worth, and an ability to get things done. I put those qualities to good use trying to turn this country around and stop the killing. I don't feel that anything else I could have done would have been more important.

David Hawk

A small-town boy from Pennsylvania, he was president of his senior class in high school and later an All-American diving and swimming star at Cornell. While still a college student, he went into the South to work for civil rights, and he was also an early leader of the antiwar movement. In 1969, he became cochairman of the very successful nationwide Vietnam Moratorium. Until recently, he was executive director of Amnesty International, a human rights organization for the protection of political prisoners. He is now engaged in documenting the atrocities in Cambodia for the Center for the Study of Human Rights. He and his wife, former antiwar activist Joan Libby (page 137), live with their two children in Manhattan.

I wasn't a pacifist. I would have fought in World War II, so I didn't qualify as a religious pacifist. I was opposed on grounds of conscience to participation in the war in Vietnam.

I had studied social ethics and philosophy, and I based my objections on Saint Augustine, who laid out the traditional just war theory: criteria to measure what were good wars and what were bad wars, stated back in the fourth century A.D. One of the criteria had to do with the origins of the conflict. Was it defensive in nature? Another had to do with the war's winnability. And another—and to me the most important—was proportionality. Those are key concepts. There was no question in my mind that the means we were using in Vietnam were out of all proportion to any possible good end.

When I was called in to the draft board, I made my position clear. I brought in Saint Augustine. [*Laughs.*] But they told me they weren't there to talk theology. They had a set of guidelines from the Selective Service System, which told them what the categories were, and it wasn't their role to judge the categories. Their role was to apply the categories, and I didn't fit in. Saint Augustine wasn't pertinent.

A little later I got 1-A classification and an induction order. When I didn't show up, I was indicted and was supposed to report for arrest. All this took several months, and by the time I was due to be arrested, I was staying in New York at the Union Theological Seminary and working in the antiwar movement. There were about thirty of us at Union who had denounced deferments and so forth. And we said, "Well, we'll have a church service of sanctuary," and I told my attorney to notify the FBI that I would be available for arrest after twelve o'clock noon in Saint James Chapel of the Union Theological Seminary. So we had a service of sanctuary. Reverend William Sloane Coffin came down from Yale, Rabbi Heschel came from the Jewish Theological Seminary; John Bennett, who was president of the seminary, and some other people spoke, and there was a sermon.

At the end of it, two federal marshals, big fellows, walked down the central aisle, came up and grabbed me, one on each arm, and escorted me out. I didn't resist or make them carry me, I just walked along. But as soon as they got outside, they put handcuffs on me, put me in a car, and took me to FBI headquarters, where they asked me a lot of questions.

What I remember most about this was that they must have done a lot of investigation on me already. They even had my high school and college athletic records. They really did. And what they were talking to me about was my athletic career. I was astounded. I said, "My goodness, you guys have a better scrapbook on me than my mother." Anyhow, they finally finished asking whatever questions they had, and then they took me downtown and booked me.

Later the dean of the seminary came down and posted my bail, and I got out on my own recognizance. He said I was a good fellow, and I wasn't going to skip the country, and that I'd show up for my court appearances and all that. I had done this as an act of conscience—

resisting the draft in an immoral war—and I fully expected that I was to get a two-to-five-year jail sentence, which is what they were giving out at that time.

While my case was winding through the courts, I figured I had time to work for the antiwar movement. So I threw myself into that wholeheartedly. I participated in many of the demonstrations and marches that occurred in the mid-Sixties, every spring and fall, but it didn't seem to me that they were getting anywhere. I wanted to mobilize opposition to the war, and to broaden it. I got involved in the McCarthy campaign and went up to New Hampshire and did advance work there for him. . . . It was exhilarating when we almost won in New Hampshire, and later won in Wisconsin. Then there were the terrible assassinations of Martin Luther King and Robert Kennedy. And then the national convention in Chicago, with the police riot at the end, and Humphrey's nomination. It was an emotional, exhausting roller coaster of a year.

Then I went to Washington to work for the National Student Association. We organized a letter that got two-hundred-fifty student-body presidents and student-newspaper editors to state that they were going to refuse induction as long as the war continued. These were campus leaders—not just from the Ivy League and the Stanfords and Berkeleys and the Big Ten, but from state teachers colleges, small schools, a huge variety of institutions. We wanted the new administration to be aware of the depth of feeling on the college campuses, and we asked for a meeting with President Nixon so that we could make him aware of this.

Well, we didn't get to meet with President Nixon, but in May or June of '69 we did get a meeting with Henry Kissinger, and, oh, my—what was his name?—John Ehrlichman. [*Laughs.*] At that time, none of us really knew who he was or how important he would become later, but we knew he was one of the White House hard-liners.

The meeting took place in the Situation Room in the basement of the White House. They'd pulled all the curtains down in front of the maps so that we couldn't see them. Kissinger spoke first, and he was very professorial. He acted as if he were back at Harvard, you know, with some of his graduate students. He refused to discuss the origins or the merit of the original U.S. involvement, but he said the fact that our country was there meant we had a commitment, and that U.S. credibility was at stake, and therefore we couldn't lose. He went on to say that the administration was going to wind down the war. He asked for patience. "Come back in a year," he said, "if we haven't made any progress." The student-body presidents said, "We're graduating. We have to decide what we're going to do about the draft next month. We don't have a year to wait."

Ehrlichman sat there stone-faced all the time Kissinger was talking. Then Kissinger excused himself, and Ehrlichman took over. He said, "If you people think that you can break laws just because you don't like them, you're going to force us to up the ante to the point where we're handing out death sentences for traffic violations." [*Slams hand on table.*] He was a real hard-liner. The student-body presidents' jaws just dropped open, and that was the end of the meeting.

We had to leave the Situation Room by going out through the Press Room, and the press knew we were having this meeting. The student editors and presidents and the NSA people caucussed on the stairs, and then went out and faced the press. Our statement said, "We hate to say this, but on the basis of our discussions, it's clear that this administration will be as bad as the last one." The war policies were going to continue, and they weren't going to end it except on their terms.

At this point, there were lots of discussions going on among the antiwar people as to what to do next. Sometime during these discussions we came up with the idea of a strategy for calling a strike that would start off with one day in October, two days in November, three days in December, and keep getting bigger and bigger. It would focus the public's attention on the antiwar movement, and we hoped it would grow and grow across the country. Sam Brown, who'd worked with me in the McCarthy campaign, called me about this idea, and I organized a followup—got some of the student presidents to come back and meet with us on it.

The idea was that the students would leave their campuses on the day of the strike and organize opposition to the war in the community. At some point, Sam and I decided that strike was the wrong word, because starting from campuses a strike sounded like something that was against the institution, and that wasn't the connotation we wanted to have. We were against the war, not against the campus administrations. We finally decided on the name "The Vietnam Moratorium." It was to be a moratorium on business-as-usual, and we hoped that it would be effective.

The student leaders were pretty favorable to the idea, as people would be then to any coherent strategy that sounded like it might work. By that time we were pretty good organizers. We rented a little office, and we spent the summer calling up dozens of deans of students at universities and colleges all over the country to find the home addresses of student newspaper editors and student presidents, calling their home numbers and finding out from their parents where they were and telling them what we were planning.

In mid-September we had announced that we were going to have this Moratorium on October fifteenth. Nixon was asked a question about it the next day: What was his opinion about the Moratorium against the war? And that's where he made a very famous mistake. He said, "In no way will I be affected by what people think." It sounded like he was completely callous to the opinion of American people, as if he didn't care what the American people thought. Of course, it turned out that he didn't, but he probably didn't mean it to sound that way.

Because his answer sounded so terrible, it became the lead news story, and it gave us the most extraordinary opportunity, because if the president says he doesn't care about what the American people think, that's news. The press started coming around to us for a response, so we called a press conference for the following Friday, timed for the Sunday papers. We had all that figured out. We were good on the timing by then. It was one of those rare occasions when you get a chance to respond to the President of the United States.

At the press conference, we rattled off all the Republican and Democratic congressmen and senators that were behind us, and pointed out that we had the endorsement of the larger community, not just students. We got a lot of attention, and we had our pictures on the front pages of a number of papers.

The press realized they had a major story on their hands. Previously we'd been covered by newspaper people who were assigned to cover the student beat, but now we became a national political story. One of the leading political columnists wrote a column saying, "The kids are out to break another president." Actually, all of our literature had been couched not to attack Nixon, but to demonstrate for the new administration how widespread the support was for an end to the war policies. That's what we were trying to do, to give a political opening for him to negotiate a settlement.

By this time the thing was just snowballing. We didn't have to try to generate news. People were calling up. We were on the television, we were in all newspapers. And it wasn't just in Washington; the activity was everywhere. People were calling from all over. "Can we have a statement on this? Can we have a statement on that?"

We were essentially a control room. We had a huge logistical problem in furnishing speakers for all the rallies around the country. There'd be congressmen and senators who were willing to speak, and we had to figure out how to fly them to six different places on the day of the Moratorium. At that point, we had the capacity to get what we said heard by millions of people in the newspapers, on television. It was amazing: We were the leaders of the opposition in the United States, and we were all in our twenties. It was really an awesome sort of responsibility.

We didn't want the demonstrations to center in Washington. We wanted them to be all over. We wanted marching on the green in small towns in New England, silent vigils in Iowa; church bells rung all over. It was symbolic; you didn't have to say anything. People would know what the church bells were ringing for. And people could do it anywhere.

There was a terrific outpouring. There were mayors all over the country, Mayor Lindsay in New York, senators and congressmen. An awful lot of people who had not come out against the war before took this occasion to come out against it. There was even a demonstration on Wall Street.

By the morning of the Moratorium, it was clear that we had achieved the first time around what we had hoped to do in another six, seven, or eight months. We had made our contribution and had shot our wad. We had accomplished it all at the very first go-around, and demonstrated the depth of antiwar sentiment.

There were hour-long television specials on the Moratorium. I remember I went to one, and Sam went to the other. The administration had set up a Republican right-winger to red-bait us, and I was continually asked questions about were we getting instructions from Moscow? Wasn't the plan for the Moratorium hatched at such-and-such a meeting in Czechoslovakia? And I was able to say it was homegrown.

While all this was going on, my draft case was still dragging through the courts. As it turned out, I got away scot-free. There was a ruling by the Supreme Court on a case very similar to mine that the procedure of the Selective Service System—to order draft resisters for immediate induction punitively—was unconstitutional.

The response of the president to the Moratorium was to announce that on November 3 he would make a major pronouncement on the war. And in that speech he laid out two things: One was he announced Vietnamization of the war, and the other was this thing of the Silent Majority versus the Noisy Demonstrators. He unleashed Agnew to attack us. Those were really bitter attacks on the kids and on the pro-peace people and on the media.

We had no idea of this at the time, of course, but it's clear now that the administration took what we were doing very, very seriously. Nixon had planned to do that fall what he eventually did on the Christmas of '73: massive bombing, pulling out all the stops. He had planned a major escalation of bombing in the North to show how tough his administration was going to be. But because of the outpouring of antiwar sentiments in the October Moratorium, they decided not to do their escalation then. We didn't force them to stop the war, but we did delay the escalation, and that's why they were so mad at us, and why they had such a calculated strategy of how to deal with the opposition. So we were, in fact, more successful in a way than we thought we were.

. . . The outcome of the war was appalling not only in terms of how long it was prolonged, but also in terms of what happened to the peoples of Indochina. Vietnam is an extraordinarily repressive nation from which hundreds of thousands have fled in leaky boats.

And what happened in Cambodia was a bloodbath. I had thought the outcome there would be bad, because the war had destroyed its traditional society. But I had no idea of what the Khmer Rouge was going to do. I didn't imagine it because it was unimaginable.

None of this retrospectively justifies the United States' intervention there, because I still believe that the war was untenable and unwinnable—and that our intervention did nothing but harm. But a lot of things turn out differently from what one expects. There are always too many unknown variables.

Joan Libby

*M**arried to former antiwar activist David Hawk (page 130), she has worked with him on many projects since they met in the heady days of the Vietnam Moratorium. She is now director of public relations for the District Attorney of New York City.*

What I remember most is that we used to be sort of glued to the TV when the news came on, and it was really dismaying, because, of course, we remembered the kind of optimism that we'd had earlier during the Kennedy years. That optimism may or may not have been justified, but it had certainly been in the air.

And then you're sort of watching these same people, the same "best and brightest"—McNamara and Bundy and all these people who were going to bring you sort of a better world, a more humane world. You know, the rhetoric and the sort of Peace Corps atmosphere that a lot of this stuff was clothed in. And now, to watch these same people go on day in and day out justifying and rationalizing and trying to sell the war—it was dismaying.

I organized a couple of local demonstrations while I was at Mount Holyoke, and we helped with some of the things that were going on at the University of Massachusetts and at Amherst. I don't mean that it was a heroic effort, but I was part of it.

My father had been in the Army in the Second World War, and he was a kind of old-line American patriot. That was the stuff we were brought up on. So we used to have great arguments about whether the war was justified or not. He was sort of into the notion that it was justified, because we were fighting Communism. And I was sort of into the thing that our security wasn't at stake, so how could you sit by and just let these things go on over there? I mean, isn't that what people did in Germany?

That was a low blow, a low blow. Both my parents were Jewish, and one of the things I had had to learn about, of course, was the Holocaust, and one of the lessons in that always is that you shouldn't stand by and think somebody else is going to do it. That's a serious lesson, I think, for susceptible young people like myself—a powerful one. It becomes sort of an imperative. There's always a double-edged sword when you bring people up with the notion that you should take more positions on things. You never know where they'll come out.

I was a member of the steering committee of the National Student Association, and I went to their national congress in 1969 in Texas.

While I was there I met David. He was one of the serious ones. He told me right away about the plans they had for this thing they were going to do to stop the war, the Moratorium, and I thought, "Oh, this sounds like a great idea." It sounded concrete and it was simple. You know, a lot of ideas that organizer types have are sort of pie-in-the-sky. This may have had an element of pie-in-the-sky in it, God knows, if you think it could stop a war. But it seemed to me manageable. They'd lucked into the right idea and the right climate and the right timing. And there seemed to be some intelligence that went into for-mulating the whole notion.

I thought, I want to be part of this. David was recruiting people to come and work for him in Washington at the end of the summer. He wanted people who would be good organizers, and he wanted them to be able to work tirelessly for sixteen or eighteen hours a day for basically seventy-five dollars a week. He figured I was a live one, and he asked me if I'd like to come. I thought, Okay. It sounds right, and I'll do this. . . .

The war was on my mind a lot then, and the notion of accountability. Do you watch these things go by you like a newscast, or do you try to do something about them? And, of course, so much of the Sixties had to do with trying to go out and do something about what you thought was wrong. I didn't want to have to sit back and watch all the Vietnam series that were going to be on TV and have my kids say to me, "Well, what did you do?" I felt like this was one of those things that comes along, whether it was futile or not, that I didn't want to be passive about. So I said yes to the Moratorium. I packed up my things in some cardboard boxes, and I went to Washington.

I moved into an apartment there with a couple of other young women who were working at the Moratorium, and I was assigned to be regional organizer for the South. Just like that. I arrived in September, and the Moratorium was to be on October fifteenth, so there was a lot of work to do. We'd get in at about eight-thirty or nine in the morning and work until eleven or twelve every night. Some days we just stayed on the phone all day long talking to student-body presidents, talking to student editors, or getting referrals from them about whom to talk to. We kept little file cards on the people we called, and we got back to them to see what they were doing and sent them material on how to do the organizing. We had lists of people from the National Student Association, names of student-body presidents, editors, local peace groups, the Quakers, and we just called everyone that we had any lead to.

The response was really phenomenal. I think one reason that it worked was because we were asking them to do something that they could actually do: staying out of school for a day, putting up posters, making a small demonstration in their own locality. I'd call one of these small Catholic women's colleges, people who've never done anything, and they'd say, "Yes, yes, we will." The notion that it was going to come under a kind of a national context was something that they could be comfortable with. It was respectable, and that was the key to the success, I think.

I did the calling and I helped put out a lot of the printed material that we sent out. We used to write organizing manuals, because at that time people weren't so used to doing local organizing. It's all so old hat now. We told them how to get permission from the local police department, what sort of people to ask, how to get a meeting permit, how to write a release—all the details that go into organizing a single day's rally and making it successful. We sent out hundreds of thousands of pieces of paper. They went out all over America, and I suppose some of them are still out there somewhere.

We were all pretty busy then, but things developed with me and David during that time, too, and at some point we decided to live together. He asked me to move into his apartment. I mean my apartment was sort of right around the corner from him, and it was silly having two apartments. So I said okay. Those were the Sixties, you know, and it seems quite funny, because I don't feel it's done quite like that anymore. It was done with no sense of expectation of a long-term relationship, which sounds a little silly in retrospect. [*Laughs.*] But in those days it seemed fine. I mean he was not attached to anyone else at that point, and neither was I, so there was no real complication. I just said okay, and we started to live together. Of course, we hardly lived together at the time; we worked such long hours that all we did was come home and collapse, and get up and take a shower and make it to the office for the next day. Occasionally we'd go to the movies, but most of the time we just worked together.

When the day of the Moratorium finally arrived, I remember going out in the streets and thinking, People are *really* here. The people are *really* doing it. It was an astounding sense of having helped make something happen. You know, you stay in this office day after day and talk to people on the phone, and now all of a sudden you're seeing what you've been talking about. I remember walking through Lafayette Park and thinking that there were a lot of sort of "Washington-type" people there. You know, people in business suits, very regular-looking suits—not just hippies and not just college students—but people who work in the bureaucracy.

There was an excitement in the crowd, sort of like the Fourth of July. It kept building all through the day. The news media were into it, and they were televising things from, you know, little places like Pocatello, Idaho, and the ringing of the bells there, and the people on the Boston Common and in California and Iowa and New York. People really went out and did these things which we'd planned. Maybe now they seem a little silly, but they were making a statement.

We knew we were affecting public opinion, but what the administration response would be we didn't know. Reading the memoirs of Ehrlichman or Haldeman or Nixon now, you realize how nervous we were making them. I never would have predicted that we were cutting so close, that it would lead them to the level of paranoia that led to the Plumbers and Watergate and all that. I had no idea that they were so scared of us.

William Sampol

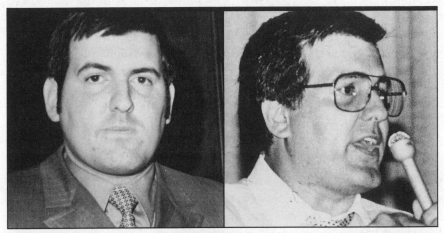

In 1969 President Nixon called for the support of what he called the Silent Majority to counteract antiwar protest. Not long afterward William Sampol organized a rally in the Wall Street area that resulted in some violent confrontations between construction workers and peace demonstrators. Today he is an administrative assistant in the New York State government. He has twice run unsuccessfully for Congress.

As soon as I heard Nixon call for the Silent Majority to support him, I went out and I incorporated the National Silent Majority, and I organized the Wall Street rally, and I organized the motorcade in support of the president. My purpose was to show support for the boys who died in Vietnam. Most of them had been drafted. They didn't want to go there, but they had gone to serve their country. And yet, when they came back, they were treated like criminals. None of the people who were involved with me were actually pro-war. We were just supporting the boys who had gone to fight.

The first thing I did was go to New York City from Brooklyn, which is where I lived then, and I rented a hotel room in the Park Sheraton and I held a press conference. I asked all those people who supported the president and our boys dying in Vietnam to join me in a major rally. I asked them to contact me, and all the papers printed my phone number.

I got an absolutely unbelievable response. Avis Rent-A-Car, for instance, when they heard I was having a motorcade, donated ten convertible cars: three red, four blue, and three white. And the man who'd been the keeper of the George Washington Bridge for years donated the largest American flag at that time, which had flown over the bridge for about ten years. Different groups, like the Knights of Columbus, the American Legion, and this group and that group, political groups, hard hats, all got involved. The response just kept escalating every day.

It was interesting. Almost more foreign-born people got involved than American groups: Cubans, Byelorussians, people from Afghanistan, Lithuanians, people who would never normally demonstrate or picket showed up, for whatever reasons. Maybe it was because they came from foreign countries where they were oppressed, and they couldn't believe the freedoms in this country. I'd been born in Cuba myself, and my parents came over with me after Castro took over.

I used to get in a lot of arguments when kids were burning the American flag, because I thought they had no right to do that. The flag represents all of us; whether we agree with what our country's doing or not, it's still, you know, our country, and we're still Americans first.

In the beginning, the police said to me, "We're not going to give you any permits, because you only have five thousand people." But in a short time I was able to say to them, "Look at the response I've got," and in about three days I got a personal appointment to meet the police commissioner and the deputy commissioner in charge of traffic and everybody else. And they said, "We're going to close the streets and do this and that, because now we figure that you might have close to a quarter of a million people."

On the day of the rally, the *Daily News* estimated four hundred thousand, and the *Times* estimated between two hundred fifty and three hundred thousand. It was all just spontaneous, and it grew so fast. I couldn't believe it. I think I spent like fifteen hundred dollars from my own pocket to make up the flyers and leaflets and that sort of thing. It was just on my own, with some people who felt the way I did who helped me.

Unfortunately, things had built up to the point where there was frustration, and a lot of people were hurt in the demonstration. But there was nothing premeditated or planned, you know. Both sides just reacted spontaneously. I remember one of the incidents where the rally passed Pace College, and the kids and students were chanting and, you know, cursing at the hard hats. And then there was a rock-throwing incident, and things went back and forth, and a few hard hats and a few students were hurt.

Everything happened very fast during the rally. There was one instance where I saved one of the kids. He was delivering coffee, and he just happened to have long hair and a beard, and when everything started to get rough, the hard hats grabbed him and started to beat him up. This kid was just a delivery boy. He really had nothing to do with anything. He happened to be in the wrong place at the wrong time. I got out of the car with a couple of the other organizers, and tried to calm everybody down before it turned into a riot, and eventually they backed off. Quite a few people got hurt in the course of the day. There was just too much strong feeling in the air. . . .

I had mixed feelings about the war, myself. But those boys who went over there to fight were fighting for us, whether the war was right or wrong, and they didn't have the choice, and I felt we should support them.

Philip Berrigan

D *uring the Sixties, the Berrigan brothers, Philip and Daniel, both priests, became a symbol of Catholic resistance to the war in Vietnam. They participated in a number of demonstrations and actions, culminating in the burning of draft records in Catonsville, Maryland. After their conviction, they both served several years in prison. Philip Berrigan, the younger of the two, has been called the "Gary Cooper of the peace movement." Tall, handsome, and rugged, he played semipro baseball and fought in some of the fiercest battles of World War II before becoming a priest. He is now married to Elizabeth McAlister, a former nun in the Order of the Sacred Heart (page 152). They have three children and live in Jonah House, a small religious commune in Baltimore, working in the inner city and participating frequently in antinuclear actions. They take turns on indictable offenses, so that one of them will always be available to be with their children.*

My instinct is, if a person hotly objects to what his or her government is doing, then it's necessary to take a position against it—to resist. You have to say *no*. After that, the only question you have to put to yourself is: Is your action responsible? Is it just? Is it decent? Is it effective? For the ramifications of your action are going to have an impact on other lives.

I learned early that the obedience required of me by my church arose from the needs of the institutional church, which were not necessarily the needs of the poor or blacks or war victims. The church is a bureaucracy, and like other bureaucracies, it's interested in its own survival. It's the old business of Caesar and God.

I first ran into this when I made a speech before the chamber of commerce at a luncheon in downtown Newburgh in 1966. I was teaching at a school for our order there, and I had been very concerned about the war, and I made the point that the war in Vietnam was a racist war, and that we wouldn't conduct such a war in New Zealand or Denmark against white people. I also pointed out that a third of our combat soldiers were black, and that the casualties among black troops were disproportionate. I had all the statistics, because I'd done my homework. The chamber of commerce took it all right. There was a pretty heavy question period that lasted about an hour-and-a-half, and I thought that was an end of it.

But I went back to the school, and *whambo*, things started to pop. Very soon after that, the archdiocese had me transferred to a black neighborhood in Baltimore, where I guess they thought I'd be out of the way and wouldn't be able to cause any trouble. I was told, "Under no circumstances are you to address the war. This is not your work. Your work is for the evangelization of souls." I heeded that for a while, but I was learning something about the politics of not only the state, but the church.

From that point on, I never told my superiors beforehand what I was going to do if I was going to object to the war or to racial discrimination or to do a nonviolent action. I'd inform them after the thing was done, when they weren't able to do much about it. On the way to the action I'd always post a letter to the cardinal or whoever was in charge, and explain what I was doing and why.

By this time I'd gone to a number of antiwar demonstrations, and it was clear that they hadn't had any effect at all. I was morally outraged by the escalation in Vietnam. I was ashamed that we would be doing something like this, because I had believed in the history books, and I expected better of our country. Here we were, a superpower, you know, chewing up an agrarian society—a bunch of peasants in black pajamas.

And then you'd see the young soldiers in uniform in bus stations and train stations and airports when you traveled along, and you knew that they were being used and that it was wrong. Some of them questioned the war and didn't want to be sent to Vietnam. They had sense enough to say, "No, this isn't right. And if I go along, I'm liable to come home in a tin box." And others were gung-ho for the war. They were all victims. They were eighteen, nineteen years old, babes in the woods.

There were several people in Baltimore who felt the same as I did, and we pondered long and hard. We felt that something more was being asked of us. We'd followed civil disobedience, and the war still continued. It was really fierce by '67 and '68. So we decided on stronger action.

The records of the Selective Service board in Baltimore had all been gathered together in the Customs House, because they knew feeling was running high against conscription. They thought they would be safer if they were consolidated in this one mammoth room, instead of being in the little communities around Baltimore, spread about.

We watched the Customs House over a period of time, and we found out what time the guards were carrying guns and when they left, and how we could get into the building. Our plan was that we would hide in the building in, say, a restroom, and after the place was cleaned up by the cleaning woman at night, we would make our way to this room where the records were, and we'd wipe them out. We'd do as much damage to the files as we could.

We took this idea to a noted civil rights lawyer down in Alexandria, who had done some work on draft cases and who we knew would be sympathetic. We laid out the plan, and said, "This is what we have in mind." Well, he threw up his hands and said, "My God, don't do that. That's very, very serious, destroying records." Then he said, "Why don't you get yourself some paint or blood or something like that, and pour it over the records?" And this appealed to us.

We caught on the word *blood*, you see, because this was a *symbol*. There was a religious aspect to it, in that the blood of Christ has been shed again, since people were doing this to people. You know, "Whatever you do unto the least of my brothers and sisters, you do unto me." And there was the bloodshed in Indochina, which we were so aware of. So we decided on blood, and this was one case where we got good advice from a secular figure. It was the right thing to do, we felt, both in a practical and a symbolic way.

We knew that we might end up in a federal penitentiary, but we felt we ought to be doing more against the war, and we weren't particularly put off by the idea of going to jail. Some of the people who were with me had been jailed before in the civil rights movement, and that was nothing new to them. But I'd never been jailed prior to this time.

We wanted the action to be meaningful and we wanted people to see it being done, so we went in the daytime to the Customs House, and began talking to the head receptionist. We had some blood that we'd got at a delicatessen, duck blood. I said to the head receptionist that I'd like to talk with some of the people who had the draft card records, and she asked me what district I came from, and I told her. And she sent a message and told us to wait, and we sat down.

Finally, one of us gave a signal, and we went through a little gate into the draft hall proper, and immediately began opening the drawers and pouring blood on the 1-A files. We had studied it so well before that we knew exactly where the 1-A files were. There was one man in our group, he was a United Church of Christ minister, and he changed his mind at the last minute. He said, "No, I will not pour blood. I'll be with you and I'll support you, but I will not pour blood. I'll hand out New Testaments." He had a tough time. A couple of the draft board clerks, when he handed them the New Testaments, they threw them back, and one of the testaments hit him in the head. It was kind of humiliating for him.

I was grabbed from behind by one of the clerks, and I stopped at that point, and so did the others. We didn't resist them. They called the FBI, and the FBI came and surveyed the mess. There was blood all over the place. Then the press burst in on the scene. It had been beautifully coordinated so that the press arrived at exactly the right time, and got these key photographs, which went all over in the newspapers and on TV.

The FBI were disgusted. Many of the agents were Roman Catholics, and I was in a Roman collar and so was one of the others in our group, and I think that shocked them. They took us to court almost immediately and we went before the judge and we were put in jail and fasted for a week. It wasn't so difficult, fasting, because it was only a week. We took liquids: juice and sometimes a little milk. We had a clean place to stay, and they were very decent to us. So it wasn't burdensome at all. And after a week, we were let out.

A few months later, we were brought to trial. Eventually we were found guilty and while we were awaiting sentencing in that case, I spoke many times at demonstrations and meetings against the war. I was also planning with several others, including my brother, to take part in another action.

We finally settled on the draft board in Catonsville. It was one of those isolated draft boards that had not yet gone into a Customs House for protection. There were nine of us, and we looked the place over very, very carefully, and made our plans. We had used blood in the previous action, because we felt it was a simple symbol: War is a bloody business. Usually, you can't kill a person unless you shed their blood, and we wanted people to know that even with technology and push-button warfare and airplanes, blood comes out of people when they're killed. But blood is just not understood in this society. It was counterproductive, because it put people off.

We considered a lot of other possibilities, and finally we came up with the idea of burning the draft records with napalm. One of the other people in the group was an ex-GI, and he had a Special Forces handbook with a little section in it on how the Special Forces people out in the bush make their own homemade napalm. So we thought to ourselves, "Well, we'll try that next time."

By May we knew how to make it, and we had the floor plan of the Catonsville draft board, and we had nine people, including several priests, and we went to Catonsville.

The night before, we got some gasoline and the other ingredients, and we mixed up well over a gallon of it. We were thinking of the significance of this, because we were taking napalm, knowing what it did to human beings, and we were using it to destroy some of the machinery of the war. It seemed to us to be highly significant, and this was a symbol that caught on.

The next day at high noon, we went into the Catonsville draft board and found the whole staff there: four clerks, all of them women. They put up quite a struggle, especially the head clerk. She kept saying, "Don't you take my files!" She was clinging to them. Her name was Mrs. Murphy, and she was a Roman Catholic. I was wearing my clerical collar, and I think she was pretty well shaken by the whole thing.

We tried not to lay hands on the women at all, just to interpose ourselves between them and the files. The only time we touched them was when one of the clerks was attempting to call out on the telephone. There was a little scuffle, but they didn't manage to call out while we were there.

We took out about three hundred of the files from the 1-A drawers, and we dumped them into those wire mesh baskets that you buy for picking up leaves, and we carried the baskets outside and burned them in the parking lot. By this time we had the press there, and it went pretty much around the world, including television. I had a feeling while it was going on that this was serious stuff, and that we might get hung by the thumbs over this. But there was also a feeling of exhilaration that we had been able to make a statement against the war, and we were all extremely grateful that no one had been hurt. We gathered around the bonfire afterward holding hands and praying the Our Father together. It was a great moment.

Then we were taken to jail, and although the judge gave bail for most of the others, he refused to set any bail on one of the other men and myself, because we were awaiting sentencing still in the Customs House raid. So I was in jail for seven months in Towson, Maryland. It was a little box of a jail, with about two hundred prisoners there, and you were locked up all day. They only let you out for meals.

While we were on trial, there was a great deal of attention in the press and on television and among various activist groups, and there were debates, I know, on whether it was right to take such strong action against the war. We never denied the charges against us, of course, and eventually we were found guilty. When the jury had left the room, the judge told us that he, too, was disturbed by the war, and he wished it would be over, and he worried about his grandson who might have to fight in it. But he said we were guilty of what we were charged with, and people had to obey the law.

I was given six years, and by this time I had also been sentenced to three-and-a-half years for the Customs House raid. The two sentences were to run concurrently. I was sent to a federal prison near Lewisburg, Pennsylvania. There were draft resisters there and several Catholic workers that I got to know well, and there was a good deal of sympathy among the prisoners. There was a chance to do a lot of praying and a lot of reading. People from outside kept sending me good books. But frankly, I found jail a little boring, if you know what I mean. I mean, you live at a very high tempo when you're resisting the war, and you work very hard, and there was great activity all the time, with the planning and the carrying out of the action, and all of that slows down in prison.

Liz [Elizabeth McAlister] and some other nuns who were active in the peace movement had come down to the trial many times, and it was a great support to see them sitting there and to know they were praying for us. And as time went on, I saw more and more of her. Finally, we realized that we were, as the jargon goes, *in love*. Of course, we understood the ramifications of making any public announcement, because I was on the point of going into jail. I was just out on bond, while our case was reviewed by the Supreme Court. I knew that I was living on borrowed time, and I wasn't going to subject her to eviction from her order by announcing that we were married and leaving her to face people alone. So we were married by our own consent, with private vows, but there was no public announcement made.

My brother and certain close friends knew, but outside of that, nobody. When I was released from federal prison, Liz and I made the public announcement, got a marriage license, and were officially married at her mother's house in New Jersey. We tried to explain what had happened, but there was severe resentment in some quarters that we had handled it this way, and I can understand why there would be.

I used to think that celibacy was useful. The church has a tradition of celibacy, and I used to think that it could free people to be servants of God and of what was right. Great good *can* come of celibacy, but it has to be freely chosen.

After I met Liz, I did some reading on the history of celibacy, and found that it was only enforced from about the eleventh or twelfth century. So it's strictly a church regulation, and yet it dominates all the morality of the church. It's not in the Bible or the gospel. I still consider myself a Roman Catholic and a priest, and I'm quite sure that eventually the church will change on the matter of celibacy. But there's a lot of bureaucracy, and the church moves slowly, and I don't know that it will happen in my lifetime.

While I was in prison, we used to talk about how Christians ought to live, and we came up with the idea of a community, a circle of friends who share work and sustenance. After we announced our marriage, and had a couple of days for a short honeymoon up in Massachusetts, we went back to New York City, filled up the car with Liz's clothes and books and headed for Baltimore, where we started this house, Jonah House, with four friends.

We share everything in common here, and have a joint bank account among all of us. We have a financial meeting every month, and try to be accountable for every bit of money that's spent. Most of our money is earned by working in the community. We do a lot of house painting, and we also do roof work and masonry and carpentry work. And we've gotten pretty good at it. Altogether, we have six adults and three children, and there are four more adults who are away in prison now for various peace actions.

. . . Activism has been pretty much central to my life for many years, you know, but now I have to be different, because there are other considerations to take into account. I have to be kind of calculating for the sake of our children. Since Elizabeth and I were married, we have to think of the effects of our actions on our family. I'm responsible for our three children, you see, while Elizabeth is in jail, so I can't get into trouble. As a matter of fact, I'm pretty well denied any civil disobedience, except of the most minor sort, since she's in prison. And that's a hard pill. Sometimes it drives me slightly up the wall.

We both feel very strongly that we must disarm, that with thermonuclear weapons around, we have to disarm, because we're going to destroy ourselves if we don't. It's as simple as that. It's a weapon that God never gave us permission to make, and it's a lethal instrument against the human race. But the American people don't understand this, and consequently it has to be explained. And that's why we take part in these various actions against the nuclear establishment.

Liz is in jail now for one of these actions. On Thanksgiving Day, 1983, she and a group of women went to Griffiss Air Force Base outside of Rye, New York, and seriously damaged several aircraft engines, a B-52 bomber that was being adapted to launch Cruise missiles, and also a Cruise missile, a first-strike weapon. That's what she's in prison for now. The object was to carry out the mandate of Isaiah, to beat your swords into plowshares.

People sometimes ask, "Why are you doing these things, and what makes you do it?" And I say, "God is using our eyes and our hands and our voices, and we're kind of like material in the hands of the potter." We're doing it, but God is a silent and very powerful partner.

Elizabeth McAlister

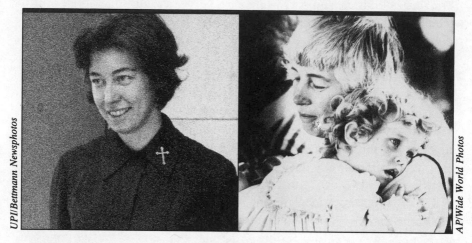

UPI/Bettmann Newsphotos

AP/Wide World Photos

A *former nun, she left her order at the time her marriage to Philip Berrigan (page 144) became public. She was interviewed in federal prison in Alderson, West Virginia, where she was serving a three-year sentence for damaging missiles and aircraft at Griffiss Air Force Base during an antinuclear action.*

When I entered the Sacred Heart of Mary as a novice in 1959, my mother was a little sad, because no home visiting was allowed. But one of her friends said to her, "Well, look at it this way, there's one of your children that you never have to worry about." In her later years, this was something Mom would bring up over and over again, perhaps a bit ruefully, and then she'd say, "There really were a few years there, weren't there, when I had nothing to worry about?"

There was something about the quality of life as a member of the religious community that was very appealing to me. There was a professional dedication in the women. There was a lot of silence and a lot of scripture and a lot of studying. The rest of the world was outside of the wall while I was a novitiate. The only newspapers I saw were the ones we put down on the floor after washing it, and we only saw TV once in the whole time I was there. That was for President Kennedy's inauguration. All in all, that period was a very happy time for me.

And in 1961, after I had completed my novitiate, I was sent to finish college, then on to graduate school to get a master's in art history, and then immediately to Marymount to replace a teacher who had left.

When I went back as a teacher, I was given a little assignment of caring for the bulletin boards in the college, in addition to my teaching duties. I used to cut out things from magazines and newspapers and put them on the bulletin board. Vietnam was in the news at that point. And I began reading this stuff as I put it up, and that's where the last years began to gel. I could not accept our growing presence in Vietnam. There just seemed to be no justification for our occupying that country. Something wasn't right. I began to question the whole domino theory, the irrationality of our fear of Communism. Nothing dramatic happened in my own life—I wasn't a participant, and it had nothing to do with me—but my views were changing.

We began having teach-ins on the college campus, and I remember being part of those and meeting other faculty members who were also committed in this direction. I began going to antiwar meetings with some of them in New York City, candlelight vigils, and fasts down in Washington Square. By 1966, I was going to a regular series of demonstrations and marches in New York City, and some of these were beyond the close religious framework. All kinds of groups would be involved.

We felt very strongly, the other sisters and I, that we were needed there. They used to put the nuns in habits on the outside of the marchers to take the heckling from the sidelines. I remember some of the hard hats, the construction workers, tossing things at the line of marchers and saying very, very hateful words. That's the framework in which they had been trained. It was important not to respond in kind—to just absorb the violence.

At first marching in a group was rather terrifying to me because of the very weird outfits some of the marchers were wearing, and you'd see some of their banners and hear some of this very, very heavy talk. It was not what you'd hear in the convent. But you're marching with them and they're sharing their water bottles and their lunches with you, and they're so happy to see you there. And you realize they're very, very decent people under their appearance.

I talked to a lot of groups, and I went to a lot of marches, and at some point I remember going to a meeting where the subject matter was, How do we move from dissent to resistance? And I thought to myself, What's the difference? [*Chuckles.*] I really didn't know what they were talking about. I felt about as committed as I could be at that point, as stretched as I could be. So mostly I just listened. It seemed to me that a young man who had a draft card could burn his draft card, but what could I do?

About this time I met Philip Berrigan. He would come around periodically to talk to us, or to meet with groups of us, and I saw quite a bit of him at that time. My feelings about him at the time were that he was a very remarkable human being, and I felt very deeply for his mind and his spirit. And then suddenly I heard about his action at the Customs House in Baltimore. I was out doing some work in preparation for a general chapter meeting of our order, and I heard on the car radio about these people in Baltimore who had poured blood on draft cards. And the tone of voice with which the announcer talked about it was a total dismissal—these crazies, he implied. Without even knowing who was involved, I began wondering why people would do that. Then I made the connection with draft-card burning, and it seemed to me that it was the same sort of thing.

When I got back to the convent, I found out from one of the other nuns that Philip had been involved, and several of us in the convent sent him a telegram in support. When the case came to pretrial hearings, there was a small group of us who went down from New York to the trial. We stayed with various Catholic workers or at houses of friends while we were in Baltimore. The trial became an occasion for me to communicate to others who were still disapproving the action or feeling that it was too violent, and I found my niche as a communicator. I felt I could help to popularize this action and explain it to people, and I began doing that to the extent that I was able. I spoke at quite a number of places in support, to explain the Customs House action, and it seemed I was effective. Now I had to think about it, and it seemed to me that it probably was something I wanted to be doing. Finally I took part in two actions against draft boards in Delaware. When we got the cards the first time, we tried to use bleach on them, and ended up burning them. These draft board actions were tremendously effective in cutting down on draftable people and quotas. We planned them very carefully.

By that time, people had gotten pretty good. We'd go in at night or on a weekend, destroy the draft cards, records, and then surface later and assume responsibility. We'd get other people to assume responsibility with us, and at one point we had two hundred fifty people who assumed responsibility for draft actions. There were no prosecutions because they didn't have the kind of hard evidence that they needed.

It's hard for the government to act when there are that many people who say they're responsible.

All this time I was seeing more and more of Philip and the relationship changed radically. In 1969, it was clear to us that we had made a commitment to one another. But he was looking down the road to six years in prison for his involvement in the Baltimore and Catonsville actions. And although the relationship was there and it was very important to us, we didn't have time to pursue it.

After Phil was released from prison, we were officially married. Prior to that, I went through a process of getting a dispensation from my vows. I would like to have seen the religious community of which I was a part include both married and unmarried people, but that wasn't the case. And I had to accept that. We went to Baltimore and began living at Jonah House, together with some other committed antiwar activists.

We have three children now—Frida, twelve; Jerry, eleven; and Kate, five—and it's been very important to us that they be in touch with the real world in which they are living. We'd all better be able to look evil in the face, or we won't be able to survive. So we're trying to help our children look at reality. It won't help them to deny it, to act like it's not there, but we want to provide them with tools for dealing with it, namely, laughter and community and joy and sharing.

Just before my action at the Griffiss air base, Phil and I sat down and talked with our two older children about why I was doing what I was going to do, about the pain and the responsibility that would be put on them, as well as on me, when I completed the action. They accepted that. They have been informed all along about the nuclear situation, and how close it is to us all. And their hope is that people who resist will make a difference, and that people can try to live together in a way that makes these weapons unnecessary. Katie is younger, and we have to explain things to her in a very limited way. She's trying to understand.

Phil brings them to see me every month, and I write to them nearly every day. They are part of my life even though I'm not with them.

You know, this place looks like a nice college campus, but it's still prison. It's a very authoritarian structure, and it's quite different from what I'm used to living in. It takes a real adjustment. There's a mix of people here, and you learn the pain that people live with. You see a lot of loneliness and a lot of anger and a lot of hatred, and that's pretty startling at times. There are outbursts, and the constant noise gets to you after a while. That's very hard for me.

But I know why I'm here. I've chosen to act, and I've accepted that as a result of that I'm in prison. But no one's keeping me here. My mind is free.

The
Generation
Gap

Nancy Gorrell

Barbara Beirne

*D*ifferences over the war drove a wedge through many families during the Vietnam years as young people questioned the official government policies supported by their parents. Nancy Gorrell, now a high-school teacher, remembers how it began for her.

Let me tell you what it was like going to high school as a girl in the early Sixties. I started in 1960 and I finished in 1964, and all that time it was as if we were encased in plastic. Girls were expected to wear stockings—not panty hose, but stockings—and girdles with garters that made holes in your legs. We wore stiff petticoats and brassieres that pushed you up and out in a very unnatural way. And we used to tease our hair and then spray it, and when we walked out in the morning on the way to school, it looked as if we were surrounded by plastic. Everything was artificial.

And then in 1964, I graduated from high school, and in September I started at the University of Wisconsin and it was as if I had stepped onto another planet. Everything was so free and loose there. In one month I had thrown away my stockings, thrown away my girdle, never to be worn again. I didn't burn my bra, because I needed it, but I wore a different kind of bra, and instead of those stiff petticoats and skirts, I wore jeans everywhere. I let my hair grow the way it naturally wanted to. It was as if I had become another person. I felt as though I was myself for the first time.

That was a very exciting time on campus. There were a million different political groups. The student union was a real center of dissemination of information. You couldn't walk to class without seeing all these little tables with pamphlets and somebody trying to proselytize you. "Here's what's going on in Vietnam!" "Read this pamphlet." "Come to this meeting." There were rightist groups, leftist groups, SDS, SNCC—each one wanted you for a reason: voter registration or whatever the cause was. You couldn't walk into the student union, you couldn't walk to classes without hearing something.

Suddenly from this little enclave of nothing in high school, in one month the whole world opened up. I flew on a plane and I went a million miles from home. I started to hear about Vietnam, and I'd never even heard of that country.

The graduate students and the professors at the university took leadership roles. I don't think I would have got so involved in the antiwar effort if I hadn't felt that there were people who were very educated and knowledgeable talking about this.

It was just one eye-opener after another. I went to all these teach-ins, and it was a very intense educational experience: to find out that your government is lying about everything, that there's no democracy in any real sense, and that in Vietnam we'd tortured and killed and assassinated.

When I went home for fall break, it was a riot. Not only did I look awful from my parents' point of view, but I started talking to my parents about what was happening in the world, about Vietnam and et cetera. And in two minutes we got into a raging argument.

My father said, "My God, I sent you out there, and within two months you're a Communist!" Which was ridiculous. I wasn't a Communist, although there *were* Communists at the university seeking my allegiance at that time.

I had violent arguments with my parents every time I went home that year. They were really disgusted with me, and they had no sympathy whatsoever. They thought I'd become a dupe of Communist propaganda. I really became estranged from my parents at that time. After a while, my father and I couldn't even talk. It was an eye-opening time, and not only for the kids.

Craig McNamara

*D*riving northeast along the highway from San Francisco, one passes oil refineries, military installations, dry brown hills: a dual aridity of civilization and nature. Yet a few miles off the highway is a little Eden, a green valley of walnut groves and wildflowers, luxuriant in the California sunshine. Craig McNamara lives here with his wife Julie and one-year-old son Graham in a rambling old farmhouse, shaded by a huge gray pine. Every morning he is up at 6:30 to do the work of his walnut farm: fertilizing, cultivating, harvesting, shelling, all in season. Slim, soft-spoken, thoughtful, he looks like a gentler version of his father, former Secretary of Defense Robert McNamara.

After we moved to Washington in 1961, my father was very busy, naturally, as secretary of defense, but he'd always been a hard worker. As a matter of fact, when I started farming, I remember talking to him one day and telling him, "I'm spending long days getting started at five-thirty or six, and not getting in until about the same time in the evening." And he said, "Well, that's nothing new. That's what I've been doing for the last forty years."

I'd have breakfast with him before school, and he'd come home in the evening anywhere from seven-thirty to nine, or something like that. He'd go around the house and adjust the paintings on the walls, and the photographs, because they were a little out of line. Sometimes I could tell how frustrated he was by the look in his eyes or the nervous hand movements.

As early as I can remember, he always focused on having family vacations together, and those were the real times when he would be there with us. But sometimes when I look back at those times, I'm not sure how accessible he was. I mean he was there, but they were such fully structured occasions that I wonder if there was really any time to sit down and chat. Days would be filled with skiing, and the nights, usually dinner all together and then to bed or on to another activity. There wasn't a lot of leisure for just sitting around and chatting or letting loose. I think that was built into our life and built into our relationship.

When I was thirteen, I went away to boarding school, Saint Paul's School in New Hampshire, and it was there that I first became aware of Vietnam. One of the students had brought a speaker to the school to talk about Vietnam, in opposition to the war. It was a kind of seminar, and I think there was a movie afterward or a slide show. These were my good friends who were putting this on, and I remember rebelling against their view initially, and saying, "This can't be right."

I went into a phone booth and called my father and said, "Dad, can you provide me with some information? Some written documentation of what we, as the United States, are doing in Vietnam?" He sent me some literature and flyers, but it was shortly after that that everything tumbled. It didn't make sense, what we were doing there in Vietnam. The more I read, and the more I explored it, the more I began to realize that we were in tremendous error there. There was no question in my mind. From then on, I was in opposition to the war.

When I first went to Stanford, they assigned me a roommate, and I guess they'd done it on a computer, comparing our backgrounds and so forth. I don't know how they did it, but they connected me with another fellow from the East, who had gone to another private prep school and was an ROTC enlistee. I suppose they thought, "Oh, great, here's the son of the secretary of defense, and here's this other fellow, a good military type." That's why we were put together.

I made my position clear that I was against the war, but I couldn't help but think what people at Stanford thought about me. You know, my father was known as the architect of the Vietnam War, and I knew what they thought about my father, which was basically that he should be tried and judged and found guilty and hanged. The fact that he was my father became a constant issue. I felt my actions had to be clear and defined, and that I had to state my opposition to the war clearly and strongly. I often had to defend myself as a separate person, admit his guilt, and attempt to let it go at that—let my actions speak for themselves.

You know, things were so split in the Sixties. You were either for the war or against it, and I was definitely against it. My father knew where I stood, but we didn't discuss it. I wish we had. Maybe he wishes we had, too, but that was not within the nature of our relationship. It was never brought out into the open between us. It just wasn't possible for us during those years to talk about the issues of the war. He could talk with other people about deeper things, but with me it was always, "Oh, wasn't that a great hike we had today?" and, you know, the happier things in life. I wasn't able to engage him on issues that were important to me, and yet, all through this I respected him as a person. I made a distinction between my father as a public figure and my father as a father. We just couldn't communicate on a deeper level.

Not long after I got to Stanford, I began taking part in antiwar demonstrations. One that I remember very clearly was where the group was going to put Richard Nixon on trial. It didn't take the verdict very long to come in. He was found guilty, of course, and what ensued after the verdict of guilty was that everyone took off down the street in a rampage that ended up being quite devastating: shops broken into, windows bashed. There must have been a good fifteen or sixteen thousand people there, and I have vivid memories of police cars racing up and down the streets at high velocities in all directions, scattering people, people being beaten, ourselves being cornered and running in the streets with the crowd. I remember initially shouting, "Don't break the windows! Don't break the windows!" thinking it was just something that the establishment was going to pin us with and say, "Oh, you have no responsibility."

But then I remember the rage setting in on me, and the frustration that we all felt because we couldn't stop the war. And I joined in on the breaking of the windows. What was in my mind, and what was in the mind of most of the people in that demonstration, was rage, pure rage at the war going on and on and on. No one seemed to be interested in having a dialogue with us at the time, so we had no outlet except rage.

After that I participated in a major event at the San Francisco airport. A group of students had got together to read a list of the California men who had been killed in Vietnam. We just stood in one of the main terminal buildings on a marble floor, with thirty-foot ceilings above and all the traffic of people going back and forth. It became very clear to us immediately that we were antagonizing a lot of people by doing that, because we were receiving unbelievable threats. It was amazing to realize how threatening one person reading a list of the war dead in Vietnam could be to other people. And it was a *tremendous* list. It was just thousands and thousands of men and women. Each of us would read for two or three hours at a time, and then the next person would take over.

I remember a variety of men coming up to me at various times during those hours, men maybe in their mid-fifties saying, "You son of a bitch!" or "We're going to kick your knees in!" or "You haven't been there. What do you know?" There were very, very hostile expressions, and I remember just taking a deep breath and keeping on reading and feeling sad, tremendously sad that this was where we all were. . . .

I think that is the feeling that we probably all share now about Vietnam: what sadness, what tremendous sadness . . . Last summer when we visited friends in New York, I went to see the memorial dedicated to the Vietnam dead, and I was very moved by it. The translucent stone and the segments of letters from the soldiers and people speaking—it's a softer, more profound view of Vietnam, and it made me weep. I just couldn't stop. I felt again that tremendous sadness that I'd felt in the airport in San Francisco back in the Sixties. . . .

My father must have known that I was involved in the airport readings, because there was an article about it with a photograph in *Newsweek* magazine, but we never discussed it. That was just another symptom of our whole communication barrier.

When I went to Stanford, I had refused to take out a student deferment, because that seemed to me to be just co-opting into the system. The tuition was at that time three thousand dollars a year, and if you were lucky enough to be a student you'd get a deferment. People my age who were poor didn't get student deferments, and it didn't seem fair to me. So I didn't apply for a student deferment, and I quickly got my 1-A in the mail. I was supposed to take a physical, and I went to San Jose to take the bus to the Oakland induction center because that's where the physicals were being given.

I'll tell you, if there are any days in my life that I remember, that is one. The feeling of gloom, frustration, and just out-and-out doom. There weren't just Stanford people on the bus. There were people from Menlo Park and all around San Jose, black and white, Chicano and

Asian, every race. When we went into the induction center, we were basically denuded, physically and mentally. It was, for me, a horrible time, like being an animal caught behind wire. That was the fear that I felt.

Then I had to decide what to do. You know, I'd heard other people's stories. They were always talking about how you get a 4-F. Are you going to claim you're homosexual? Have you been on drugs? Are you going to claim you're an idiot? Have you deprived yourself or deranged yourself in preparation for today?

Well, I hadn't done any of that, but the fact was that, through high school and college, I'd had a raging ulcer—due, I'm sure, in no little way to my relationship to Vietnam, my closeness to it at home and my struggle with it in my own personal life. And the anticipation of being inducted just increased this ulcer tremendously. Finally I got to the last booth at the medical and there was a shrink there—you know, with a beard. He seemed like a pretty responsible and caring sort of person, and I talked with him, and told him about this ulcer, and he said, "Well, to me you seem 1-A." I felt betrayed, because here was this man trying to appear sympathetic, but playing both sides of the fence.

However, it turned out my medical records showed that the ulcer had gotten to the point where it needed operating upon. It had to be controlled. And I received a 4-F permanent classification after that. . . . Strange times, when you feel lucky to have an ulcer.

People did all sorts of things: starved themselves so they'd be underweight, anything. I had a friend who had claimed he was a homosexual drug user, and later on, after the war was over, he started a winery in New York State. And when it came time for the FBI investigation of his alcohol license, he had a hell of a time. It came back to haunt him. It wasn't fair, what we had to go through, but on a scale of fairness, it's nothing compared to what we did in Vietnam. You shudder to think of it. And when you think of the guys that had to go to Vietnam . . . I don't believe in guilt, but there are times when there's a feeling of guilt that I didn't go to Vietnam. It's just one other burden the war put on us. None of it was fair.

All this time I felt, in a way, that I should be taking a leadership role in the antiwar movement. Perhaps I was trying to combat or stand up to the legend of my father. But I wasn't able to do it. I just couldn't get up in front of a group and talk. I didn't have the figures. I didn't have the facts. I just knew that we were right, and that the war was wrong.

I was tremendously alienated. I felt gutted, as if I had no center. It was at that point that I decided to leave the country to get some perspective, to try to find my inner self. I realize that I was lucky to have the freedom of choice to leave and to explore and to find my center. I mean, my God, I was lucky to have an ulcer. I'm still struck by it.

In addition, there was a part of me that wanted to get my hands in the soil. I was very attracted to the simpler side of life, which to me was represented in an agrarian society. And so I left for South America.

Two friends and I went on motorcycles down to Texas with our shoulder-length hair and ponytails and leather pants. Nobody stopped us. We just kept going until we got into Mexico, and started the long journey to the south. When we got to Bogotá, my two friends decided they'd gone far enough. They were going to stay, and I was on my own. I decided to send my motorcycle home. To me it represented imperialism. I set out, myself, into the unknown, and traveled for the next few months on trucks, buses, trains, hitchhiking.

It was just a wonderful experience—of colors, of flowers, of language, of people, being part of humanity. People were very friendly. Simple people or educated people, they all seemed so open, so warm. I remember in Ecuador once, in a little village, I was looking through the window of an adobe house, and there was a weaver weaving ponchos, and he said, "Come on in," in his language. Then as dusk came on, he said, "If you'd like to come up to where my parents live on the mountain in the hills, you could spend the night with us." We went up through golden-thatched cornfields of incredible beauty, found their little, very simple, humble home, and I had dinner there and slept on corn husks and talked and talked with them. That happened all the time.

I remember long discussions with all these people. They were so interested in the United States. And answering their questions allowed me to realize the good in this country that I had been estranged from. In an amazing way, traveling through the incredible beauty of Peru and Ecuador and Bolivia and Chile just increased my appreciation of everything. I realized how beautiful they were, but I also realized how beautiful our country was. It was a remarkable journey through life, and it brought me to an understanding so that I could begin to look at my own country, slowly.

While I was in Santiago, my father came down to a big United Nations conference on trade. He was head of the World Bank at that time. I was staying probably a mile away from where he was, but we didn't see each other. I think it was probably a decision on both our parts, that we were in different worlds and those worlds couldn't seem to come together at that time. It seems bizarre to me now, but it was probably best then for us not to see each other. In any case, neither of us made the move.

I wanted to work in Chile, but I realized after a couple of months that if I took a laborer's job, I'd be taking a job away from someone who needed it, and that if I volunteered to work for no pay, which I was willing to do, that took work away from people who needed it, too. So I decided to keep on going south, down to where the road ends. At that point, there is a tiny little island a kilometer or so out in the ocean, a beautiful island with a latitude sort of like Seattle and a pleasant climate. I went out there and began walking around the island. I passed a family who were bringing in their hay crop, scything it and putting it on wooden sleds for oxen to pull to the barn. I was looking at that, and the woman of the farm saw me and asked me if I wanted to help cut the hay. I ended up staying nine days with them.

It was one of the most beautiful places I've ever been in—an old house that they had made themselves. We'd work all day, and at night we'd have a big stew, like a chowder, with milk and shellfish and potatoes, cooked in a big cast-iron pot over an open fire in the kitchen. We'd sit around the table and talk about their lives and my life, and I'd practice my Spanish and play with the kids. I can see to this day the room where I slept. It had a beautiful high ceiling and a wooden bed and an enamel washbasin to wash in. It was very important for me, being there. I felt I'd journeyed a long way to get there, and that it had been worth the journey. . . .

I stayed with them until they got their harvest in, and then I went on. Got on a boat that was going to Easter Island—it's just about the most remote spot in the world, I think. It's twenty-three hundred miles off the coast of Chile, and there's another eighteen hundred miles to Tahiti, and a long way up to Hawaii. So it's far away from everything: remote and beautiful. I ended up staying there for a year and a half.

An island family took me in, and since it's customary there for everyone to address women who are of the age of, let's say, fifty or so as Mama, I called the mother of that family Mama. It must have been hard on my folks at home, when in my letters I'd refer to the woman of the house as Mama. I was so far from them. I was isolated from my family, and I was calling another woman Mama.

I felt incredibly at home, more than at home. I felt almost like a new person, because they gave me an Easter Island name: Toukoihu. Tou-koihu is a legendary figure who made the statues that are carved out of stone, so it was quite a compliment to be called Toukoihu. After a while, very few people knew I had another name. I had a new name, a new family, and a totally new society.

Then I found work to do. There was a little agriculture on the island, some sheep and a small herd of cows, maybe three or four cows. Nobody was milking them. So I thought, "Well, why don't we milk the cows?" The island population was importing milk from Chile at that time, so why not build up the dairy herd, and the island would have its own milk? I thought we could do it on a cooperative basis, rotating the work. Families could come and milk, and then receive milk free for the next week.

We built up the herd to twenty-five cows. Of course, I had to learn how to milk a cow. I'd never learned that before.

But what happened was that the island society wasn't really interested in a cooperative milk venture. What they really wanted to do was buy the milk. They wanted me to milk the cows and sell the milk. It was frustrating for me, because I wasn't there to make a business or a profit. I was there as sort of a one-man Peace Corps, but instead it turned into a moderately lucrative business for me.

At first the island seemed almost mystical to me, so remote from modern life, so peaceful. The statues were there, of course—those strange statues—and it seemed to me that the islanders had such a different perspective of life. They were so accepting of everything. If it rained, they'd just say, "Oh, it's raining. Isn't that funny how it's raining." And to me this was a very satisfying way of living. My ulcer healed up during this period, and I lived at peace with nature and with the people around me.

But, you know, once you're into a society, things change, and you understand more of what's going on. And that's what happened on Easter Island. I began to see the more material side of their nature. I'd come from a tremendously materialistic society, and they wanted what we had. We'd gone to the moon. We had telephones in every room, we had TVs and new cars and all of that, and how could I deny these Easter Islanders any of these same things? It became no longer possible to romanticize Easter Island. And so what happened was that my love affair with the island became a more realistic relationship.

I ended up buying a ticket home with some of the thousand dollars or so I'd made from the dairy, and I came back through Chile. When

I got to the United States, I remember trying to get back to my family—I hadn't seen them in two years. I was going north from Miami. My bike was in bad shape and overloaded, and it was late at night, and a rain set in. I stopped at a gas station and asked the attendant if I could just sleep on the seat there until the rain got a little better, and he said, "Oh, all right." A few minutes later, I woke up to hear the owner saying to me, "Buddy, you get the hell out of here with your long hair and all of that." I hadn't heard that for a long time. I was back in my own country.

My mother had been ill, and I spent some time with my family. Then I thought about what I should do next. I'd always wanted to be a farmer and to sort of combine farming with cooperative living. So I went down to Mexico to look at some of the old cooperative farms down there. But the farms there were not doing well, so I decided to come back to the United States and get a degree in farming and then see what I could do. I got a B.S. at the University of California at Davis, and went to work for a wonderful Chinese farmer in California, who had a large farming operation. After a while I became his partner in a fresh vegetable market, and I worked at that for four years.

Then I bought this walnut farm together with my father. We're partners now, and obviously I'm not doing cooperative farming. This is a private operation. Although my goal in the beginning was to grow fresh vegetables for low-income people and to get a quality product to grocery stores in poor areas, what I'm producing is a luxury crop: walnuts. I have two employees who help me, and although we do work and toil here, it's very mechanized. We have three different machines just to harvest the trees. It's a little different from what I planned, but it's important to me to be close to the soil, and this is an environment in which Julie and I can look forward to raising our children.

It's been a long journey getting here, but I feel that each step I took along the way had to be taken, hard as it was at certain points. I'm farming, and I'm close to the soil, and I'm happy with what I am doing. I'm involved in the antinuclear issue too, and although they're separate activities, they're equally important to me.

One of the things that's made me happiest is my father's involvement with the antinuclear effort. I saw him on a television show the other night explaining in such a logical way that the nuclear arms race must stop, and I was just so *proud of him*. It's funny, you know, to compare the recognition factor in the name McNamara in the Sixties with what it is in the Eighties. Back then I had to constantly defend myself or differentiate myself and my beliefs from my father. And now, you know, people know the name McNamara, but they know it for disarmament. It's quite a change. Hearing him on that television show, all I could think of was past experiences, when what he was saying was so disheartening, so awful. It was a great feeling to be agreeing after so many years of disagreeing.

I'm a very different person from my father. Not better, not worse, but different. And yet, there are ways in which we are so alike: the way we walk, certain hand gestures, our voices. . . . And sometimes I come in at night and start straightening the pictures on the wall just the way he used to. I guess we both like square corners.

Four Women

Lynn Ferrin

In the early Sixties she moved to San Francisco and settled in the Haight-Ashbury district, which became a mecca for the counterculture. She works as a writer for a small travel magazine in California.

I guess I could be an example of somebody who, because of the Sixties, got to do what I wanted to do. I was raised in the Fifties, in an atmosphere in which my mother had to do what my father wanted. She was the corporate wife. She had to live where he wanted. She had to entertain people she didn't know and didn't particularly like. She was not her own person. She was "Mrs. Him."

I'd hear quite a bit from my mother about these poor women who were schoolteachers and not married. That was living death. It was funny, because I admired those women very much, certainly more than the housewives around me. I wanted to talk about books and ideas, and the teachers were the ones who were talking about that.

We lived very strict lives. We were watched. I was beginning to go through sexual awakening, and my mother was afraid I was going to go all the way with my boyfriend in high school. There was all this guilt around that. So I didn't. And I wasn't really encouraged to develop my writing. I was in my room crying all the time, and my mother constantly told me, "How can you be so unhappy? Look, these are the best years of your life!" That was a big lie. Those were the *worst* years of my life, because I had no freedom.

Even in college, women had a curfew. You had to keep it. You were punished if you didn't. It was enforced by the dean of women and the house mothers who were hired by the school to maintain moral order and also by fellow students. Everybody bought into it. I was a virgin until I was twenty-one. The week I graduated from college, I lost my virginity. That was a statement: "Okay, I'm free now. I can do whatever I want."

I always pictured myself with a career, although that was not the standard among women my age at the time. All the women in college were looking for husbands. Usually in their senior year, they'd meet someone and then be married right upon graduation or that summer. I graduated in 1959, and I wasn't engaged. I really wanted to pursue a career.

I arrived in California just as the Sixties were beginning. I went to Stanford and got a master's in journalism. I got in trouble my first day, because I wore slacks. I went marching into the library in white slacks—after all, I was in California—and people stared at me. Later somebody told me that women students weren't allowed to dress like this. Women had to wear skirts on campus. I worked really hard, so I had my master's in nine months. I wanted to get out of there.

When I first tried to get a job in San Francisco, they made all women take typing and shorthand tests. Even if you went to work for a company as a professional, they made you do it anyway. You had to submit to this stuff. I found a job opening when I got out of school: working for a magazine, writing about travel. I had always loved to travel, and I was fortunate enough to have a job traveling and writing about it. I loved being able to roam at will.

During my childhood and teenage years, I wasn't allowed to go camping, except in a couple of very organized groups. But here in California, I began to discover the pleasures of backpacking: that I could carry a pack on my back and wander through the wilderness alone.

That was in a period when the ecology movement was also starting. It turned out that I could experience this beautiful country and share it with people in my stories. That seemed important to me because I felt that too much of the energy was going into legal battles and hard-core fighting, and not enough going into trying to make the general public aware of what they had. So that was my mission: writing about the things I loved.

What I found I loved to write about most were the wild lands of California and the West, so I would do stories on the national parks and how to experience them. As part of that I would spend time in the front country, hiking nature trails and going to campfire talks and so on, and then take off with a backpack and wander in the back country and camp out alone.

I found that when I was out in the field, when I'd go interview, for example, the superintendent of a national park, people would be a little surprised that the reporter was a woman, and that I'd say, "Well, I brought my backpack. I'm going out for a few days on the trail." I just had a feeling that they were *impressed*.

And I was impressed with myself. I was real proud that I learned those kinds of skills that had seemed to me to be male skills. I learned rock-climbing skills: belaying and rapelling and how to place pitons. I learned how to put up a tent. I learned cross-country skiing. That was amazing to me, that I could actually do this. Here I was, going out alone on skis with a pack on my back, camping in a snowfield somewhere, building a snow cave and sleeping in it. I was just living the most magic life, beyond my wildest dreams as a child.

It took me years to have my own expense account. In the beginning I would have to put my travel on one of the men's accounts, and then he would reimburse me, because the accounting department couldn't handle a woman traveling on an expense account. It sounds amazing now, but it was true. They wouldn't give me business cards because women in the company didn't have them, which infuriated me because quite often I was asked for my business card when I was out on assignment.

Because of my job description, the company had to keep raising my salary. I remember the payroll department being outraged because I was being paid more than other women in the company. To them, what I was doing had no bearing on it—just the fact that I was female and making too much money. I remember the payroll clerk saying to my boss, "Don't you think you're paying that little girl too much?" It took many years for me to battle through all that.

In the early Sixties people were not open about their sex lives. You even lied to your roommates about what you were doing. Nobody was a virgin, but nobody admitted it. I remember when I'd spend the night with a boyfriend, I'd either try to get back that night so my roommate wouldn't know what I was doing, or I'd just lie to her: "Well, I stayed at Barry's house, but I slept on his couch." But little by little that began to change.

There was always the fear that you could get pregnant, and then you would have to "pay" for it. Since abortion wasn't legal, there was that possibility. It happened all the time, and I saw many lives ruined. Women had to have their children and give them up for adoption or marry someone they didn't love. The idea of the single mother hadn't begun at all. Of course, when the Pill came out, that fear lessened. But there was still that moral thing going on—you weren't married and you were asking for the Pill! You would look for "friendly" doctors.

I started taking the Pill, and I was allergic to it. I began to hemorrhage, my tongue and lips were all swollen—classic allergy reaction. So I was terrified, and the doctor said I had to be put in the hospital. And the whole way I was handled was as a single woman who had been taking the Pill. I was disapproved of. I was bleeding a lot, growing very weak. The doctor said, "Frankly, we don't know what to do. We've never had a case like this." I said to him, "Well, I hope you don't just do things to try them, especially if they're expensive, because I don't have a lot of money." Already I was worrying about the hospital bill. And he said, "My dear, you have expensive hobbies."

I was among the women in that whole vanguard of sexual freedom who were very excited by being free women. For me it was like, "God, this is wild. You can have lovers. You don't have to be married. You can have different men, and experience different men's lovemaking." It seemed really avant-garde and exciting; we were in the front lines. In my circles, you wouldn't think of getting married, settling down with one person. The suburbs and the station wagon full of Cub Scouts became something you didn't want anything to do with.

Here you were enjoying your sexual freedom, but the moral order was still against it. You would still never think of telling your parents what you were doing. You wouldn't let people at your workplace know what you were doing. And only the really far-out people were living with the opposite sex. At that time, that was really radical. That was tearing families apart, when daughters would move in with a man. The mothers would break down, the fathers would want to kill the guy. That was something I would never do in that period of my life, move in with a man. That was something I didn't think my family could handle. If I did that, my mother would check into a hospital.

And then around that time, Helen Gurley Brown's book came out, *Sex and the Single Girl*. It seems like a silly, frivolous book today, but it had this message that "it's okay." The whole spirit of the book was, "Wow! You're single. You're free. You can do whatever you want. Have a good time." The book was excerpted in newspapers and magazines everywhere and was a big, hot bestseller. I still feel that book helped change public attitude toward single women enjoying their sexual freedom. And the book wasn't just about sex. It was also about having your own career, having your own place to live, having your own money and doing with it what you wanted.

I lived in the Haight-Ashbury in those years. I moved there in 1965. I just happened to like the neighborhood. It was very pretty, near Golden Gate Park, on the edge of the black ghetto, and you could get apartments fairly cheaply. The hippie thing hadn't really quite started then.

The Haight-Ashbury was full of these beautiful old Victorian buildings, and people would rent flats that had a lot of rooms. There would be mattresses on the floor, and it became the thing for people to come and go, wander in to meet friends, and they would accept you into their crash pad. And communes would develop. And the neighborhood began to attract great numbers of people who were on the road.

I remember the first time I smoked pot was in the really early Sixties. A friend of mine said he knew where he could get some. It wasn't easy to get then. It was still very much contraband. You had to go down to the black ghetto, and he knew someone who had a contact. He showed up at our place and he had three joints in a little matchbox.

My roommate and I were terrified we'd be caught, but we were so excited. We pushed bureaus up against the front door and hung bedspreads over the windows and smoked those joints and got high. I had just hysterical giggles, and my roommate went into a deep depressed funk, and the young man was very horny and interested in both of us. Neither of us was interested at all.

Of course, after that, marijuana was everywhere. People were raising it in their houses and quite openly smoking it. You could just smell it in the air. I learned very early on that I didn't like the effects it had on me. That first time I giggled a lot, but mostly it made me depressed, and I didn't sleep well. So I really didn't smoke much pot at all.

I was a weekend hippie. I always had a job. Here I was in a very conservative job, dressing up every day to go to work, putting on stockings and so on. And then on weekends, you could wear long dresses and go barefoot. Everybody strung their own beads out of everything they could find: abalone shell, buttons, juniper berries, eucalyptus seeds. And people would paint their faces a lot, as if they were dressing for tribal rituals. We went around with flowers in our hair, acting like children. They called us flower children. I found it just wonderful. You could do anything you wanted, wear anything you wanted.

I remember one typical wedding of the Sixties. My best friend was a man, and he was going to marry the woman he'd been living with for a long time. He wanted me to be best man, because I was his best friend. They had planned to go home to Oregon to be married, but both families declared war on this situation. They said, "You absolutely cannot have a female best man. It is not done in this town." And that issue made them see that they didn't want to be married at home in a traditional ceremony with their parents trying to run it. So they decided to be married here.

We all went out to Golden Gate Park. The woman had her best friend as attendant, the man had me as his best man, and the minister was a professor of theology at San Francisco State University. The women wore long ethnic dresses and the men wore embroidered Mexican shirts. The couple had spent a day looking through the park to find a beautiful place, and they found a tree they loved in a meadow. They wrote their own ceremony and memorized it and said their vows directly to each other, so they weren't repeating after the preacher. They just faced each other, held hands, recited the ceremony, and then said the prayer of Saint Francis for peace and love and hope.

Then we all went to their house for the reception. Most of the people were Haight-Ashbury dwellers who didn't have much money. The wedding gifts were things like a basket of strawberries, a tray of fresh mushrooms. One guy gave them a poem, which he read. And those were the wedding gifts. Every one of them came from the heart, and all of them were symbols of the good things in life, as we had begun to see them. No appliances. No silverware. But the biggest, most beautiful strawberries you'd ever seen. I thought it was a wonderful wedding of the Sixties. However, the marriage didn't last. It was also a *marriage* of the Sixties.

There was a part of Golden Gate Park called the Panhandle. It was just a block wide, but it was this beautiful area of grassy lawns and fine old trees that stretched for maybe ten blocks. During the summer that they called the Summer of Love, people would gather in the Panhandle and in the big meadows in the park and listen to music. Almost every

Saturday and Sunday afternoon the big rock bands would play there. You could hear Jefferson Airplane or Janis Joplin, free. We'd prepare these wild picnics, spread out a blanket, wear flowers and long dresses we'd made ourselves, and listen to the music all afternoon.

There was a paper called the *Berkeley Barb*, which had wonderful essays and antiestablishment writing and movie reviews and poetry. In those days, it was *the* newspaper for the alternatives. In fact, it was fun to sell the *Berkeley Barb* on Haight Street. I'd go buy a stack of *Barb*s and then walk along the street selling them. Then on the way home, I'd just give the money to the interesting people asking for spare change. That would make an interesting morning for me. It was my entertainment.

Then the following year, it started to get ugly. Word got out in the world. Tour buses would come through, and there were all these Midwestern tourists pressed to the windows, looking at the hippies. People were heading here from everywhere on earth. So it became overcrowded. A lot of people were literally beggars, living in crash pads, getting weird diseases. You could see lost kids in rags, hungry and barefoot and hollow-eyed. I wasn't happy walking down Haight Street anymore. People were on hard drugs, being really freaked out, ODing on stuff. And of course crime came along with that. My apartment was robbed.

In 1970 I moved from the Haight-Ashbury. I'd outgrown the neighborhood. I bought a little old house, built in 1910, in Noe Valley, where I live today. That was where all the hippies moved, and the house was very cheap when I bought it. It was rare then for single women to buy houses. I sort of met with doubt and derision. Realtors said, "Oh, what are you, a little schoolteacher, buying a little house? Why would a single woman want a house? You'll just get married, and you'll want a bigger place, so why even bother?"

Well, I've never married. I didn't feel I needed it. I never loved anybody I wanted to marry, and I never wanted to marry anyone I loved. I felt that the permanency of bonding with another person seemed to come through friends. For people who are never married, your friendship group becomes your family, although your sexual partners come and go. Sometimes *they* become part of the friendship group later. Compared to a woman who has been married all her life, I feel that my sexual life has been a lot more intense and interesting. There were a lot of men of different kinds: surfers, rock climbers, authors.

Those men have changed my life, opened up exciting things to me. . . . Even at forty-seven, I have a pretty active sex life. For one thing, old lovers keep coming back. If you get enough of those, you can stay busy for a long time.

Annie Popkin

*M*any of the radical and activist groups of the Sixties observed traditional sex roles for men and women that might seem surprisingly
old-fashioned by today's standards. All too often, women made
the coffee and stuffed the envelopes, while men made the decisions and led
the marches. Annie Popkin was among the women who were active in
changing this and making the women's movement itself a cause. She now
teaches women's studies at a state university in California.

From maybe five years old on, when I blew out my birthday candles,
I would wish for justice and brotherhood and peace and those kinds
of things. I was kind of unhappy as a teenager, and I think at a certain
point I just said, "If I'm not going to be happy, at least I'm going to
change the world." That was how I was making peace with my suffering:
by making things better for other people.

Civil rights was the first issue that gripped me. I remember being
very moved and horrified by the pictures in *Life* magazine of white
people putting cigarette butts out on people in sit-ins in Woolworth's
in the South. I went on a picket line around Woolworth's in Freeport,
Long Island, to support the sit-ins. I worked with CORE in New York.
Freshman year at Radcliffe, I worked with black teenagers in a settlement house in Roxbury in Boston. I went on the 1963 March on Wash-

ington, and the next summer I went south to Mississippi and worked with black voter registration.

I was in SDS at Harvard and in the antiwar movement, but I always felt like a number. We had chants like, "Hey, hey, hey, LBJ, how many kids did you kill today?" but not the same kind of moving spirit of togetherness as the civil rights movement had. And there was sexism. I was definitely second-class—a sort of "Movement chick." Personally I never did mimeographing or brought anyone coffee, but I didn't feel valued. I never talked at meetings, I didn't feel my ideas were sought out.

The men did most of the talking. All these Harvard guys would argue facts and statistics about Vietnam: how many numbers of our forces were being sent over, how much ammunition. I don't even know if they were actually convincing anyone, but they sure liked to argue a lot.

I could never remember the facts and figures, and I hated to argue. If I thought I had a good idea, I would show people and talk about it. If some of them didn't respond, I wasn't going to try to hammer it into them. I'm not a person who likes to argue. It's not my personal political strategy. But at the time, I thought there must be something wrong with me, because isn't that what you're supposed to do if you want to change the world?

I remember about two years before the women's movement started, 1965 or '66, this friend of mine said, "You know, you'll never be a radical as long as you don't see how the system affects *you*. You always think it affects other people." And I sort of agreed with him, but I didn't get it, surely not as a *woman*, because we didn't have that category yet. It still seemed worse to be poor and lynched and all the other things, so I didn't quite understand.

I just wasn't ready yet. Sometime in '67 or '68 this friend said, "You know, these women are getting together to talk about what it's like to be a woman in the Movement. Don't you think you'd want to join them?" "Oh, I don't know," I said. I didn't think I was oppressed or had any reason to want to join.

Then three months later, by the middle of '68, I was helping to form the women's movement. Everything started to come into place.

My silence in political meetings, which I had attributed to some personality fault, I could now see as part of a system, in which men are at the center. We're not encouraged to talk. It explained so much. And it was marvelous—the relief of being able to talk about it and see it *wasn't just you*. It was the system.

I remember so many times in the first few months we would make comments to ourselves about how exciting it was to be a woman with just other women. . . . We really all wanted to talk and listen to each other. There was something about all of us being equal and not having to be in the background. It was just so *liberating*. I was excited, too, by the places we dared to go and the things we dared to raise and question. The women's movement was definitely an idea whose time had come. And it just took off.

We started forming a group in Cambridge that would become Bread and Roses, one of the earliest women's liberation groups. At first we called ourselves "a radical women's liberation organization." We didn't yet call ourselves feminists. We had to do some reclaiming work on that term, because feminists were people like spinsters, like Susan B. Anthony and those weird people who were related to that century. And we called ourselves revolutionaries, because it was still the Sixties and we thought the revolution was around the corner.

All of us in the founding forty were from SDS or civil rights or some kind of activism. So in the beginning a lot of what we criticized was how we were treated in the Movement: the contradiction of preaching egalitarian politics in a movement that was not egalitarian. We talked about not being valued as theoreticians or spokespeople, and in many places doing all the shitwork. So our Movement brothers may have gotten a disproportionate amount of anger in the beginning, because we expected more of them than we did of American society.

The men were charging us with dividing the Movement. Weren't the Vietnamese and the blacks and everybody else more important than we were? And why did we want to weaken the Movement by bringing up our issues, which weren't that important anyway? I remember a friend said, "Do you honestly think the issues you're raising are as important as poverty in the South among blacks?" And I was so glad to have an answer to that: "It's not a question of who's worse off. We don't believe in a hierarchy of oppression."

We purposely had our meetings on Friday nights at Bread and Roses— the night you're supposed to go out on a date—to counter what women were supposed to be doing on a weekend. And we had small groups— collectives or consciousness-raising groups. The collectives would be five to fifteen people, and we would talk about everything, from what it was like to walk down the street in front of a construction site to the sex roles you learn from your mother and father. We'd have a topic that would go around the room, and everyone shared her personal experience, and from that we made some generalization about society and about how to make changes. And we tried to figure out a strategy to change *everything*.

We talked about everyday life. We talked about institutions. We had a media show and billboards critiquing the Rolling Stones and their sexism. We criticized the Weathermen for having "pseudo-bravado"— trying to point out the confrontational politics of the male sex role. There was nothing too big or too small to issue a manifesto around.

It was a time, also, when we were doing zap actions, like guerrilla theater. One collective had an ogle-in in front of a boutique in Harvard Square. They ogled men, instead of the men doing the ogling. Little gangs of women made comments like, "Hey, look at those balls," to counter the usual way of doing things.

We did an action on a radio station that called women "chicks." They ran an advertisement for a secretary, and it said, "If you're a chick and can type, we need you." We were very offended. A group of us went to a place that sold baby chicks and got a basket of baby chicks and stormed the station saying, "These are chicks. We are women. There's a difference." And we said, "Besides, if you had a job opening for a janitor, would you say, 'If you're black, we need you for custodian'?"

We had no personal relationships that didn't get touched by sexual politics. There was Ann Koedt's *Myth of the Vaginal Orgasm*. We passed around dog-eared copies like crazy. Women stayed up all night reading it to themselves and to their boyfriends. We didn't want to carry our politics in a suitcase and then come home and live something different. We had our politics all the time.

It helped me break up my long-term relationship at the time. Not that my collective encouraged me to break up with him, but I expected more and wanted more. It was harder sometimes to make the change within an existing relationship rather than start anew. It wasn't as much over a particular issue that we separated as the fact that he couldn't really see my point of view. He was not that crazy about the women's movement.

We often half-jokingly talked about kind of "training" men, both sexually and emotionally, for the next woman who would come along. So they would know how to be emotionally present, they'd know where her clitoris was, things like that. We felt very altruistic for the women who came after us. Especially when you got frustrated, and it wasn't working for you, you'd say, "Well, at least the next woman will have a lot better try at this." . . .

In a year and a half, I think over five hundred women came to Bread and Roses. It existed such a short time for all the things that came out of it. We started women's health collectives—the whole idea of women working to provide services for other women in nonsexist, safe, and supportive environments. The ideas for battered women's shelters and rape crisis centers also had their origin in that time. And the health book *Our Bodies, Ourselves* started with women in Bread and Roses. That's a lasting legacy.

It's exciting to be in the forefront of a movement, to make a movement happen. You don't get that chance often in your life. And it's funny. Until the women's movement came along, I was going to help *other* people have better lives. Well, I'm glad that changed, that I could make it better for myself, too.

Kay Anderson

A *suburban housewife in her late thirties, she is the mother of two active young sons. She also teaches part-time in a nursery school and serves as a PTA officer, Fresh Air Fund chairman, and den mother for the Cub Scouts.*

I was raised Catholic, and I remember all of the Catholics being very proud that we had a Catholic president. His Inauguration Day was a snowy day in January, and I was out shoveling snow and building snowmen. My mother called us to come in and watch the inauguration on television. I remember the clothes very well. I remember Kennedy had a top hat on, and his wife had a pillbox. Mrs. Kennedy looked so sophisticated. I thought to myself, "My dress is going to be like that someday."

I didn't go to Catholic schools but my next door neighbor did, and from the time he was a freshman I can remember admiring the boys from Xavier Military Academy in their blue uniforms, with the buttons and the hats. They had to salute everything, full military style. I just thought they were gorgeous.

By my junior year in high school, I was dating one of the neighbor's friends, and I was invited to go to the Xavier military ball with a senior. At the military ball, you march under an arch of crossed swords. I was just looking forward to it as an incredible opportunity. It was to be at a hotel in New York City!

I went out with my mother for three or four trips before I found the perfect dress. It was very sophisticated. It had a black velvet bodice, very plain, and satin off-white on the bottom. I thought it looked like Jackie Kennedy's kind of style, you know: simple but glamorous. [*Chuckles*] All the style was in the fabric, not in any detail or anything like that, just very simple. I loved it and I'd been looking forward to the dance for a long, long time.

Finally, the big day came. I went to school with a note saying, "Please dismiss my daughter at noontime, because she has to get her hair done." Oh, it was so exciting. I got out of school early and went home on the bus. My mother was working at the time. I had just taken a shower when my mother called me. She said, "Are you sure they're having the dance? Have you heard the news?" I said, "What news?" And she said, "The president's been shot." I said, "The president of what? Xavier? They can't call this dance off." My mother said, "President *Kennedy*. Just calm down. We'll have to make a few phone calls and find out if things are still going according to plan."

As it turned out, I was lucky, because the school didn't cancel the dance. They'd already made all the commitments, hired the band, and everything. The Hotel Commodore probably wasn't going to give them refunds or anything, so they went ahead. It was done very nicely. As a Catholic prep school would, they stopped and said prayers that felt like they were going on forever. But then we marched through our arch of swords, and they presented the class officers with their honors, and we got on with the dance and all the rest of it.

Some of the people, especially the instructors, seemed rather saddened, and there were some girls who seemed pretty tearful. But I was too self-centered to get teary-eyed. It was my night, and I wasn't going to let anything ruin it. The only drawback to the whole evening was that all the places where we'd planned to go after the prom were closed down. But luckily one girl's mother had thought of this and had told her she was allowed to have as many friends back to the house afterward as she wanted. So we had a big breakfast party at a private home.

My parents were house hunting that weekend, and I remember we were in somebody else's house that we were looking at, when suddenly the murderer was shot on TV—Oswald. And everyone just stopped where they were and looked at the television. And they showed it over and over. I was kind of amazed that one would follow the other. Things seemed to be happening so fast. Later on we got more used to the assassinations—Martin Luther King and Bobby Kennedy, you know. But that was the first.

By the time the Vietnam War was on I was going to college at San Diego State. I was still very apolitical, but I melted into whatever group I happened to be with. There were a lot of people at the college who were wearing beads and whatever, and if I was going with them, I'd put on some beads and be a flower child. I'd go to a concert that Joan Baez was giving about boycotting some Navy ship, and then the next weekend I'd go to a Marine Corps officers club.

San Diego was an interesting place to be at that time. There were a lot of Navy and Marine officers in San Diego because of the war in Vietnam, and there was a lot of social life revolving around them. It was like Saint Xavier Academy all over again. I mean, at San Diego State drugs were kind of big, but if you went to the Marine recruit depot to meet your dates, it was guys who were out of school and had a respectable salary, wanted to see the town and do nice things and go to nice places. So it was a different class of date than your fellow student, who didn't have any money, and whose idea was to sit around somebody's apartment smoking pot or something.

I dated a lot of Marines, and I was writing to a lot of them in Vietnam at the time—four, at least, quite seriously. I remember there was one guy who spent a week with me right before he went overseas. He was a Marine officer, and I wrote to him all the time he was over there. We agreed that we would talk about anything but the war. He'd write about his buddies, and I'd write about the weather or what was going on at college and that sort of stuff. We just didn't write about war things. It was kind of an unstated agreement, you know. I didn't want to hear details of threatening kinds of happenstances.

I had a wonderful time during those years. As I said, there's something about a uniform. . . . I liked the idea of dating those officers, but when it got down to the point of really marrying somebody, and thinking of moving every two years, and him being on a ship for eight months at a time, I'd say to myself, "I don't think I can live like that." What I really wanted was a veteran who was out.

I met my husband on a blind date in New Jersey, and on the first day we discussed our different backgrounds. And I heard that he'd been in the Navy, and even had been in San Diego when I was, although I hadn't met him. By the time I met him, he had a job as an executive with an insurance company, and he was commuting on the Erie Lackawanna with a little briefcase. I used to say, "Someday my knight in shining armor is going to come along on a big white horse." And I thought, The Erie Lackawanna is close enough, and the shining armor is a three-piece suit.

. . . I'm still apolitical. My husband and I don't agree on voting issues or anything like that, but we just kind of agree not to discuss it. I'm not knowledgeable enough to discuss serious political issues anyhow. And rather than open my mouth and put in my two cents, when I could be putting my foot in my mouth, I'd rather just not discuss it at all. I stick more to the social side.

Marilyn Laurie

*B*ack in the Sixties, she was one of the small group of environmental activists who launched the first Earth Day, coordinating a hundred details from her kitchen table in Manhattan. Today, she is vice president in charge of public relations for AT&T. Her large office overlooks the rolling wooded grounds of the corporate headquarters in New Jersey. Despite appearances, there is a cause-and-effect relationship between her two roles.

I had watched the early Sixties go by with great sympathy. But I had two kids who were consuming my time, and maybe that was why it took me a while to get personally involved. By the time '68, '69 came around, I was starting to feel deeply guilty at not having taken part in what was so obviously a thrilling sweep of history. I couldn't bear to close out the Sixties and not have done something worthwhile. I was looking for an outlet. I was looking to make a difference. And then came this bizarre glitch.

I was in my kitchen one Saturday morning, and I was looking at *The Village Voice*. My husband had brought home a copy because he had run an ad in it for his commercial art studio. I was looking through the ads. I read his ad, and I looked through the other ads. And there was a little classified item that said, "Anyone interested in coming to an Earth Day, come to such-and-such an auditorium in Manhattan." I had no idea who placed the ad, and I had no idea of what an Earth Day would really mean, although there was some environmental sentiment certainly building in me.

Perhaps because I had small children, I was personally distressed by the air pollution within the city. The threat of smog and air pollution at that time was really frightening. Remember all those stories about the "Killer Smogs"—the invisible enemy that was spewing something into the air that was poisoning your lungs? These were in the back of my mind, but I hadn't done anything about them. I just came in off the wall. I was looking for something to help with, and I found a cause. Or the cause found me.

It seemed to me that here was something starting up fresh that maybe I could make an impression on, because I would be on the front end of it. So I said to my husband, "Look, this meeting is this afternoon. I'm going to go. Stay with the kids. I'm going to go."

What happened was an absolutely incredible exercise in how things really work, which I didn't know anything about at the time. The auditorium was crowded with people. There were at least four hundred, maybe more—total chaos. A lot of young people. And you know, in the Sixties everything was undisciplined, so there was certainly no order in the meeting. The only thing that anyone could agree on was to meet again.

Next week I went to the second meeting. The numbers involved had dropped to less than half. Again, there was no plan, no real action, other than that we wanted to get something accomplished, and we decided to meet again. Well, the third meeting the numbers were reduced by half again, and by the fourth or fifth time that we met, there were only five of us left. I got my first lesson, and possibly one of the most important in activist politics, which is that *leadership goes to those who are willing to go the distance.*

At that point, I never would have dreamed that the five of us would have brought the city of New York to a halt a few months later. But that's what we did. The seedbed was there, of course, because the climate of the Sixties encouraged community responsiveness. You can see, looking back in history, that a very few people and a powerful idea can change society. And we had the advantage of knowing that we were right. Pollution was a bad thing. There was no equivocating. We were the good guys, and we knew it.

The five of us began to organize for a consciousness-raising event, built around this plan of an Earth Day, and one of the linchpins of the plan was that we were going to have no traffic on Fifth Avenue on that day. That was to be our symbol.

It's not so strange now, when parts of New York are routinely closed and turned over to the people for various festivals and celebrations. But that concept just did not exist at the time—that people would take over the streets, and that the automobiles could be stopped. It turned out to be a very difficult feat to accomplish. We had many battles with the Fifth Avenue Merchants Association. I remember at one time the head of the association screamed into the telephone at me, "Streets are for cars, and sidewalks are for people!"

Then we had companies who felt we were going to bomb and sabotage them, because in those days that was the kind of terms that people thought of when they thought of demonstrations. The store owners were terribly worried about people breaking windows and beating up on cars, and all the violence that was associated with the activities of the antiwar movement. We spent days and days and weeks and weeks meeting with businesses to try to calm their fears. We kept saying, "Hey, hey, we're just nice guys."

We had problems with the blue-collar workers, too, when we started talking about the stench coming out of the smokestacks. I remember one blue-collar worker saying, "That stench smells like bacon and eggs to me," which symbolized the argument. They were afraid we were going to try to close down some of the companies that were creating the pollution. We were also accused of being elitist. There were bumper stickers around saying that we were interested in protecting trees, not people. We did a lot of soul searching. But we knew that we were right.

While all this was going on, we were putting out brochures and doing fund raising and attempting to get people alert to the long-term implications of environmental problems. I was the one who was assigned to handling all the public relations because I'd done a little advertising copywriting before. Someone had to do it, and they seemed to feel I was the one who could take a stab at it.

The most surprising point for me was when we decided to call a press conference to announce Earth Day. I had never called a press conference for anything before, but it seemed to me that the way to get the press to come was to have some celebrities there. Earth Day didn't mean anything at that point, but celebrities did. So we called some show business people and some politicians and some folk singers, and we let the press know that they were invited. And we just hoped that somebody would come.

On the day of the press conference, *everybody* that we asked came. We had Pete Seeger, we had representatives from the mayor, all the networks came, *Life* magazine came, *Time* magazine came, the newspapers came. We were totally overwhelmed, and we suddenly realized that we'd made it. Now we were on the tail of the comet, and we were being swept along with this event.

The movement was just exploding around us. Mayor Lindsay came down on our side very quickly. He recognized that this was a better thing to be in front of than to be either behind or against, and he responded accordingly. Ours was really a positive movement, and one could say, in a sense, a conservative movement. We wanted clean air and a clean environment. So it caught on and swelled, and most people perceived it as nonthreatening.

By the time the great day came along, we shut the city down. We had a quarter of a million people in Union Square, and I can remember standing on a platform there with universes of people in every direction. On my left was Paul Newman, and on my right was John Lindsay—a pair of very blue eyes on either side of me. I remember thinking it was probably the most glamorous moment I would ever experience. It was a great coming together, a soaring celebration. In those days, you didn't have that kind of congregating of people in a peaceful context very often.

Afterward, of course, we were faced with the problem: Where do we go from here? In the year after Earth Day, I worked on the Mayor's Council on the Environment, and we were trying to focus attention on recycling. Remember, we were at the height of a throwaway society then. There were even paper dresses that had a short period of popularity. Recycling was the key to so many of the problems: to air pollution and water pollution, the defoliation of America. All of those issues could be attacked through recycling. And it turned out to be an idea that really worked. In fact, it's hard to imagine that twenty years ago there wasn't any such thing.

We introduced industry to the idea that not everything had to be made out of totally virgin material, and that it was cheaper, and that it would work—fabric, paper, glass. And now, you know, it's almost routine to get materials recycled. But then it was a radical idea.

As the anniversary of Earth Day began to roll around, *The New York Times* came to us and suggested we have a Sunday supplement in the *Times* for Earth Day's first anniversary. They asked me to work on it, and being young and naive, I thought I could do it. I got a friend of mine to help me do the writing, and we wrote a twenty-four-page environmental supplement that spanned all the issues. We had little sidebars with celebrities commenting on what they thought the environmental issues were and endorsing various actions. My husband did all the photography, and we did everything on a volunteer basis.

And we printed the whole thing on recycled paper. It was the largest recycled paper job ever printed at that time. Back then, people said that recycled paper would jam the presses. Can you imagine? And this was a wonderful demonstration that it would work.

Shortly after that, it came to the attention of AT&T that I had edited this supplement, and they asked me if I'd like to come to them and work doing environmental education for their employee organization, which at that time had over four hundred thousand members. So I worked on getting people involved all over the United States in all sorts of projects, including river reclamation, planting—and recycling.

. . . You know, we have a phrase in the telephone business called the Golden Relay. It's the ultimate mechanical device that's inexpensive and will click on forever and will never need any fixing. We're always reaching for the Golden Relay. And when you think of the problems of pollution, defoliation, energy, recycling is the solution to all of them— or at least part of the solution. It is the key solution. It may not be the Golden Relay, but it's the closest thing we've got.

The Counter-culture

Jason Zapator

*I*n the summer of '69, the Woodstock Music and Art Fair and Aquarian
Exposition drew hundreds of thousands of young people to a farm in
upstate New York to hear dozens of the top rock bands of the time. In
spite of rain, mud, and overburdened facilities, the crowd was remarkably
good-natured throughout the three days of the festival. Jason Zapator describes it as one of the most important experiences of his life. Now married
and raising three children, he works in advertising sales and spends his free
time writing and playing music. He is currently putting together an album
of original compositions.

I turned nineteen at Woodstock on Friday, August 15, 1969, and that
was a very interesting coming of age. I was into what was happening
at the time, the whole gigantic social kaleidoscope of events, ideas,
feelings, and music—everything that contributed to me going out on
Route 46 in New Jersey, sticking my thumb out, and putting a sign
around my neck that said "Woodstock."

Personally I didn't even know how to get there, but I just started
picking up rides, one right after another, like a chain reaction. I don't
think I waited more than five minutes between rides. It was like there
was an energy in the air that just kind of carried me up there. There
was a sense of community that stretched from down here all the way
up there.

Somebody picked me up in a van, and there were all kinds of strange, long-haired creatures in it, myself included. It turned into a caravan of cars and vans, and there came a point where everything came to a standstill, and everybody just parked their cars. The police were there, trying to wave people on, but the cars couldn't go anyplace, and it didn't matter. There was a camaraderie, even with the state troopers who were directing traffic, that was amazing. People were smoking marijuana and doing things like that, and the state troopers weren't batting an eye. I had never seen anything like it.

I got out of the van and started walking where I saw everybody else was going. Pretty soon I got to the gates. There were these nominal ticket booths there, and some people were buying tickets for a while, but that didn't last very long. Everybody kind of felt like we were going to get in. Finally they made an announcement that from here on it's a free concert, and everybody just went right through. There were no more barriers.

I guess you could say love was in the air. There was a lot that we put up with for those three days, because at times it was packed like sardines. The valley was filled with people just trying to get around. I mean, it took me two days to get to the bathroom. Maybe it wasn't two days, but it seemed like it. But there was a mutual feeling of wanting to have a good time, of everybody being for each other. What it was is basically I think the way anything works: Everybody agrees on it. And when we were at Woodstock, we just made up our minds that this was the way it was going to be. As long as nobody was getting hurt, and everybody was having a good time, nothing was open to question. Peace was the ideal.

Even the Hell's Angels were cool. Of course, anyplace the Hell's Angels wanted to go, they went, and they went right to the front of the stage. They had front-row seats. But they didn't do anything bad. In fact, they were almost like the police, the security forces, making sure everybody would stay cool. They appointed themselves, and nobody gave it a second thought. Nobody had to say it, because we understood that's what they were doing. Well, everybody has something in them that's good if they want to concentrate on it. It just so happened at Woodstock that everybody was aware of it. Even the Hell's Angels understood it.

I just brought me and the clothes on my back, but it didn't matter, because everything was freely shared. It didn't matter whether the thing was food or if it was smoke or if it was conversation or if it was attention, or whatever it was that humans do with each other, whatever kind of intercourse it was. There wasn't really a second thought about, "Well, I'd better hold on to this," because everybody was all there together anyway.

If you wanted to get something to eat, you'd go to the top of the hill, where there was a commune from California called the Hog Farmers, and they had all kinds of things going. Anybody that needed something to eat was welcome to eat for free. And there was a lot of free living going on. People weren't particularly uptight about wearing clothes. There were a lot of beautiful ladies there, and you got to see a lot of their beauty.

As for drug use, it wasn't a thing where all of a sudden, "Oh, now there's nobody here to stop us, we're all going to go crazy." It wasn't really like that. If somebody wanted something to smoke, it was there. If they didn't want to smoke, it didn't matter. Everybody took it in stride.

The music was another whole thing altogether. So many great bands played there—forty, fifty bands—one right after another. There were times when there was some rain, but then as soon as the weather broke, it would be going on again. It didn't matter what time of day it was. We're talking like two o'clock in the morning, five o'clock in the morning. Something was going on constantly.

The music wasn't just something that you listened to. It was something that you felt inside. It would be as though it could come out of you, out of everybody who was there. I remember the night when Melanie came out and sang that song, "Lay down, lay it all down." What is it? . . . "Let your white bird smile . . ." Something like that— a very peace-oriented song. It was beautiful. Everybody lit up candles, and the whole valley looked like a sea of stars in the dark.

I also remember when the Who came out and played, especially Peter Townshend playing guitar, because he jumps all over the place when he's playing. But what he did that day I'll never forget. It was like in the middle of a song, and he was playing and strumming really, really aggressively, and then he took the guitar and threw it up in the air. It went end over end at least twenty feet in the air, and it came back down end over end, and he caught it right in the exact position he needed to make that chord that came in at the right time. He just grabbed it *exactly right*. Not only was it a spectacular performance, but it was excellent musicianship.

And the way he was bending the neck as he was squeezing the strings, it was like he was wrenching the sound out of the guitar, and it was echoing all over the valley. Finally he put it over his head until the feedback finally died out, and then he took the guitar, and he threw it out into the audience. And some lucky guy or girl out there ended up with it. Everybody loved it.

The grand finale I was waiting for was when Jimi Hendrix came out. There were rumors, a sense of expectation that, "Okay, Hendrix is coming, Hendrix is coming." Everybody just kind of knew it. They brought him in a helicopter, and as soon as he came off and hit the stage, he just took over everything. He was wearing his turquoise shirt with all the streamers hanging from it and a headband, and he was very, very serene. And everybody just focused on him.

He was playing so fast at times, it looked as though his hand was passing through the guitar neck and going out the other side. He was playing on his back. He was playing with his teeth. He was playing upside-down. He held the guitar in the air and played with one hand. He did everything. But the way he was doing it, it was just part of his natural way of playing.

He played for a total, I think, of two-and-a-half hours. I remember I got a pair of binoculars from someone and I was looking at him, and his eyes were closed just about all the way through. It seemed like he was from another world, and it was immaterial whether his body was there or not.

When he played "The Star Spangled Banner," it was incredible. I don't know if anything quite equaled it. I mean, it was ringing and echoing all over. It was like it filled the entire valley—a bowl of sound that stretched for miles around your hearing range. It just electrified everything.

It was probably the truest rendition of that song I've ever heard, because Hendrix was using sound effects through the guitar to complement the lyrics. I mean, you definitely *heard* the bombs bursting in air, you definitely *heard* the rockets going off when he played.

At the time, of course, if you were thinking of war, you were thinking of Vietnam, so Hendrix was calling up revolutionary feelings in us. His playing was reminding everybody that "the rockets' red glare" and "the bombs bursting in air" was really the napalming of the villages. Like this was the supreme irony that the lyrics and the song were supposed to be about the defense of freedom. . . .

Of course, after Woodstock people became very radical. It was like we finally made our statement for peace and love, but now it became a thing of putting your fist in the air. The next concert up in that area, about a year later in Connecticut, was called Powder Ridge, appropriately so. A lot of the same kind of bands played there, but you didn't get the feeling it was like Woodstock. People were flying American flags upside down, and it felt like an armed camp. Everybody was ready to go to war.

I took a long journey, and I ended up going all the way out West. I was getting involved with a lot of Eastern religions—Hinduism, Buddhism. I was looking into the American Indians, their beliefs. I was looking into ancient mythologies. And I went through a period when I got into Christianity, where the only thing I looked at was the Bible. Only the Bible—everything else, forget it.

I guess I've come full circle now to the Woodstock way of thinking and conducting myself: sharing, banding together. That's really where my heart is. And I'd like to do something that will bring about a constructive way of life for others.

What I'm doing now is preparing for my final statement before I depart this scene. I earn a living like anybody else, but I've been working on my music a lot, putting it down on tape. Right now I have a drummer I'm working with regularly. I've been doing all the other parts. Like I'll lay down the bass line, and then I'll lay down the guitar line, and then I'll put down the vocals and the harmonies, and the drummer plays the drums, and we're able to build the album piece by piece.

We hope to have that wrapped up in the studio before too long. I'm going to share artistically what I've been given, as much as I can, with everybody, and hopefully I'll leave it here after I'm gone. Just like Jimi Hendrix isn't here, but his music is. That's the way to really live.

David Malcolm*

*H*e is an editorial writer for a medium-sized suburban daily news-paper.

I went to Woodstock. It was not the new millennium. It was not the new society. It was a lot of shit. It was three days in a muddy cow pasture with the toilets blocked up.

I did drugs and I smoked grass and I wore my hair a lot longer than I wear it now, but I was not a hippie by any means. I never wore beads or adopted that sort of wide-eyed naive ethic of the hippies. I was always completely turned off by this kind of Dionysian spirit of the times, you know, where they said, "Turn your mind off and let your emotions run free." I never said, "Oh, wow." Also, hippies were sloppy. I'm a very neat person.

In some ways I was more redneck than the worst rednecks. I was more hostile to the hippies than the worst pot-bellied Southern sheriff. I did not admire the generation of the Sixties very much, or anyone who was stupid enough to think that Woodstock was a blueprint for modern society. I mean, there were people who lived in a pasture for three days without toilets or food. This is not a new society. This is a bunch of people wallowing in the mud. It was sick.

I remember running into some woman, some space cadet, and she told me she was going to San Francisco. So I said, "Well, what are you going to do there?" She looked at me like I was crazy. She said, "I'm going to *live*." I thought that was ridiculous. I thought that was really stupid. I'd decided that people were on the world to do things, not to just exist. You know, we aren't just sort of flowering plants.

So we'd lie on bales of hay and listen to them play music. The music was all right. It helped. But I don't think that music has held up terribly well nowadays. I mean, if you put Janis Joplin on the record player today, it's lousy stuff. I think Jimi Hendrix is unlistenable today. Let's put it this way: I'd rather go to the Metropolitan Opera.

---

* Not his real name.

Kevin Compton

*H*e was still a student in high school when he made the trip to Woodstock. Now in public relations at AT&T, he recently took his twelve-year-old son to his first rock concert.

I remember them telling us at one point that we were then, at three or four hundred thousand, the third largest city in New York State. They got a big cheer out of that. That was the first time, I think, that we actually knew how widespread the countercultural movement was. Most of us came from rather small towns where long hair was the exception instead of the rule, fashionwise. To see that many people who looked like us—or worse—from all over the country was very striking.

I had already experienced a lot of prejudice because of that, having the greasers or jocks back at the high school or in town pick on you and try to start fights, just because you had long hair. They'd say things like, "Are you a boy or a girl?" It got to the point where, "God, can't you guys think of anything else?"

And this was not just kids, but adults in authority. I remember I got pulled over a lot of times for having my license-plate light too dim. Even my physical education teacher threatened me physically, pushed me up against a locker, and said, "You'd better get a haircut." Even if you believed in rock music and love, peace, and understanding, that many people putting you down was going to give you some doubts.

Woodstock made you think, This counterculture has taken a lot of knocks, but it really looks like it's capable of great things. Some of the artists would come on and talk about how large groups like this show that it's possible to get together and to do things without violence and without hatred.

I think there was a certain leftover glow after Woodstock, a camaraderie, although that didn't last too long. We very quickly realized that you couldn't tell whether another person thought the same as you did just by virtue of their hair or anything like that. We had plenty of occasion to find that out.

Jane DeGennaro

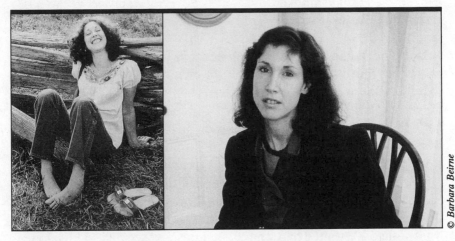

*A*fter a succession of jobs including farm caretaker, bartender, and Head Start teacher, she is now an account executive for a graphic media firm. Divorced from her second husband, she lives in Bound Brook, New Jersey, with her daughter Elissa.

After I graduated from high school in 1967, I wanted to have all the experience and pleasure and inspiration that I could possibly accumulate. I wanted to explore the new world. So I went to Ohio State University in Columbus.

There was a clash of cultures between the sororities and fraternities and the hippies and the freaks. I was being courted by the established sororities, but that didn't inspire me. I had no interest in beer and necking and humiliating initiations, like men in go-go outfits and women in togas. Right away I wanted to learn more about the freaks. During high school, I had been initiated into the drug culture—marijuana and hashish—and I wanted to see more.

Especially I wanted to see some LSD. The media were advertising it, saying things like "heightening your perception," "seeing things like you've never seen them before," "getting to the roots of religion and ritual," "playing with madness." All that was just fascinating to me. I thought, Wow! Give me some.

One day I met this guy Dan in my theater class. He was attractive, and I just sensed an affinity. We had a lot to talk about. His major area of interest in school was psychology, and mine was too. That was my minor. He had smoked pot, and we were interested in the same music and the avant-garde. And we were also interested in making love.

Dan and I had a very nice relationship, and we decided that we wanted to move in together. A bunch of students had this apartment together, and we rented a room there. And we were all exploring the universe: Carl Jung and synchronicity and anthropology and religion, be it the religion of the American Indians or the Zen Buddhists. We were looking for whatever transcended barriers, for freedom, and drugs were part of it.

The first time we did LSD, Dan told me that he had done it before. So he was going to be the guide. We had a mattress on the floor, posters on the walls, incense. We dropped the LSD—little orange barrel-shaped things—and we waited and waited, and nothing seemed to be happening. Then we just started feeling silly, which wasn't unlike us. We started chasing each other around the room, and at one point he admitted that he had never done LSD before. It was about that time that we realized that we were off.

It was so funny. We had been studying the *Tibetan Book of the Dead* and books by Alan Watts and others about Zen Buddhism, and there seemed to be a theme running through a lot of them about the death of the ego. Leary also talked about breaking out of the restrictions of your concepts of yourself into a greater self—a greater awareness that transcends the temporary, including the body, perhaps. At one level we were scared of it, and on another level we were fascinated by what, we had read in the literature, was the possibility of ego death and expansion of awareness beyond the limited ego. So we were trying to prime ourselves to go through a psychic death experience while we were tripping: "Okay, now I'm going to die. Now I'm going to know what it's like."

A friend came visiting, and she had her flute. She played for us, and it was just miraculous, just gorgeous. I cried, it moved me so much. There was so much soul in the music. It was just so touching. We ended up going out in a Volkswagen, out into the streets, driving around, and I had a strong sense of myself as a cell in a bloodstream. You know, one cell in the flow of things, zipping along. And that was our first experience. It was terrific.

There were some other great experiences on LSD trips that I just cannot forget. One day I was tripping at a party with Dan. I was in the living room, and the music "And Thus Spake Zarathustra" by Strauss was playing. Unconsciously, automatically, Dan and I and another fellow, who later became a friend of ours, came together. People were walking in and out of the room and sitting on couches and chairs, and we were *drawn*, without thought, onto the floor on the center of that room. It may have been where the acoustic vibration was the strongest, I don't know, but we just sat there in a little circle. I closed my eyes and what I saw was a spiraling tunnel. At the end of the tunnel there was an eye, and I knew, somehow, that I had the choice of whether or not I wanted to move down that tunnel. And I decided to go.

I started traveling down that tunnel, and the eye became, you know, an eye and a nose, then another eye, and a mouth and a beard, and dark hair, and laughing eyes, and it was the most magnificent man I ever saw in my whole life. I don't know who it was—I've hypothesized—but I experienced religious ecstasy. I got a communication from that man. Basically without words he said to me, "We made it. You're here. We did it. Here we are. We're together." And there was no greater goal. That was it. I was absolutely, completely, one hundred percent satisfied. If I had died right then, I wouldn't look back. Not at all. That was it. That was what life was all about. I cannot express how fulfilled I was, how absolutely, totally happy. . . .

Dan and I had an open relationship. As soon as I had got to college and counseling was a service at the health center, I decided that I might as well take advantage of it and construct my own personality. So I went to this psychologist, and when Dan and I got together, he joined me.

The psychologist seemed like a very conservative figure, but by today's standards he was radical. Dan and I expressed to him that being so young, we found ourselves attracted to other people and didn't know what to do with our sexual impulses. Both of us had a hunger for more experience, and we didn't know how to handle it. So the psychologist suggested that one option was that we have an open relationship, meaning we allow each other the freedom to explore other partners. He even gave us some literature. So we did.

And I had my first and only experience with group sex. I know there's all that kind of stuff going on today, but when it happened to me there was an innocence about it—a purity—that I think was unique to the time.

We were at a birthday party with old friends, something like fifteen people. We were doing a variety of different drugs—Quaaludes, marijuana—and all of a sudden this one woman took off her clothes, and everybody just followed suit, or unsuit. Everybody started dancing together, and then some people went to bed and some people took baths together, and they were just doing everything they always wanted to do—together. At one point there were a lot of people lying on a bed, and it was just *undulating*.

Dan was doing fine. He jumped right in. He had a good time. But at one point he got jealous. When he didn't have anybody with him, he came into the bathroom and found me with another man in the bathtub, and he wanted to drag me home by the hair. He asked me to come, and I was ready. We said goodbye to our friends, put on our clothes, and went home.

Actually I learned from that experience that I don't really like orgies as much as I do one-to-one experience. I didn't get that much satisfaction out of it. But I was hungry for experience, and I got it.

In 1968, we ended up getting married, but we didn't want to imprison each other. Our feeling was that all through time people have been *cheating* on each other. Everybody wants to do this, but why do they have to *lie* about it? We should be able to be honest with one another, and not destroy what we have by sharing ourselves with other people as well.

But it was difficult for us to accept. It was an adjustment every time you knew the other person was with somebody, and little by little we started getting more and more discreet, you know, to spare the other person's feelings.

Everyone knew we had an open relationship. I remember there was a girl who was after Dan. She would ask me, "What's he like?" and they would sometimes talk on the phone. Once we had a party, and I turned around, and there she was kissing Dan passionately in the doorway of our bedroom. Right then and there I put my foot down, and I said, "That'll be enough of that." She said, "But you told me you guys both have this open relationship." And I said, "I don't care what I said. Don't you kiss my husband now, in front of me, no. That's it."

Ultimately, I guess, the open relationship broke up our marriage. It was just too easy to look elsewhere for intimacy.

. . . Today I'm learning that my happiness and satisfaction are to be found within myself. I'm just grateful that I'm here and now. I don't have the financial security that I'm working toward. I don't have the abundance that I'm working toward. I don't have a family, and it's not easy being a single parent. But Elissa's a gift, and I'm grateful for being able to take care of her. I'm aware of what I have as opposed to what I don't have. It's a balancing act, and I'm learning.

Bruce Hoffman

*D*uring the Sixties, Timothy Leary popularized the use of LSD for greater spiritual awareness with the slogan "Turn on, Tune in, Drop out." Bruce Hoffman was one of thousands who responded to this message. He is now a professor of English at Rockland Community College in New York.

I never wanted anything less than the "infinite." I can recall in my high-school years reading books on yoga and Zen Buddhism. Of course, back then, in the Fifties, people had not even heard of yogurt, much less yoga. If anything, they thought that meant you had aspirations to walk on burning coals and sleep on beds of nails.

I went off to college, during which time I think, looking back, that it's a wonder I actually did my course work, because so much I saw around me seemed so absurd. I looked at philosophy faculty people, knowing full well that philosophy meant "love of wisdom," and none of them seemed very wise. They certainly didn't seem very happy, and it seems to me that something that would have to be part and parcel of wisdom would be happiness. And I looked at English teachers, teaching literature, talking about the social concerns of Tolstoy, for example, and saw at the same time that they were very annoyed when someone came to class late. The gap between the mind and the heart astonished me.

I graduated with an M.A. and in 1964 got a job teaching literature while going for my Ph.D. I found that teaching sort of pacified my spiritual yearnings, because I was able to deal with a search for meaning and share the confusion and hopes of students who were not much younger than I was at the time.

I yearned so much to find that center within, to gain a hold on something that seemed to me authentic. I was spending hours a week meditating, basically in the Zen Buddhist tradition, and at times being amused that I was doing it, because to me it so often seemed to be so much posturing.

But during one rare moment in meditation, I had an incredible experience in which suddenly the whole of the world, everything, seemed to be simply various aspects of God playing hide-and-seek with himself. Everything was so absolutely illuminated with the joy and presence of this underlying divine unity that I must use the word *God*, although *God* is a term that is so soiled by misuse that I don't really like to use it. But that was a remarkable experience.

During Christmas break, I went down to Florida to visit my parents, and I ran into a woman friend. I described my experience to her, and she said, "Well, have you ever used LSD?" And I said, "What is it?"

She explained that it was this wonderful chemical that a teacher, a professor, mind you, at Harvard was experimenting with. In fact he was using it to assist divinity-school students to experience Christ more directly than in the classroom. Indeed, *Life* magazine had a major feature on this man who was helping to awaken spiritual awareness among Harvard Divinity School students. The Harvard professor was, of course, Timothy Leary.

Well, she was getting this remarkable substance in the mail from the psychedelic underground, with Timothy Leary at the heart of it all, who felt that it was all too good to limit just to the students that were supposed to be experimenting with it. He was willing to share it with all those who were at all willing to try it.

She said, "Would you like me to send you some?" I said, "Sure." You have to realize that at that time it was not even illegal. It had none of the negative press that came into existence later, and it seemed wonderful and exciting. Yet, had she offered me some marijuana, I would have been horrified and refused it. Pot was illegal, and I didn't want to be around anything that was illegal. Well, needless to say, after several LSD trips I didn't feel that grass was such a terrible thing anymore, but I never really smoked very much. I probably have smoked a total of ten joints in my life. It never really appealed to me.

When the LSD was sent to me, one of my colleagues at the university was very eager to share this with me, and I said, "Fine," because I certainly didn't want to try this by myself. He had some friends who had already been involved in this vast growing psychedelic underground, and he had tried mescaline, so he offered to sort of help me go through the trip.

Back then we used sugar cubes, with a drop of liquid that contained the LSD in it, and these sugar cubes were being mailed all over the country from Cambridge.

Tom, wanting to have a good trip, carefully programmed, made sure that everything was in place that was needed for the weekend without us going out again. The trip was arranged to take place on Saturday morning, giving me Friday evening to recover from the work week. It started around ten in the morning, got deeply intense two hours later.

That first trip was pretty much the archetypal trip: the tingling in your extremities, a strange taste on your tongue. You knew it was working when you moved your hand and you had twenty images of the hand in your mind at the same time, like fifteen stills of a motion picture film at one time. And, of course, there was an enormous sense of being a space traveler. You felt you were entering the frontiers of consciousness.

Really, some remarkable perceptual changes take place. At a certain point, you'd have the floor dissolve beneath you, the walls would be acting more like jello than like masonry. Your senses seemed much more acute. You imagined you could hear people at a great distance, and I think that to some degree one could.

You certainly were able to look at things that were normally almost too small to be seen with the naked eye more clearly than would ever be imagined. I was always amazed by flowers, the gorgeousness of the stamen and the lines that make up the various structures of the plant that were almost invisible in normal day viewing. It was all beautiful. It was all to be cherished.

During that year, I took about six LSD trips, and they were basically a replay of that marvelous meditation experience I had prior to LSD, with all sorts of additional phenomena thrown in, such as melting into the woodwork and getting lost in the patterns that cells form in cup-cakes.

The trips were exhausting. It took that night and all of Sunday and Sunday night to recover. When you reappeared on campus, you felt like you had reentered the historical past that was still alive, and you really wanted to share this marvelous experience with everyone. You knew you had to be discreet, because that was no way to maintain a job, but it was really the fervor of those who had a vision.

At the end of the year, I decided that it was time to change my life a bit, sold everything I had. I didn't go off to India, I went off to France. I needed a language competency for my Ph.D., so I just felt, Best to do that in France, since I'm using French.

When I came back to America from France, I had been over there for five months or so. I went to visit this colleague of mine who had been my guide for my first trip, who had arranged for records of Ravi Shankar, the marvelous sitar player, and Napoleons from the pastry shop and candles and all the paraphenalia that went into a "good trip."

Much to my dismay, he was now experimenting with heroin and shooting up speed, and so was his girlfriend, his wife having left him in the meantime, and he was also engaging in shoplifting for the fun of it. He was one of the first clues I had that something was going wrong, because at that time I still had a rather utopian ideal of what psychedelics could bring about in our culture. I really had hopes that it was going to result in an awakening to inner values.

Shortly after that, as drugs became popular, I heard a conversation in the street between a couple of kids I would have to call teenyboppers who must have been sixteen and seventeen. Of course, now I suppose people experiment and get out of drugs by the time they're thirteen, but I was shocked to hear these kids talking about using LSD that weekend. They weren't searching. They were going to have a great party, and they were going to have great records, and they were going to have great sex.

I said, "My God, is that what they're using it for?" I mean, I saw it as a sacrament, and they were going to drop LSD for the sheer partying of it. But I still didn't completely give up my own use of LSD. I said, "Well, they're abusing it. I won't abuse it."

The following year I got a job at Oglethorpe College in Atlanta, Georgia, continued to work on my dissertation, and continued to take an occasional trip, about once a month. It was at that time that I became more and more distant from what I was beginning to characterize as "straight society." My hair was growing with great abandon and I had a marvelous beard.

I bought a Yamaha 250 motorcycle, and I was painting on my helmet a psychedelic design with the yin-yang on the front—you know, that black and white design, with the black dot in the white and the white in the black—but I was painting all this with Day-Glo colors, and where was I doing this? I was doing this while teaching British Lit in the classroom.

I would take my helmet with me to class, my five or six Day-Glo bottles and brushes, and while I was lecturing, I'd be painting away. I remember the chairperson of the humanities department coming by and looking in the door window. It was a sight to behold, his absolute shock. And I, so oblivious to it all, just looked at him and his shocked face and threw him my most loving smile and a wave of the hand. I'm sure he thought, "Well, nothing we can do now. We'll just have to wait out the year."

In the madness of those years, we really thought that we were the chosen, the ones to lead everyone to the truth. Our egos were having free rein, and we basically had a very simplistic vision: the straights versus those who knew—comrades in the psychedelic quest.

My relationship with my parents really went downhill. Not due to any fault of theirs, but due to my feeling that I didn't want to be around people who were not sharing *my* world. I offered them the opportunity to take LSD, and to my great astonishment, they refused. I told them that I had found a wonderful substance which enabled one to experience God more deeply, and I'd like them to share it with me. They had seen some press on it, and I think they were so perturbed, they simply said, "No, we don't wish to do that, and we don't think it's very good for you to do it." I just felt, They can't understand.

In April of 1967 I heard via the grapevine that there was going to be this marvelous Great Easter Be-In in Central Park, a sort of celebration of the whole counterculture. It just spread by word of mouth throughout the entire East Coast, and it has to be one of the great historical events of the whole psychedelic movement.

I stayed with the same woman who had originally told me about LSD. She had an apartment in the East Village, and one day I noticed how dismally dirty the sidewalks were on the block. So I took a broom and started to sweep down the sidewalks. Shopkeepers came rushing out telling me to stop, because they thought I was going to then ask for money for cleaning the street in front of their store. Well, it was just like, "Oh, no, no, no, I'm doing it for free. I want to make this a beautiful street." And they'd just look at you, of course, and think you were totally out of your mind, and, of course, they were to some degree quite on the mark.

The Be-In was a massive gathering. We thought it was the springtime of a whole new age. It took place in Sheep Meadow in Central Park, and there were literally tens of thousands of us: chanting, dancing, hugging, kissing, outrageous costumes, Day-Glo paints on the skin, people—I being one of them—giving out daffodils to businessmen and policemen. I think everyone was stoned out of their minds on hashish or grass or mescaline or acid and/or all of the above. It was truly a type of Edgar Allan Poe phantasmagoria of sights and sounds and colors.

While I was there at the Great Easter Be-In, I ran across some people, an older couple, who were handing out pamphlets called "God and the Pill?" and "The Universal Message" by Meher Baba. They told me that Meher Baba was born in India in 1894, made a number of trips to the West, and that he was an avatar, a God-man such as Buddha, Christ, or Mohammed.

And they told me that Meher Baba said, "If God can be found in a pill, he's not worthy of being God." While the imbibing of psychedelics had led certain people to an awareness of deeper reality, continued use is harmful physically, psychologically, and spiritually, and that if one knew of other paths, other alternatives to drugs as a means of greater consciousness awareness, one would never even dream of trying to use chemicals to achieve it.

I thought, "What a bunch of loonies," but I took their pamphlets, read them and threw it all away, dismissing anything that Baba had to say about LSD, because one of these people who followed him had said that Meher Baba had never used LSD. I figured if he had never used LSD, what did he know? How can he speak on this issue? So I thought that was that, and had a wonderful time at the Easter Be-In.

I flew down to Atlanta, Georgia, to continue my teaching job. Several weeks later, I went off on a motorcycle trip up to the north of Georgia to the parks by myself. When I was up there I took some acid early in the day. It was about a two-and-a-half hour drive, and as late afternoon was approaching, the acid still was having its effect on me. Rocks still were very mobile, clouds had a great ability to become particular figures without straining on my part, and I realized that I was not in very good shape to ride home, but it was getting chilly. I knew I had to get back.

So I got on my motorcycle, and on the way back to Atlanta, these mammoth trucks roared by me with a sound that seemed to be a thousand dinosaurs roaring, and the trees along the side of the road seemed to shape themselves into beautiful Japanese cliffs, and the lights on the backs of these huge trucks, behind which I was often traveling, were in themselves a disco light show. I mean in every way I realized that my senses were not what they should be for safe riding on a super-highway.

Here I was, you know, this frail body on a two-hundred-fifty-cc motorcycle, surrounded by huge dinosaurs and cliffs and light shows, and found myself saying, "If I survive this, dear God, it's only by your grace. If I get home alive, I will never ever take LSD again." I mean, I wasn't bargaining for my life so much as, spontaneously within me, I found myself saying that. And needless to say, I got home alive, because I'm here today; and I didn't take any more drugs.

What happened was I ran into a part-time librarian at the college who had a book by Meher Baba called *God to Man and Man to God*. As I read the table of contents—titles about the evolution of consciousness, the separative ego, the nature of karma—I was suddenly struck with the fact that I had come in contact with something that was far more a manifestation of truth than anything I had ever known. It was more than just the titles. There was something on an inner level.

There was a center that Baba established in Myrtle Beach, South Carolina, and when I first went there, I was absolutely overwhelmed by Baba's presence. It was like being dissolved in absolute joy. It sounds almost as nauseatingly sweet as some of those born-again experiences you hear from fundamentalists. I felt that I had come home. There was nothing strange or alien. It was my beloved Baba. When anyone tried to tell me about him, it was like if someone tried to tell you about your dearest, your wife, your lover, whoever is more intimate to you than anyone else in the whole world. That is how I instantly felt about Baba.

I went back to Oglethorpe and announced that I was going to give a talk about the spiritual path and drugs. At that point, drug use at the college was rampant. To the student body, I was this very hip professor who was aware of LSD and who, indeed, seemed to take trips. I think the administration was horrified, not knowing what I was going to say. And in the audience, I noticed two gentlemen of ample proportions who were dressed very properly, who turned out to be narcotics agents.

I think everyone was truly shocked when I got up there and gave a talk about the danger of drugs, that people seeking truth must realize drugs to be an obstacle rather than a help, that actually drugs will only lead one to greater illusions if one continues to use them.

My line was, "Only in America would people try to use drugs to find God, because it's part of our general cultural belief in 'Better Living Through Chemistry.' You know, if you're nervous, you take Compoz." I was giving them an alternative.

I went to Woodstock, and I remember looking at all these beautiful young girls and boys and seeing how sweet they were and yet how deluded they were. And simply hoping that their beautiful dreams would find a way of being transformed into something more practical and more real. Some of us Baba lovers were active helping people off bad drug trips. Most of it was simply holding hands until people came down.

And we distributed at least ten thousand cards with a picture of Meher Baba and his universal message, "Don't worry. Be happy." It rained constantly during Woodstock. The whole area was one great big mud swamp, and a lot of people were getting very downed by that. I remember going from tent to tent, with the rain falling and smoke rising from each tent. The whole place looked like a foggy scene on the moors.

I would just sort of knock at the tent, and people, somewhat with a sense of annoyance at being disturbed, would say, "Yeah, what is it?" And I'd say, "Hi, I just want to give you this," and we'd give out this lovely picture of Baba smiling. The responses were always, without exception, "Oh, wow! Hey, he's beautiful, man. This is wonderful."

Of course, they were so bombed, I suppose you could have given them a picture of Godzilla, and they'd say, "Hey, he's beautiful, man. This is wonderful." At any rate, Baba's picture has this unique ability to touch hearts and make people smile, whatever they might think he is. And then they'd say, "Hey, let me turn you on."

I didn't want to put them down and make them feel like I was being judgmental by saying, "I don't smoke." So I said, "Oh, no, no thanks, I'm just fine right now," and let them assume what they wanted to. I guess they all assumed I was flying high; and, of course, they were right, I was, but not on drugs.

. . . I'm no longer a seeker. I have found the answer. Now it's simply a matter of living it. You know, when I first came to Meher Baba, I thought, Well, now I'm going to just wear a nice little robe, and live in a little room and probably eat rice, but one of the things I have found fascinating is how very much Baba has us involved in the everyday.

I mean paying a mortgage, cleaning up the cat litter, or grading freshman compositions. Seeing everything ultimately as a channel through which people grow closer to knowing that they are one with that incredible mystery that many call by many names, as Christ or Buddha or Baba. While enjoying the Jets game, you know, and Arthur Miller's *Death of a Salesman*, and a silly Stephen King horror movie.

In fact, I enjoy all these things far more than I was able to when I was searching. That's why I feel my whole life right now is just Baba's gift to me.

Alex Forman

*L*ike many other young people, he headed out to San Francisco in 1966 *with a guitar and not much else. It was a time when the city seemed to offer an alternative to the escalating violence at home and abroad. He still lives there and now works in a holistic health clinic, practicing acupuncture, biofeedback, and nutritional counseling. In his spare time, he is active in the nuclear freeze movement.*

When I came to San Francisco, the city was just exploding with this counterculture movement. I thought, "This is it!" It was like paradise there. Everybody was in love with life and in love with their fellow human beings to the point where they were just sharing in incredible ways with everybody. Taking people in off the street and letting them stay in their homes, breaking free of conventional morality. You could walk down almost any street in Haight-Ashbury where I was living, and someone would smile at you and just go, "Hey, it's beautiful, isn't it?" It was like people were high on the street and willing to share that energy. It was a very special time.

It was a whole other vision of what was possible. Rents were cheap and people were living in big communal groups, and we didn't have to work very hard. There was a sense that you didn't need very much, and that people who worked hard were just trapped into trying to acquire more and more possessions. People should just begin more to enjoy life, play music, dance, experience nature. We were going to raise our kids communally and all that stuff, and such attitudes would flourish even more. I thought this was the new world beginning right here—an alternative society—and this was where I wanted to be. So I stayed.

The first human Be-In was in January of '67 in Golden Gate Park. That was a very high moment. People went and just kind of experienced. A lot of people were on LSD or peyote or marijuana. They played music, shared food, played drums, did American Indian chanting. You know, tie-dyed clothes, the whole thing. It all seems very trite now, but at the time it was all new. People were coming from all over the world to research it, to experience it. People from Czechoslovakia, Australia, Finland. It was a real phenomenon.

For a while I worked with a group in the Haight called the Diggers, who had a kind of a primitive communism view that was just "share all the wealth." The Diggers set up a free store, and people could just come in and take whatever they needed, and we fed people for free in the park.

At one point I realized the absurdity of that when these people from the neighborhood, these older black women, came into the free store and said, "How much do these clothes cost in here?" We said, "Oh, it's all free. You just take what you need, and then if you have extra, you give." They said, "What do you mean, you just take what you need?" "Well, you just take what you need, that's all." They said, "Really?"

So they came back with these big boxes and they started just taking tons of stuff off the racks. We said, "What are you doing?" They said, "Well, you said take what you need." We said, "Yeah, well, you don't need all those clothes for yourself." They said, "No, but we need the money, so we're going to take the clothes and sell them."

They were in real scarcity, you know, they needed money, and here we were saying just take what you need for your own personal, immediate needs. But for them, that wasn't reality. Their reality was, "How are we going to get some money, and here's these foolish white people just letting us take whatever we need. Well, we need it all. We don't have anything."

That was the illusion of the whole hippie ethos, that there was this abundance. I think the hippie movement started in California—and was most powerful here—because there is this illusion of abundance here. Fruits were falling from the trees, rent was cheap, there were places to stay, the weather was tolerable even in the winter, there was a community of people who were into sharing. But there wasn't an abundance. There was an abundance at a certain time for certain people.

In early 1967, people would just give things away. On every street corner, there would be somebody giving things away, free food, a free place to stay. Then in the summer of '67 was the Summer of Love. People started storming in by the thousands, and within three months there were people begging, "Do you have free food?" In other words, so many came that the surplus changed to scarcity. It got very ugly very fast. People got into really bad drugs like speed and heroin. There were ripoffs, violence, guns being drawn, people really malnourished, hepatitis, people living on the street with no place to stay.

I quickly saw then that the counterculture wasn't going to make it. It wasn't going to work. It was an illusion. And meanwhile the war was going on. It became more and more clear that you couldn't just set up little islands of peace and love in the middle of the Vietnam War.

On the
Campuses

Jack Weinberg

"*D*on't trust anyone over thirty" was one of the most widely quoted slogans of the Sixties. It was first uttered by Jack Weinberg, a leader of the Free Speech Movement at Berkeley, which, in the fall of 1964, set the pattern for campus political activity throughout the decade. Now forty-five and graying, the former activist lives with his wife in Gary, Indiana, where he worked in a steel mill until he was laid off in a recent economic slump.*

I was a graduate student in mathematics in a Ph.D. program, and I was beginning to figure that I might end up as a college professor. I didn't think I'd be tops in my field, but I thought I'd be at a large university and be relatively successful. But by the summer of '64, those of us on the Berkeley campus who were involved in civil rights were working full-time.

I dropped out of school because the civil rights movement was just so much more important to me at the time than doing the kind of esoteric crossword puzzles we were doing in the mathematics department. I had been a graduate teaching assistant, but after I dropped out, I really didn't have any regular source of income. I gave up my apartment and all my possessions, and I just sort of slept on people's couches and worked in the movement.

We held dozens of demonstrations protesting hiring discrimination at places in the San Francisco and Oakland area. We helped welfare mothers and public-housing tenants who were having problems. We had picketing, arrests, and we sent all kinds of students south for the Mississippi Summer.* It was a really active summer, and everybody was saying, "In the fall when the students return, things are *really* going to happen."

This was also the point of view of the university administration, because the business community had been putting on the pressure. They felt that the campus was being used as a base for organizing all these tactics, and that this was intolerable. We saw the movement as something that was beneficial to society, but they didn't, and they wanted it stopped. The university had been let to know that if they couldn't stop all this organizing on campus, their funding was going to be affected.

And so, at the beginning of the fall semester, the administration issued a set of rules saying, in effect, that political and social activism on the campus were not going to be permitted. There was a large sidewalk area at a corner of the campus where traditionally people would stand and hand out leaflets, or if you had a cause you'd set up a card table and collect money, or get signatures for a petition. You could sign up recruits, you could sign up volunteers. We'd signed up a lot of people for the Mississippi Summer there. You might call it the free speech area on the campus.

It always had been thought that this was city property outside the campus, and so you could do things there that were prohibited on campus. Well, now it was suddenly discovered that the free speech area was part of the campus, and the rule went out that there would be no fund raising and no advocacy on campus. You couldn't urge a particular issue, you couldn't raise money, you couldn't mount a demonstration, you couldn't hold a rally, you couldn't give speeches. All this was prohibited.

This was a real shocker. All the student groups, a real cross-section of the students, joined together and opposed the new rules. Our reaction was, "They may prohibit it, but we're not going to stop doing it." The university tried to start negotiating with us, but the student groups said, "Any agreement that fundamentally limits our doing what we've done in the past is not going to be honored." This limited the

---

* Summer 1964 during which hundreds of young, Northern civil-rights workers went south to help register blacks to vote.

options of the negotiators. Then very quickly we expanded our definition of free speech rights to the rest of the campus, because if that strip of land at Bancroft and Telegraph was no different from the rest of the campus, then there was no reason to limit our free speech rights to that strip of land. Actually, in our minds, this was to give our people something to negotiate with, because the feeling was we'd settle for what we *used* to have. We had law students and all sorts of people advising us, and in their terms, the *status quo ante* was what we'd settle for, but at that point it was a tactical escalation. From the administration's point of view, it was a serious escalation.

We put tables in the center of campus in front of Sproul Hall, and the dean came out and said, "If you don't take these tables out, you'll be cited." The first day the students took the tables down, and then we had a meeting, and we decided to have people sitting there the next day with the tables. We weren't going to take them down. As soon as the dean came by and said, "Take the table down. We instruct you to take the table down," the student was to say, "I'm sorry, my organization has not authorized me to take the table down." Very comforting to respond to authority with some sort of equivalent bureaucratic jargon. [*Chuckles.*] Then the dean would say, "You are being cited for disciplinary action. You are instructed to go into the administration building at three o'clock and meet with Dean So-and-So." As soon as that would happen, the dean would go to the next table. The student at the last table would get up and someone else would immediately sit down in his place.

The next day a big crowd gathered. It was clear to the dean, after about five people had been cited, that someone was always taking their place, and he stopped. This went on all that day, and the next day, too. We wanted to continue to escalate the thing.

A few minutes to noon on the second day, our group brought up a twelve-foot-long table, and got a dozen people, including me, sitting around it, shaking cans and saying, "We're raising money for an off-campus cause." Seven students had been suspended and thrown off campus the last night. They were the ones who had been manning the table the day before, and we were raising money for their defense. That was our off-campus cause. We were saying it and doing it provocatively, because we wanted a test.

Well, in a short time the dean came out and approached our table, and asked me to leave, and I refused. Then he asked me to identify myself, and I refused. He said, "In that instance, you're going to be arrested." From our point of view, he was doing all the right things. He went off to call the police to come and arrest me—at exactly the right time: It was approaching twelve noon, when thousands of people come through this area, and people were gathering around.

I gave a little speech to the crowd about how the university had become a factory and they want to turn out a standardized product. They just want to produce people who will fit in, who will fit the specification of their clients, who are the businesses and the state. They don't want square pegs that won't fit into round holes. But *we're not going to be a standardized product*. It was that kind of speech.

Right at that point the police came, and they picked me up. Now, of course, as a civil rights activist, I'd been trained in all the nonviolent methods, so I went limp, and they dragged me into the police car. By the time I got into the police car, there were students sitting around it, and that was the beginning of the police-car event—the big event that got so much media attention at the time. People kept getting up on top of the car and making speeches. By the time it was over, I had been sitting in that police car for thirty-two hours, surrounded by thousands of students.

Of course, I didn't know how long I'd be in there. By the evening of the next day, the whole Alameda County Sheriff's Department was mobilized. They were there with hundreds of motorcycle policemen. Their plan was to set up two rows of motorcycles and sort of pull the students out between the two rows. Things were getting tense. People in the crowd were saying, "If you're wearing earrings, take them off." "Take off your jewelry." People were getting prepared to be arrested. There was a large crowd around us who were with us, and lots more people standing up watching, and people were saying to them, "Join us, join us." In the end, I would guess there were several thousand people sitting around the car. I was in the middle, and the police were mobilized.

All this time, negotiations were going on with the administration, and in the final hour an agreement was reached. These were the terms: one, I would be booked and then released on my own recognizance, and then the charges against me would be dropped; two, a committee would be set up with representatives of the students, including the demonstrators, and representatives of the faculty and administration, to resolve the issues. With that agreement, it was announced that the demonstration was over. I was booked and released.

That was on a Friday, and over the weekend, the Free Speech Movement was formally created. During the next several months, the university tried to back down on the agreement. The first big battle was that they set up a committee in which the students representing the Free Speech Movement were automatically outvoted, so we refused to participate. Then, when we got a committee that we could work with, they wanted to reserve the right to discipline on campus any student who was engaged in mobilizing activities for an off-campus action that subsequently led to civil disobedience. Well, from the civil rights activist point of view, that was a fundamental question. If we gave in, the university couldn't continue as a base of support for an activist civil rights movement. So that was a big battle, which couldn't really be settled to the satisfaction of both sides.

Students started setting up tables again on the campus, and again the administration started citing people. At this point, the graduate teaching assistants organization became involved, and about half the teaching assistants at the university manned tables in violation of the rules. Basically, they realized that the university couldn't function without the teaching assistants, as the majority of the undergraduate education was being done by them. Nobody came out to cite anybody, at which point the teaching assistants hoisted the American flag and marched into the administration building and presented the administration with a list of all the teaching assistants who had been sitting at tables. And from that point on, the issue of sitting at tables was moot. The administration capitulated. We had a de facto victory.

Naturally, the administration wasn't satisfied to leave it at this, so over Thanksgiving recess they sent letters to the seven people who had been cited earlier, telling them that they had been expelled or were about to be expelled. So we were back to square one. Seven people's heads were about to roll as a result of something that thousands of people were involved in, and everybody felt a real obligation to those people. The result was a sit-in, with the administration building jammed on every floor with hundreds of people. The police were called in, and over eight hundred people were arrested.

They sent in a squad of police to get me special, so I was picked off early. The police were somewhat rough, but in terms of what happened after that, I would have to say, looking back, that it wasn't the worst police brutality imaginable. I gave a little speech to the people around me, about how not to resist arrest, how to go limp and be nonviolent, and all that. The police came to get me and I went nonviolent, and they pulled me down the stairs by the ankles, on my butt. I can't say it hurt too much, but it was upsetting. I grabbed two policemen by the legs and pulled them down on top of me. They started whaling me. All I could think of was, "I hope they're going to beat me bloody, because they're going to help our cause if they do." I was willing, because that's what I was in it for. And I was too mad to feel any pain. But, of course, one of those policemen's superiors saw this and stopped them before I really got hurt.

After the eight hundred student arrests, there was a student strike in the university, and a big majority of students honored the strike. The university shut down, and at that point the faculty voted overwhelmingly that the students were right in the things we were asking for and called on the administration to honor our demands. So the administration finally gave in, and the Free Speech Movement had an unmitigated victory. Nobody was disciplined, and we had the right to organize on campus.

The President's Commission later reported that our success, and the attention it got in the media, made the Berkeley Free Speech Movement the pattern for the later student movements at universities in the Sixties. But, of course, we didn't know that at the time. We were just interested in our own issues, not in setting a pattern for the country. But the right of students to engage in social and political action on campus was won in our battle, and it quickly became the norm at large universities throughout the country and even percolated to the junior colleges and smaller colleges. And since this was at the beginning of the Vietnam War and the protest movements against it, this was an important victory.

While all this was going on, I got quite a bit of attention in the media, as a result of the thirty-two hours in the police car. A couple of weeks after that incident, I was being interviewed by a newsman from the *San Francisco Chronicle*, and he was pursuing a theme that many people were pursuing: Who's really behind the Free Speech Movement? What's going on? Who's telling you what to do? You know, there was this theory that it was a Communist conspiracy. Those questions were getting me quite angry, if what he meant was that somebody was behind us, because I was on the committee that was doing it, and I knew there wasn't anybody behind us. We were calling the shots.

This reporter was really getting under my skin with the suggestion that we were being manipulated, and finally I said in real exasperation, "You know, we have a saying in the movement: Don't trust anyone over thirty." I'd never heard it before. I think I made it up right then, but I don't mean that it's anything original. Ever since Plato there have been variations of this generational thing.

I just said it, and it clicked, and it came to sum up the feeling that we weren't going to turn our fate, or the fate of our movement, over to anybody else. We were in control of our own situation. It caught on as a way of summing up, encapsulating what this was all about. Kids who were in high school or grade school around the country were watching this stuff on television, not knowing what to make of it. Suddenly we were quoted as saying, "Don't trust anyone over thirty," and the kids would say, "Aha! Now I understand."

I think that in the way that I meant it then, it would be valid today, too, and I'd be on the other side of the generational line. Young people respond differently to change. They don't have the scars, they don't have the history of defeat and failure and caution and conservatism that flows from experience in life.

There's something else, too: At that point, I don't think I actually believed I was going to live to be thirty, or I didn't care if I did, or I wasn't doing anything to prepare myself for it. There was a real existential sense in the early Sixties of living for the moment, defining yourself through your actions. You knew that if you got arrested you were risking your future and you might be hurt. But the idea was: Let the future take care of the future. The years ahead just didn't seem real.

After the Free Speech Movement victory, the Vietnam issue was beginning to heat up, and in a fairly short time I became very involved in the antiwar movement. Throughout the rest of the decade, I threw myself into that.

After 1968, the movement that I had been part of was hopelessly fractured. If Berkeley were a country, we would have had a revolution in Berkeley, and it would have all been over. But Berkeley wasn't a country. It had played its role, and I'd been part of that. But now I felt that the radical movement that I had been part of was committing suicide on every level, and I was very torn up by that. We were just alienating ourselves from American society.

I remember talking with my friends and saying that we have to reach the working class. The antiwar movement was not going anywhere, because there was a whole group of people out there who were more important than we were, and we were not swaying them. Tied up with this was a lot of Marxist theory and romanticism—a feeling that the real part of society was the working class, and a further theory that there were going to be hard times coming, and that this would lead to a radicalization of the working class. I felt that those who had been through the early Sixties movements should be part of this radicalization. It was a romantic theory, because it wasn't based on a real understanding of what was happening or what was going to happen, or even on a very real theory about the working class.

In any case, I decided to go to Detroit and take a job in an auto plant. The idea was to get involved in union activities, to contest the current union leadership, lead a rank-and-file revolt, and end up with a more progressive union. The theory was half right and half wrong: There was an economic crisis, but there wasn't any rank-and-file movement against the union leadership. The result was I got caught up in a wildcat strike, and I was fired.

During this time, a lot of the radical and theoretical views I'd had began making less and less sense. It became possible that I was not on a mission from God. And I was tired. I was living with a woman, now my wife, who had also been active in the Movement. She had an M.A. in English, but she'd been working as a union organizer. She was tired, too. We decided we just wanted jobs. We put in applications in a lot of places, and got hired in the steel mills in Gary. At that time, the steel mills paid well, and it was one of the last places where you could get a good union job, with the possibility for long-term employment. A lot of things about that kind of work were appealing to me. I didn't have to turn over my creative energies or my personality to an employer. I didn't have to sell anything. I just had to work for so many hours. I made enough money; it didn't take any great effort to do the job in the mill, and it left my mind free. Whatever was me was left to do my own way in my own time. So I came to Gary, and my wife and I both worked in the mill.

I was set to spend the rest of my life here. I bought a house, I had a car, and I had a not overly demanding job. I care about nature, and I liked watching the birds on the water in front of my house.

But the economy and its effect on this industry didn't work out that way. I was laid off a few months ago; everyone at the mill who had less than eight years of service was laid off. Now I'm trying to start a new life, and I'm not sure where I'll go from here. I'd like to get an organizing job that I could live with, in which I'd have a degree of freedom, because that's what I'm good at. But organizing isn't a job with tenure, and that's one of my problems.

You know, I did a lot of things during the Sixties that I feel were significant. But I'm almost a nut to even remember them, let alone think they're significant, because in our society, if you don't make money or establish an institutional position, whatever you do is not valid. If it doesn't lead to position, to power, to money, then it didn't really happen. In retrospect, it had no value. I feel good about the things I did. I think I did the best I could under the circumstances, and the mistakes I made were honest ones. But none of it's like money in the bank.

Still, you played a key role in a historical event.

Yeah. That and ten cents will get me a cup of coffee—or maybe thirty-five cents now.

Amy Ross*

*U ntil recently she was associate director of a large philanthropic or-
ganization in the Midwest. She now spends her time caring for her
new baby son and entertaining for her lawyer husband. They live in
a spacious, elegantly furnished apartment overlooking Lake Michigan. In
1984 they both voted for Reagan.*

I went to my first SDS meeting the first quarter I was on campus. I was
a freshman, barely eighteen, and I was sort of getting myself oriented.
At that time, SDS was a very small group at the University of Chicago,
maybe ten people who would come out for the regular weekly meetings.
It was really just a bunch of people sitting around talking, not so different from a bull session in the dorm. The focus of the discussion was
usually how to find something that would get people out.

We wanted an action or a cause that would get people interested and
involved, and we wanted something that would dramatize the university's connection with what was going on in the greater world out there.

We tried a couple of causes. One was protest about the university's
involvement with the neighborhood to the south of the university and
the housing problems that were being caused by urban development
there. But that didn't seem to arouse very much interest. Another effort
was to connect the university's research activities with the science and
technology used for the war. And that one went absolutely nowhere
as a major interest on campus. We kept trying to find a way to reach
out to a broader group of people. But everything we tried seemed to
fizzle out.

The women's movement was getting started right then, and there
was a lot more excitement and activity about that than there was about
the official SDS meetings. Women in SDS decided that they were sick
of stuffing envelopes while the men were being leaders, which was pretty
typical of what was happening in other places, too. So they organized
a group of their own, and *that* very quickly became a much larger group.
There were lively discussions in the women's meetings about whether

---

* Not her real name.

women, per se, were oppressed in America or whether this was really a class issue.

I remember one meeting in particular that became an enormous fight over whether Jackie Kennedy was oppressed. Well, you could say that Jackie Kennedy was oppressed, because, after all, she was a woman, and that was all it took. On the other hand, she obviously wasn't part of, you know, the masses. We also spent a lot of time comparing our own expectations for ourselves with our mothers' lives, and that sort of thing. I guess you would call it consciousness raising.

Finally, there was one meeting where the women decided to invite the men to the women's group. After all, the men in SDS had been kind of wondering, "What have our girlfriends been talking about all this time behind our backs?" And at that co-ed meeting the attendance was really enormous. People went around the room, as we usually did at those meetings, talking about why we were there, and what we thought was important. It was a pretty heavy evening, after which a men's group was formed to talk about how chauvinistic they were, basically. That petered out after about three or four evenings. They weren't too enthusiastic about it, I guess.

So most of the activity and intensity was going on in the women's group, and SDS itself was not much of a powerful force for a while. But we were looking for a cause. There was a definite desire to do something more than write pamphlets. And then we got an issue: A sociology professor named Marlene Dixon was denied her promotion, which meant that she wouldn't get tenure. The feeling was that the decision was based on the fact that she was a Marxist and a woman, not on her academic credentials.

We felt that she was such a popular teacher that students should have been consulted about it. She was one of the few people in the social sciences who was teaching from a Marxist perspective, so her particular following was especially upset about it. I, myself, hadn't taken any courses from her. I was still taking the basic common core of required courses, so I would have had no occasion to take a course from her; but I thought it was a good issue. And it was.

Her case sort of galvanized everybody in SDS, and we managed to get a lot of interest in it. The women were interested in it because she was a woman; the Marxists were interested in it because she was a Marxist; and there was a graduate-student group that was strongly behind her. Up until then, very few graduate students had been involved with SDS. But now they felt *they* should have had some say in the decision on Marlene Dixon. We were all brought together by this. The people involved in the women's group were especially excited, because it was the first time at any university in the country that there had been any action on the women's issue.

We finally had our cause, and it was something that brought all these groups together. In a short time we'd grown from an SDS group with weekly meetings attended by about ten people to this very large group, which was excited about the Marlene Dixon affair—men, women, graduate students, Marxists.

At that point, we had to decide what to do. A lot of the communication with the university at this stage was just in writing letters back and forth. They didn't seem to want to talk to any of us in person, which I think was frustrating for all of us. We knew we had to make a decision soon. The big decision was whether to occupy the administration building or not. I don't remember that any other alternatives were being bandied about. It was a very dramatic meeting, because it was a question of, "Well, are we going to do something?" And then all of a sudden, there were the logistics. I mean, after all, it's not something that we ever had done before. You know, how do you feed everybody; how do you sleep everybody; how do you get in; what do you do after you're in? It was exciting, it was intense, and I had just turned eighteen about this time. I was ready to do anything.

One thing that seemed to me to have a lot to do with the decision to do something dramatic like occupying the administration building was that the Living Theater came to campus shortly before the sit-in. They were a radical theater group who did a kind of participatory theater where they revved everyone up. They got the audience involved, and it became a kind of real mob scene, actually.

I went to almost every one of their performances. At the end of one of them, half the audience was on the stage, and many people had taken all their clothes off. The idea was to liberate yourself from the confining conventions of life, and to celebrate the irrational side of your nature, kind of let yourself go. And at a place like the University of Chicago, this was really the opposite of every message that you'd been getting from the moment you stepped into the place, which was, "One discusses things reasonably; that's what life is about." This was the counterculture coming to us, and it stirred people up and made us feel like doing something dramatic.

I had a really ambivalent reaction to it. I was kind of scared by how quickly a group of people that walked into the theater as ordinary people could end up after two hours doing these wacky things. I thought it was kind of frightening, but it was stimulating, too. It stirred things up—and it stirred me, too.

I don't think any of us were terribly realistic about the consequences. We just thought, "Let's do it, let's do it," and so we did it. There was an appointed time, and there wasn't, as far as I know, any physical attempt to stop us. The building is an open building, always had been. We just walked in. They hadn't planted security guards in the place to keep us out or anything. The whole thing was, in fact, rather strange, especially if you compare it with what happened at places like Columbia, you know. After we got in, the first thing I did was make peanut butter and jelly sandwiches. [*Laughs.*]

There was at least one security guard in the building all the time, and we didn't try to physically remove them. In fact, relations were rather cordial. It was really quite civilized as compared to what happened at other places. It wasn't a siege. You could come in and go out of the building at will. I mean, it was a sit-in, but some students went home. I remember I left once to go to a birthday party, and people left to take showers, and to bring in more food. A committee was organized to offer some sort of an alternative curriculum, and we asked people to come and join classes or organize them. We wanted to get people interested and involved in what was going on, and to go beyond the particular issues of Marlene Dixon's situation.

There was sort of a festive air about it at first. People brought sleeping bags, and there were all these posters we'd put around: a big poster that said "The Winter Palace," and there was another that said, "Sit-ins Cause Cancer." That was for the people who were sitting in meetings and smoking nonstop. And we had letters and telegrams from people at other universities. Pete Seeger gave a concert in Hyde Park and came to the building and sang for us in the lobby. It was festive and exciting, but most of the time we were all extremely serious. We felt that this was for *real*.

Then, of course, there were divisions in the group, because five hundred people is not a coherent group. Once we had the sit-in, the list of demands kept growing. It was headed, of course, by the "Rehire Marlene Dixon" demand. But there were a number of groups or factions that thought this was an opportunity to bring up other issues: urban renewal, student participation in university decisions, a variety of things.

The biggest issue was whether we were going to go into the files, because obviously we could have. I felt it was extremely important that we not do that, because it might discredit the action. There were a lot of meetings about that, intense meetings. People were saying, "Look, why should anyone have any respect for them?" Other people were saying, "We're here for certain reasons and not for others." And others, "We shouldn't just trash the place."

There was an issue at that time about whether the university should cooperate with the draft board by giving academic-standing information to them, and I think that was one of the things we were interested in finding out: Were they doing it? More than that, there was just a "Gee, there must be something in there, you know. Imagine what we could find out!" But the final vote was against it.

How did the university react to the sit-in?

The administration's tactic was to kind of divide and conquer. They felt that if they could identify the leaders and send them disciplinary notices while the thing was going on, they could really divide up the group. This was fairly effective. You know, people were sitting in the building with a disciplinary notice that said, "If you don't come to a hearing tomorrow, you're going to be kicked out of school." And there were four hundred seventy other people in the building who weren't facing any consequences, so it was difficult.

They got the faculty to come into the building and identify students who were sitting in. They would say [*snaps fingers sharply*], "I see you, and I see you, and I see you." And they'd give the names of students they knew to the disciplinary committee. Many of us considered that a real betrayal. They identified us from photographs, and from these kinds of encounters, and some people probably identified themselves. It got to be divisive.

I learned something about strategy from the way the university handled the situation. Basically, they were able to outwait us, and in the end the whole sit-in petered out, well, not with a bang, but with a whimper. In fact, I remember our talking about wanting to put a huge chessboard out on the quadrangle in front of the administration building, because it seemed as if everyone was waiting forever for one side or the other to make a move.

Basically, I think the administration decided that the best thing was to do nothing. You know, don't call in the police, don't do anything dramatic, just kind of pick away at it. Call people to the disciplinary committee, one at a time, in small groups, and pretty soon we would decide that we had to go home. And that's what happened. It was clear by the time the sit-in ended that they were not going to reinstate Marlene, but actually they said, "We'll appoint committees to talk about it." And they appointed a committee, and they did a lot of talking.

There's a momentum to these things, and finally we wore down. In the end we decided to leave the building. There was nothing left to be gained by staying any longer, and we all felt a little defeated.

Afterward, of course, there were the disciplinary committee meetings. I had to go to those. And some people were expelled. At the hearing you were allowed to state your case, and if you said something like, "I think I was right, and you guys are a bunch of schmucks," you weren't going to be treated very generously. I had what was considered a very stiff sentence, because I wasn't apologetic. I wasn't expelled, but I had a four-quarter suspension.

Eventually, on appeal, which was allowed, my sentence was reduced to a three-quarter suspension. One quarter was the winter quarter, which was already past; that was the quarter of the sit-in. The second quarter was the spring quarter, and the third quarter was the summer quarter, when I didn't expect to go to school anyway. So it wasn't a big deal. I ended up graduating in August instead of in June, the same year that I would have graduated. But at the time, for a very short time, it seemed like a very dramatic thing.

I'm not a left-wing or a liberal now. You might call me more moderate-to-center. I wouldn't say conservative, but comparatively conservative. I think one of the things that changed me was seeing some of the people who had been at the sit-in become Weathermen, partly in reaction to the outcome of the sit-in. Some of them participated in the Days of Rage in Chicago, and we began seeing their pictures on the wanted posters in post offices. That was rather sobering.

Politics isn't a very big part of my life now, although I understand a lot more about it. I went back to school and got an advanced degree in the social sciences, and I've taught at the university level. And I must say, if the same situation came up today and the students were occupying the administration building, I'd side with the faculty. But it was right for me to do what I did then, because I felt it was right.

Eugene Goldwasser

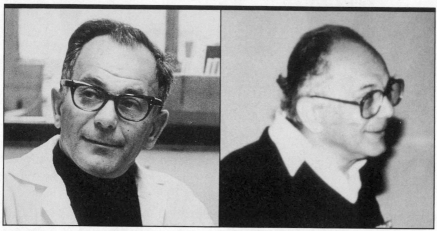

He is head of the department of biochemistry at the University of Chicago, an authority on the structure of hemoglobin.

During the sit-in at the university, a few of the other members of the faculty and I met with the student group that was involved in the sit-in, around a table in one of the classrooms. Among the things that the students were insisting on as part of their "Support Marlene Dixon Movement" was a voice in the appointment and promotion of faculty members. And the question I raised with them was the appropriateness of students being involved in that kind of decision-making: Could they, for example, qualify to pass on the credentials of a solid-state physicist or a neurosurgeon? The answer being sort of evident in the question.

That turned them off completely. They were clearly at the meeting only to hear opinions that agreed with their own. They were not listening. They were unwilling to indulge in any kind of discourse. They wanted support, and if you weren't for them, you were against them. At least that was the major impression I got from all these meetings.

I felt very depressed at the whole thing—largely because it seemed to me to symbolize a failure in the educational process. Here was this group of really highly selected, perhaps elite, students coming to a small, high-class university, and they had given up on rational discourse.

They knew what was right. There was a kind of zealousness—an absolute surety in what they were doing. They had no doubts whatsoever. And so, since my view of education really is that it should inculcate doubt about everything and question everything, it seemed to me to have really failed in that case.

Charles O'Connell

*N*ow *provost of the University of Chicago, he was the brand-new dean of students there in early 1969 when the main administration building of the university was occupied by a group of students. It was a time when student takeovers of university buildings had become commonplace across the United States, and a large percentage of university administrators' time and attention was taken up in deciding how to deal with student demands.*

Right after I became dean of students, we had a meeting at this university attended by administrators from a number of colleges, including Columbia, Harvard, Rochester, Middlebury, and others, discussing the student situation at the time. That was 1968. Of course, none of us could read the future. The general feeling was, "We don't know what the next year will bring, but it looks bleak. It looks as if unrest is mounting and there will be excesses on every campus." It appeared to us then that there was an attempt to change the nature of the way universities were governed, and that this went beyond Vietnam, beyond the immediate goals.

After everyone had had his say, the man from Columbia said he couldn't help but agree with us to some extent, but that at his institution things were good, students were happy there. He had very close relations with the students. In fact, it was not uncommon for them to come into his office and sit on his floor and talk. He had his finger on the pulse of what was happening at Columbia, and although other institutions might be headed for trouble, he certainly didn't see anything coming up there.

Well, within six weeks I picked up a copy of *The New York Times* and saw him climbing out his window onto Broadway or Amsterdam Avenue or one of those New York streets, pursued by people who were invading Hamilton Hall or the library at Columbia, whichever building it was, and I·thought, "Well, so much for foresight."

For the first year I was dean of students I don't think I knew that I was supposed to be thinking about student housing and planning for the next decade, or trying to improve the quality of student life. We were so busy wondering whether there was going to be *any* life on campus—manning the trenches and fending off disaster, all day, every day. We were so totally preoccupied with holding the place together that we couldn't think about any long-range planning.

The first indication I had that anything was brewing was a series of letters protesting the failure to reappoint Marlene Dixon. It was really a decision of the department of sociology, but we did meet with the students and explain the university processes for making decisions. We explained that it hadn't been a discriminatory decision because she was a woman or because of her political beliefs. But that didn't satisfy the students. The leaders of the group couldn't really have cared less about Marlene Dixon. They just wanted an issue, and she became their issue.

On the night of January thirteenth the students voted to occupy the building the next day, and we knew we were facing a confrontation. The next morning, at seven o'clock, I was here at the administration building, and my staff was pinning up notices announcing the university's policy on disruptions and warning students that they were risking penalties if they should occupy the building. We distributed 8½-by-11 sheets all over campus repeating these warnings. There was a rally here at noon, and about twelve-thirty they began coming into the building. I left my office at noon on the thirteenth of January, and I didn't come back until the middle of February.

We made a decision at the time not to call in the cops, which was a policy different from that which most institutions were following, and it was a difficult policy to maintain. I recall that as the sit-in went on, the *Chicago Tribune* published an editorial which suggested that the president of the University of Chicago should undertake a spine transplant, and they would provide the money for the necessary surgery, because he had obviously no backbone. Later the paper apologized, but at that time there was only one answer that everybody was urging: Call the cops. But we didn't, and we had to go to enormous lengths to avoid it.

The students wanted to bring down society, to change society fundamentally, and the university was the closest thing they could get hold of. They really didn't want to talk, and their demands kept escalating as the occupation went on. In the course of the month, the Marlene Dixon demand escalated into a catchall for everything from Third World courses to a change in the governing structure of the university that would have involved student staff, professional staff, union employees, and community people making all the decisions.

We decided to wait it out, and call students in for disciplinary action a few at a time. The president made it clear that he would not call the police unless there was physical danger to anyone, but that he meant it when he said there would be disciplinary action. So we had to follow through with that while the occupation was going on.

One of my jobs was to get the faculty to agree to come into the building and identify specific students and warn them to come out, and say, "If you don't leave, I'm sorry, but I have to turn you in." There was nothing covert about this, but it was unpleasant for many of the faculty members to have to identify somebody and know he's going to be called up for action. There was a group called the Chickenshit Brigade—students who weren't occupying, but who were supporting the occupation—and they put on makeup with blackface and purple paint and followed these faculty members around, shouting and annoying them.

I think students would have preferred to have a paddywagon pull up and to be photographed while they were being put in it—to be arrested and be told, "If you stay free of problems for the next six months, there'll be no record of your arrest." That way you get everything. You get the pure feeling that you've sacrificed and you get the publicity and you won't suffer. Whereas if you get something on your academic record, it's there and it stays there, and you have a constant set of explanations to go through to anyone who wants to see that record before admitting you to graduate school or professional school. We felt this was an appropriate course of action, and better than calling in the police.

It was a funny kind of occupation, because people would be leaving to go to class and all that sort of thing. Some of them would stay two days and leave, some of them would stay into the second week, and some came in in the second week, and there were people there from the beginning until the end. There were speakers coming in, and they had music, and they had some kind of entertainment. At the peak I would guess there were perhaps three hundred fifty or four hundred of them in the building.

At one point during the sit-in some really weird characters—I think they were called the White Knights of Cicero—came cruising down to the university with the express intention of defending the university against the students who were sitting in. With friends like that, you need no enemies. Our security force came out and protected the students against these people and then withdrew. I don't think the students ever recovered from that paradox: that we were furious at them for doing what they did, and that we were going to discipline them, but meanwhile, they were ours, and we weren't going to let them get clobbered by some nomadic airheads from Cicero.

After they'd been in about a month, the students announced that the next day they were going to walk out. By that time there were only about seventy-five left in the building. They wanted to make it seem as if they'd made their point, but obviously it had petered out. Our feeling was just joy, joy that it was over and that no one had been hurt. There were no heroes and no martyrs, and we hadn't had a confrontation.

As soon as the students left the building on February fourteenth, then the call came for amnesty, and that was much more difficult to deal with than the sit-in in some ways, because there's something terribly appealing about that call for amnesty. Everybody's so glad to have the heat of it over, and they say, "Let's forget about it. Boys will be boys, girls will be girls." There was no serious physical damage done to the building—some catsup in the dictaphones and that sort of thing—and the files, as far as we know, were never touched. So there was a push for amnesty. The students wanted it, and some of the faculty, but the president made it clear that we said there would be disciplinary action, and we meant it then, and we mean it now.

So we had the season of disciplinary committees. Every student who had been identified as being involved in the sit-in had to appear. They were allowed to have their say, and I must say some of the defenses were rather unusual. There was one student who told us he'd been out that day, the first day, listening to the rally, when the students announced they were coming in. He was caught up in the fervor of the moment, but he didn't go in right away. He went to a telephone and he called his psychiatrist, and told the psychiatrist his feelings, and the psychiatrist said, "Well, if you really feel that way, you've got to act. Yes, you ought to go in there." "So," said the student, "I did. I wasn't in there more than an hour when Professor So-and-so came around and said, 'You're Johnny Jones, aren't you? What are you doing in the building?' " And so the student got up to go out, and then he said, "But I kept remembering that my psychiatrist told me it was good for me, so I stayed. I was acting on medical advice." I don't think it was an invented excuse. If it was, it was extraordinarily ingenious. We were easy on him.

Many of the people who organized the strike never showed up at the disciplinary hearings, or if they did, they just denied the jurisdiction of the review group. A good number of them went on to become leaders in the Weathermen, and they took their cause to the streets in the Days of Rage. But other students accepted the disciplinary action, waited out their time, and came back and finished at the university.

. . . You know, there's an awful feeling when you get involved with something like this. You don't think about what's happening at Harvard. You don't think what's happening at Columbia. You think about what's happening in your own place. But at the same time you're conscious that this is very, very much a national thing. I don't think anyone here *really* thought of it as an international conspiracy, but when you see something happening here and here and here and here, it's terribly tempting to say it must all be masterminded somewhere. We didn't really think that, and, of course, it turned out not to be so. But we were never sure. We were never sure.

Tom Jones

*I*n spring 1969 newspaper front pages across the country ran a photo-graph showing black students carrying rifles on the campus of Cornell University. Two days later a black student, addressing a mass meeting on the university campus, used the chilling words, "Cornell has until nine o'clock to live." Tom Jones, who made that speech, is now a senior vice president and comptroller of the John Hancock Insurance Company.

After I got to Cornell, I learned that this was the first year where the university had made a concerted effort to increase the number of black students attending Cornell. They had a program called the Committee on Special Educational Programs, COSEP, but I wasn't really part of that program. My grades had been good and my SATs were not out of line for Cornell. The reason I chose Cornell was because I got a good scholarship there.

I'd come from a middle-class background, and, for the most part, the COSEP students were from an either all-black or predominantly black environment and were more likely to be inner city or Southern rural. Perhaps they felt a little bit uncomfortable and a little bit intimidated by the atmosphere at the university, and therefore tended to be more clannish, seeking support from one another, and turning inward, as opposed to turning outward.

But I felt like I was part of this university, and was having fun right from the beginning. I channeled a lot of my activity into extracurricular projects in student government, and I felt very accepted there. My dorm relationships were good, and I had black and white friends, and I also developed good rapport with some of my professors. In many respects, I probably was one of the students that the university would have pointed to as what they wanted to have happen with integration.

The person who was head of the COSEP program had identified all the students who were enrolled, and he called me and invited me to come to a meeting. Frankly, my first reaction was to be offended, in the sense I didn't think I needed any special consideration. At that time, I felt a natural part of the university. But after a while I began to gravitate toward social relationships with the students that were in the program.

Some people started to organize a black awareness group, and although I was not part of the effort to start it, I became an active participant. There were noticeable differences in attitudes between the COSEP students and the regular students. People like myself were more oriented toward integration, almost in an unquestioning way. To a greater and greater extent the COSEP students were moving toward Black Power and black identity. The articulation of these concepts made people like me think a lot about certain issues, and to become cognizant that not everyone enjoyed the same experiences that I did. As a result of this, I started to read more and more black literature and black history, so that I could understand what had been the economic underpinnings of slavery.

I had thought that I was a rather smart and well-informed person, but I found out that I had never really been taught anything about myself, and I was appreciative of the Black Power thrust for making me want to inquire into these subjects. I had to go outside of the curriculum to read these books, and I felt that there was something wrong in that process, so I began to believe very deeply in the need for black studies. *Knowledge is power*, and people that have an awareness and a sense of self, of where they've been, where they are, and where they want to go, those are the people that can make a difference.

Suddenly this became a common ground for me with those who in the rhetoric of the time were called the more militant students, who were using the arguments for black studies primarily as an organizing mechanism. Their idea was: Once you can get these poor, blind, black people to realize that they just don't belong in this society, they will

be open to ideas such as a separate state, and they'll be open to trying to be part of a class revolution. Theirs was a different agenda, but
we had the same immediate goal: that the university introduce black
studies.

The first reaction was a knee-jerk negative reaction. Professors would
say, "We have a whole history department. How can you say black
history isn't being taught? There's no such thing as black history that's
different from American history. We teach American history, and you're
part of it." But then you ask, "Where did this professor teach about
what was intentionally done to the black family in order to weaken the
slave population; about the breakdown of husband-and-wife relationships and parent-child relationships through intentional sale to weaken
the bonds, because then you have a more passive slave population?
Where was that in the sociology books?" So the first reaction from the
university led students to feel that confrontation was probably necessary.

Actually, I believed at the time, and I believe now, that no confrontation was necessary. The president of the university and I could
have sat down across a table and worked out an entire program, but
there were people on both sides who preferred confrontation for their
own purposes. There were those among the black community who
felt that confrontation was necessary because it would lead to more
rapid politicalization, and there were some hard-core faculty who
really felt that the whole concept of black studies was intellectually
illegitimate.

To this day I believe in the validity and legitimacy of black studies,
but I don't think it's something that a lot of people should try to major
in. The black community needs help from engineers and scientists and
business people, doctors and lawyers and teachers. Each of these needs
to have the perspective that comes from having had the kind of intellectual grounding you could get in half-a-dozen good black studies
courses, a couple in the economics, history, sociology, perhaps some
literature—let's say fifty books altogether. But I don't think it should
be the only major.

One of the things that I found was that as my black peers in the early
years at Cornell began to read more and more economics and history,
often the reaction was bitterness or anger. I was never able to convince
many people of my own point of view: that what's happened is a fact.
There's a vast difference between being knowledgeable with history and

being a prisoner of history. I mean, you can be perfectly aware of what somebody has done to you in the past and say, "I won't tolerate that in the future, but I would like to have this type of positive relationship in exchange."

You see that every day in the relationship between nation-states. What ally of the United States of significance haven't we had a war with? Think about the top countries: Japan, England, Germany, Italy. France would be the only one we haven't fought a war against. After all, you don't carry the baggage of what your ancestors did any more than I do; that's unreasonable. All that any of us can do is to address today and tomorrow. None of us can change the past.

But that wasn't the attitude of many of the black militants then. By spring 1969, the divisions over the black studies program had become so heated, and the movement toward confrontation so strong, that Willard Straight Hall was occupied by the black students as an act of defiance. I wasn't part of the leadership and I didn't want to do it, and I didn't think it was necessary. And I'd been voted down in the meeting that decided on that. But the kids felt they needed to feel they had done something.

Then they began to lose control of the situation. The university wasn't knuckling under, and it appeared there weren't going to be any concessions. Things came to a head when some white fraternity jocks came in through one of the back windows to clear us out. In the milling about and confusion, I became involved, because I said, "Even though this is stupid and we don't belong here, there's a point where you draw a line, and I'm ready to draw a line at these guys deciding they're going to be the ones to take us out. If it's worth our blood, it's going to be theirs, too." Sometimes events take on their own dynamic, and you have to take a stand in places where you'd rather not be, and this was one that I had to take. And so we got the guns.

After the decision to bring arms in, the talk was over. Now it was the time for action. Who's going to walk out the door and get the guns and bring them back? I was one of the people who did that. Actually, it was surprisingly easy. The university hadn't established a very large police presence around the building, so it was just a matter of people being willing to go out and bring them in. One of the reasons I took part is that if I was going to be involved with upping the ante, it was necessary to be responsible for the adequacy of the planning and to be present whenever trouble might occur.

[After a weekend of negotiations with the university administration, the black students left Willard Straight Hall—still with their guns. The crisis continued as the administration and faculty debated what to do about the students' demands, which included amnesty for those involved in the take-over.]

I knew that our chances of success depended on involving the white students, and here one of these absurd arguments developed where the militant leaders wanted to have nothing to do with the white students. This was *our* struggle. I argued that we can't count on people at the university to give a damn what happens to *us*, but I know they care what happens to the general white student population, and to the extent that the white student population stands between us and them, nothing happens to us. And so I became involved in what was probably the turning point of the whole crisis.

I gave a speech to an assembly of about ten thousand white students who had gathered because of this crisis atmosphere. Guns were present on campus, and what was going to happen? Is the National Guard going to be called up or what? It was a powder-keg situation. I think I was effective before those white students, partially because many of them knew me. It wasn't like looking at somebody strange. A lot of them had voted for me a couple of years earlier to be their class president. They knew I was a member of the student judicial board and a member of a fraternity, and they knew I was not an angry person; so suddenly it was, "Why is Tom taking this stand?" They understood the theme that I was establishing: that our blood would not be the only blood that was shed if the university took a hard line. And they listened.

The issue wasn't worth shedding anybody's blood for, but if the university said it was worth our blood, then it was worth their blood, too. When you state things in straightforward and clear terms like that, and people trust you, you can usually get a good response, and the students understood. As a result, the assembled white students declared an occupation of the main assembly hall at the university, and said, in effect, "Now we're occupying the university, and there'll be no classes or anything until the university reconsiders its position."

As a result, an accommodation was made. Some of the faculty resigned. They knew we'd won, and I think it was hard for them to accept. Afterward, I think many of the black students missed the point that the guns didn't bring us to this success. They just created an atmosphere where victory was possible, but the victory was really achieved by an alliance with the white students.

Afterward there was a tremendous high. The news was on the front pages of all the newspapers and news magazines, and I was told at the time that there were news reports on it in Communist China and all over the world, because this was sort of a symbolic episode—the black intelligentsia arming themselves. For many black students there was a kind of pride and esteem, a sense that they were somebody because they'd been part of this. That was all very nice, but, you know, there are other ways to get those feelings. This might have been done at a price that was too high.

In the aftermath, I received many invitations to speak and opportunities to do this and that, and I turned my back on them all. That wasn't what the purpose of my life was. I wanted a black studies program, and we were going to have that; and if you guys want to be a revolution, go ahead—more power to you.

After the settlement, there was an amnesty at the university, so there were no retributions. I stayed on and I began to work on setting up the black studies program. That was a real eye-opener for me, because we ran into problems right away. Certain of the radical students felt that if myself and others weren't always getting in the way, there would be much more rapid progress toward revolution. I found out I could be hated by both sides. The conservative whites hated me because of the statement I'd made about blood, and the militant blacks hated me because I was usually opposed to what I thought of as their hare-brained schemes.

For example, I didn't like the idea of a Malcolm X University which came to the fore right after the settlement. They said, "We don't belong here at Cornell. It's an alien institution." They wanted to go out and build their own alternative university. And I felt that this was now reaching a height of absurdity. We'd gained our point, and now we weren't going to be allowed the victory. I felt that the resources at Cornell had to be used. These people were not well trained and intellectually effective enough to help anybody alone, and to pretend that we were going down and teach each other, to my mind, was a case of the blind leading the blind. This was a serious parting of the ways.

Another argument developed over whether white students would be allowed to attend black studies classes. A lot of the black students didn't want that, and for the life of me, I couldn't understand why we should be threatened by somebody wanting to share this learning experience with us. Why is it bad for a white person to sit down and learn these things? But it was one of those periods of tension when it seemed like everything led to a clash. There were bitter arguments then, and it was quite an education for me. I learned that you have to be very discriminating about the caliber of people that you get close to, because different people have different agendas.

I stayed at Cornell after I graduated that spring, working on a master's program in city and regional planning. And then starting in 1971, I worked for several social planning agencies; one in Binghamton, New York, and later in Cambridge. We did a lot of federal government work, because that's when the government programs were big. There were health programs, housing programs, et cetera. I was an analyst, and then a contract manager. The head of one of those agencies had gone to the big public accounting firm, Arthur Young and Company, to head up their health care section, and he recruited me to work for them. And so, in September of 1973, I went to Arthur Young and Company here in Boston.

That was a major turning point in my life, because this was my first exposure to big-time American business and a really first-class business organization. It was the first time I'd seen what kind of work these people are doing, and what caliber of people they are, and the quality of their work. I was tremendously impressed with the discipline, the quality, the sense of personal achievement and pride in one's own work. And, you know, it began to contrast so much with the public-sector stuff that I had been involved in that I just thought to myself, I want to do *this*.

Now I had a very practical problem: I didn't have any training in business. My background had been in liberal arts and then in public policy and planning. So I started going to night school to get an MBA in finance and accounting. I really dug in, and I got A's or A-minuses in almost every one of those courses. I really wanted to master the material.

I was working full-time then, and classes were five-thirty to eight-thirty. You took classes two nights a week, and the other two nights you had three or four hours of homework, and usually you had that all day Saturday, too. But I was young enough to stand the strain, and I did well.

I went to work for John Hancock in 1982 and now I'm comptroller of its subsidiary holding company, which is the owner of all the non-life-insurance subsidiaries: a brokerage company, a casualty and insurance company, a reinsurance company, a real estate development complex, a home mortgage corporation, a leasing company, and a mutual funds complex with about five billion dollars in assets. It's exciting work, and I like it very much.

One of the luxuries of being a financially successful person is that you should then be able to choose to make other kinds of contributions. And all other things being equal, I probably would have thought about the possibility that at age fifty, fifty-five you retire from a place like this and you accept a government appointment or even consider running for public office. But those are things which I now consider unlikely because of my record. I have no apologies other than to wish the whole thing hadn't happened. But there are ways in which things can be used against you.

My son will be going away to college soon, and there are only a few things I would like him to remember: to have a sense of God, hard work, discipline, and to have the satisfaction of knowing that you did your best. Then whatever the outcome is, you can accept it. And above all, don't abdicate your decision-making responsibility to others.

Ed Whitfield

*H*e grew up in Little Rock, Arkansas, and entered Cornell University *in 1967 as part of the school's first large-scale recruitment of black students. Originally placed in an accelerated Ph.D. program, he dropped out to become a full-time political activist and labor organizer. He is now an electronics technician at a tobacco plant in Greensboro, North Carolina, and operates a small computer company.*

I guess the whole question of civil rights was pretty close to home, given the incident in Little Rock Central High School in 1957, where federal troops and state marshals were out there on opposite sides when nine black kids tried to enroll. My sister went there during the early years. She would come home with stories of having chalk thrown at her in the classroom, soup thrown on her in the cafeteria, and rocks thrown at the car on the way home.

By the time I got there, there were fairly large numbers of black students, so the conditions were different. The level of racial antagonism was generally lower, but there were some conflicts. In my presence students would say to somebody I was talking to, "Hey, don't you know you're not supposed to talk to a nigger?"

I remember when I was in my senior year, there was an exchange program with Madison West High School in Madison, Wisconsin. They were to select a few of their best students to exchange for a few of the best students in Little Rock Central High School. The principal called me into his office and said, "Now, Ed, we know you're a good student and all, and we would let you go on this exchange program, but we weren't able to find any black students up there in Madison"—he probably said "colored" or "Negro"—"to exchange you for." And so I asked him what difference did that make? He told me that if they brought some white kids down here, they'd end up staying around my home, and the school didn't want to be accused of race mixing. And so, since they weren't able to find any blacks to exchange me for, I couldn't go.

So I got irritated sometimes, but at that time my shot at doing something about it was to try to make everybody else around me look dumb. They were a little surprised, I think, by my success. I ended up graduating fifth out of a class of about seven hundred students.

By the time I went off to college, I was adamantly opposed to the Vietnam War, firmly in favor of black folks' struggle in the United States. It seemed strange to me that they'd be off somewhere in the jungles of Vietnam fighting for the right to vote for Vietnamese people when black people didn't have it in Alabama.

I remember Lyndon Johnson was giving out these Presidential Scholar medals, and I was there in the White House. I didn't think very highly of him, and my intention had been that I was going to give it back to him and say that I didn't want anything from anyone who was murdering people in Indochina. But I chickened out. And it bothered me that I had wanted to do it, thought I should do it, and didn't. So I told myself, "When you ought to do something, do it."

When I got to Cornell in 1967 I wanted to get a Ph.D. in mathematics as quickly as possible and go back and become the head of the math department at the University of Arkansas. That was the goal I had.

There was a black student organization on campus called the Cornell Afro-American Society, and I joined. I remember one of the first meetings, the vice president was giving a kind of welcome speech, and he said, "One thing that none of you should forget while you're here at Cornell is that the only reason you're in this country is because your great-great-grandparents were dragged over here as slaves, and you've got a responsibility to that." It made a lot of sense to me, and it was something I kept in mind.

I joined, and I ended up getting in the leadership of the black student group there. I think I was the one that initiated the change of the name from the Afro-American Society to the Cornell Black Liberation Front.

See, the whole thing that created activism on that campus was really the situation that existed in the communities that the people came from. You had people who had come from Watts and Harlem and the ghetto communities in Cleveland and Newark, a few of us from the South. Right while they were in college, their friends at home were struggling in a fairly concerted effort to change the way things were in those communities and give more power to the black communities there. So I think the natural response on the campus was, "What can we do like what's going on at home?"

In the spring of 1968 Martin Luther King got killed. I was not a follower of Martin Luther King. He was a bit too pacifist for me, but I was kind of shocked. I said, "They really messed up now. He was trying to get folks to stay nonviolent, and they killed him." That was my main reaction: that this was a ridiculous mistake.

If you remember, following Martin Luther King's death there were major urban insurrections all over the country. There were a lot of demonstrations that we were involved in on campus. Within the next couple of days, there were reports that some white students in a fraternity drinking club called the Mummies were out buying guns and ammunition and talking about they were going to kill some niggers. I didn't think too highly of this. I never grew up in the turn-the-other-cheek generation. That was before me.

A lot of the black students at Cornell had never shot a gun. I was from the South, where I was never a hunter or anything, but my parents had taught me which end the trigger's on, how to leave a gun on safety. So one of the things we did was to go out on somebody's farm and teach the students how to shoot guns.

There began to be a lot of discussion and demonstrations about setting up a black studies program at Cornell, to try to make the education more relevant to the needs of the communities we had come out of. And we also asked for a level of control over how the programs were established.

There were differences among the black students. Some were pretty much career-oriented people, who didn't want anything to happen that would interfere with their getting through school. There were some others who almost seemed nihilistic. I guess I was kind of in the middle. But in spite of that, there was unity around having some kind of black studies.

There was a building that we wanted for a black studies program, and some black students went in and turned over file cabinets in there and started moving stuff out. They were charged with criminal violations, as though they had simply done it as an act of vandalism. We insisted these were political demonstrations, and they shouldn't be charged the same way as if they were just pranksters. The university wanted to go ahead and charge them.

By that time, I was chairman of the Black Liberation Front, and we called together all the students and told them of our plans to have an occupation of Willard Straight Hall, the student union building. Frankly, part of why we did it was because people had talked for months about doing different things. It seemed as though the student organization would fall apart if not for some ability on our part to act in concert instead of just talking. So occupying a building was something to do at that time, and we did it.

It was on parents' weekend of April of '69. More than a hundred of us went over in the wee hours on Saturday morning. Someone got appointed to be in charge of security, and I remember my first job was writing up a list of demands. I wasn't exactly sure what we would be demanding at the time. During the day these football players broke in through a window to try to force us to leave the building, and some guys met them and tossed them back out. Then we heard that later that night they were going to try to force their way back into the building, but this time they were going to shoot us out, if necessary.

That's when we asked people who were outside to bring our guns inside. There were probably twenty-five rifles or so. I had the view: no more one-sided shootouts. Somebody's going to shoot at me, I will shoot back, and I'm not trying to sell wolf tickets. I meant it.

But I wasn't one of the more radical students there. Some students suggested that we should set the building on fire. I said, "What are we going to do when we set the building on fire, and we're in it?" There was some little tunnel, about three feet high and maybe three feet wide, and I said, "How are all of us going to get out that little hole while the building's burning?" So there were times like that when I'd have to make them put out the cleaning fluid or whatever they would light the building with.

Once the university knew we had guns there, they started doing things that were, to me, comic. A guy called up and said, "Look, we understand you all have some guns." And I said, "Yeah." He said, "Well, why don't I bring my car up behind the building, and I'll let you all put all the guns in the trunk of my car and take them away?" I said, "Huh? No. We brought them in, I guess we can take them out." He said, "Well, okay, how about this? We could get a school bus to come up to the back of the building, and you all can walk out the back and get on the bus with your guns." "Huh?" It tickled me. I said, "No, I think we really want to walk out the door."

The university finally agreed to meet whatever demands we had. It was almost like, "We're not even sure what you all want, but whatever it is, you can have it. Just leave the building with these guns." And they told us that the National Guard was mobilized downtown and was ready to come over to the campus and shoot us anyway, because the mayor would exercise his police power, irrespective of whether or not the university called for it.

What I found out later was that down near the edge of one of the lakes Ithaca is located on they had in one day's time lined the inside of a boathouse with chain-link fence and barbed wire. They'd built a little concentration camp large enough to lock us all up. There were jeeps and armed personnel carriers with machine guns downtown ready to move up the hill where we were. They were serious.

I try to have a good sense of timing, and I figured by the time they were ready to give in to all our demands, I was about ready to come out the building. I didn't want to see anyone get hurt. I didn't think it was necessary.

I naively hadn't thought about the publicity that happened afterward. At the time we walked out of the building, I had no idea there would be anyone taking pictures. In fact, we ended up saying that for our own safety, "What we'd like to do is, as we come out, we want you all to walk out with us." It was real in my mind that students can get killed on campus, and I didn't have any particular reason to trust them. So we got the provost of the university and another person we had been negotiating with to walk out with us. In fact, we told them we didn't even want them to walk out directly in front of us, because then it might look like we're holding them hostage. We wanted them to come out alongside us.

So we got all lined up. Several guys had on bandoliers and makeshift things to make them look like Mexican outlaws. There were pool cues that had been broken off, and knives affixed to the ends as spears. A lot of imagination went into it, you know, and some theatrics, probably.

When the building finally opened, there were probably several hundred people standing out in front. I didn't know who they were. They stood there in silence for a few seconds, and we stood where we were in silence, and then a cheer went up from them. It turned out that they were largely SDS supporters, who had been outside the building demonstrating in support of us. So they were cheering, and then cameras started clicking, and we walked on out.

At the point we came out, the administration had basically agreed to our demands: amnesty for ourselves, dropping the charges against the people who had been in other demonstrations, and the establishment of the black studies program. Then there were these meetings that explained this to the rest of the university. And they were trying to figure out are they really going to give these people amnesty, and there was a big push not to. Several professors resigned based on the university having caved in to the demands of terrorists.

Then the university called a big convocation to try to decide what was going to happen. They asked me to speak, but I really didn't have anything I wanted to say to them. So Tom Jones volunteered to go as a representative of the Black Liberation Front. That's when he gave his speech and said that the university had three hours to live, that pigs are going to die.

I was listening to it on the radio, and I had absolutely no idea what he was talking about. When he came back, I said, "Tom, what are you talking about? How are we gonna back that up?" It was a bluff, but the university backed down, and the faculty went ahead and approved our demands that the administration had agreed to. I guess they thought we had the campus booby-trapped, ready to start blowing things up. That was certainly not the case.

I could have graduated that next year, but I didn't go to classes very much. I didn't think much of the black studies program as it was set up. It was too abstractly academic. They had courses with cute names like Black History, Black Ideology, and Black Economics. It was pretty clear to me that it wasn't what we were talking about. But I didn't feel that any effective way existed to turn it around.

I ended up moving down to North Carolina and teaching political economy and mathematics at Malcolm X Liberation University. Black students from all over the country—mainly people who had been involved in political activity—had set up their own educational school. But it wasn't exactly clear what we were trying to do. It lasted for about two-and-a-half years, and after that people scattered.

I stayed here in North Carolina and for a while tried to help organize unions in the textile industry. It was hard. The majority of people were frightened of the company and also leery of unions. And I've done some work helping housing-project tenants stand up for their rights.

In the last election, I ran for city council. I missed being in the run-off by about a hundred votes. I used to wonder why the people with real guts to take sharp positions weren't out here involved in politics. I found out that they're there, and they run. They just don't get elected.

I guess the initial reason I got interested in computers was political. I wanted to try to find some way that young black kids can get involved in something that's got a future to it. I may never succeed, but I do it. See, if we don't watch it, in the next few years you're going to have two groups of people in the United States: One of them works with computers, and the other works at Burger King.

Irene Smalls

© Sandy Middlebrooks

*S*he lives in a renovated Victorian townhouse in Boston's South End with her children, Jonathan, age two, and Dawn, age nine. She has operated a marketing consulting business and served as director of public information for the City of Boston, and now works as a news reporter for a cable TV station.

I was lucky. I was born at the right time when the doors were opened for blacks to come in. I think the people who benefited were the black middle class, who were better prepared and were poised at the door, and as soon as that door opened, they pushed right through. And there were folks like me, from the black underclass, who were swept along with that wave. That's why I got into Cornell. They weren't taking kids like me before.

I grew up in Harlem. No one in my family had ever finished high school. My father was a pimp, and my mother was one of his prostitutes. I was raised by my godmother, who was an older black woman, the lady who had the greatest influence on me. She only had a third-grade education and basically washed floors for a living, for many, many years. And therefore college was very important to her, because she hadn't had the opportunity.

I mean, she pushed me. One of the reasons my housekeeping skills are fairly lax is because whenever I wanted to get out of housekeeping,

I'd say, "Oh, Ma, I want to read this book," and she'd say, "Oh, read the book, child, read the book."

I was fairly bright, so I was always in the special classes, and it always seemed to me that I was the only really poor kid there. I was accepted by three colleges, and Cornell offered me the most money. So for someone with the least amount of money, it seemed clear to me where I was going. Of course my godmother was just the proudest person in the world. She would proceed to tell all the neighbors, "Did you see what my baby did?"

I went off to Cornell in 1967, and the experience was traumatic. I had been pretty much immersed in a black community, and then I went to Cornell, and there were two hundred of us, the largest class of blacks ever admitted at one time, out of a total enrollment of fifteen thousand. And for a city kid, it was rural upstate New York, cows and all this.

I remember I used to call home every weekend and cry. I'd say, "Mama, I want to come home. I want to come home, Mama." And my godmother would say, "Girl, you've gone too far to fall back." I'll never forget those words. I would give her a litany of things that were happening. I'd say, "Mama, these people aren't treating me right. They're feeding me cottage cheese up here. Cottage cheese!" And she'd say, "No, we got you this far, honey, we're not letting you fall back." And I'd say, "Okay, Mama, okay, I'll stay."

This was the first sort of wholesale importation of low-income urban blacks at Cornell, so this was an experiment, an explosive experiment to say the very least. We had this one black student, Alicia. She was a trip. I mean, this chick was fighting all the time. She had fights in classes with white women. She was having fights with her roommate. They said Alicia played her music too loud, and they didn't like the kind of music she played.

Half the time, I didn't particularly like Alicia, but I felt they weren't taking into account any of *her* rights. They were always talking about the effects on the roommate, the effects on the dorm. What about Alicia? No one was defining her in her own terms. Alicia and I had come from predominantly black environments, so I understood what she was going through. So I felt that somebody had to speak up for Alicia.

I remember they were talking about putting her out of school. I knew how much college meant to my family, and I knew how much college would mean to *her* family. It's one thing to send a middle-class white student home. The parents pooh-pooh, they complain, but they put him in another school. But for an Alicia, generations of families have worked toward this goal, and you're talking about throwing it all away. I just couldn't see that. So therefore I said, "No, you can't put Alicia out."

I decided that if they're going to put her out, they're going to have to go through me first. And they decided, Well, what's that? No problem. So I organized the girls in the dorm. We had sit-ins outside Alicia's room, and then they didn't seem to be hearing me, so the sit-ins got bigger. I started writing press releases. I finally went to the provost, and he said, "Okay, what's your alternative?" And I said, "You have to give her an opportunity to exist in her environment. What we need is a black house."

That's when we set up our black student union and started pushing as a group for a black student house. The demonstrations started escalating, and then other black students got involved. It took a while. We went back and forth and back and forth. I'd say eight months to a year. It was a lot of struggle, but the university finally said, "Okay, Irene, we'll get you a house."

They took me around, and we looked at all these houses, and then I found the house that I liked. It wasn't too far from campus. It was far enough, sort of secluded, where we could be alone if we wanted. They asked me to pick a name, and I called it Wari House. It means "home" in one of the African languages.

Once we began to deal with issues like, "We're entitled to our lifestyle, to our music, to our clothing, to whatever," then the movement began to grow. We began to say, "What about black history? What about black faculty? What about black counselors? Let's give us a full menu of options." It developed into an entire black student movement.

My attitude was that I should be able to have a leadership role. I had started the whole thing. I set up the first series of demonstrations, and it was my idea to look for a house. But as the men got involved, it became a matter of manhood. So when I wanted to run for president of the black student union, they talked me out of it.

The feeling was, "You black women have been too strong" and "You black women have held us men back" and "You black women have castrated all of these men." They said, "We want you to cook and have babies. That's your role in the revolution." I was so young, seventeen, eighteen. What did I know? I bought it. In terms of leadership, it became a man's movement.

And while we were in upstate New York evolving as a movement, there were all kinds of other events roaring around us. I remember when Martin Luther King was assassinated. I felt as if the world had ended. It was Martin Luther King and his activism that got me into school. And my godmother and those older black women revered him. It really saddens me that kids today don't know who he is. I mean he was a living, breathing god to black people.

When you look back, we were innocents at Cornell. We completely believed that we were going to change the face of the earth, and we gave everything we had. I mean we had folks burn out. Some of us were strong enough to stay, but I would say less than half of the black students in that class of '71 graduated on time.

I think we made our mark. We got more black faculty hired. We got black counselors. There's a black study center. We have our Cornell black alumni association, and it's alive and well. But in retrospect, we didn't change that much.

I've been back for reunions and meetings, and the black students following us are largely more middle-class. They acculturate a lot more easily in the Cornell environment, and these students are interested in grades. They're not interested in blackness. When we were there, if you saw a black face, you went out of your way to say hello, whether you knew them or not. The point was that they were black and you were black, and you were up there together. A lot of that sense of camaraderie and community has diminished, and I'm really sorry about that. The momentum is gone.

In 1979 I had a rally at City Hall Plaza in Boston with five hundred people, and we called it "I Love You Black Woman—A Rally." We read poems and sang songs. It was just meant to be an affirmation of black women in this society. And I put out these flyers saying "I Love You Black Woman." I was giving these flyers to black women, and I noticed that nobody was throwing them away. I thought that was really odd. I've done flyers for years and years. You know, people read the flyer, and then it goes down on the ground, right?

I thought about it. Well, maybe nothing in our society said "I Love You Black Woman," and these women wanted to hold on to that message just a little bit longer. So as an offshoot of the rally I put the "I Love You Black Woman" slogan on T-shirts. I put together this little T-shirt business. And I did "I Love You Black Man" and "I Love You Black Child." I got a contract with the military exchanges to distribute in fourteen states, and we got some national attention.

I'm really concerned about young black females. When I went to

Cornell in the Sixties, twenty-five percent of black households were headed by single females. Now it's almost 50 percent. They talk about a permanent black underclass, because black females are the poorest of all. What I say is that if there were an opportunity for some of these single black women to run their own small businesses, there'd be a means for them to maintain contact with their families and also provide for their economic viability. At some point I'm going to do something about that.

But, for me, I can't say that I've failed. I have two kids. I've got my education. I've got my M.B.A. I've got a decent job. I've got a house. I accept myself as I am. My godmother always said, "Look at the distance you've come. Don't look at the other fellow. Look at the distance you've come: where you started, and where you are now."

Orest Allen Ranum

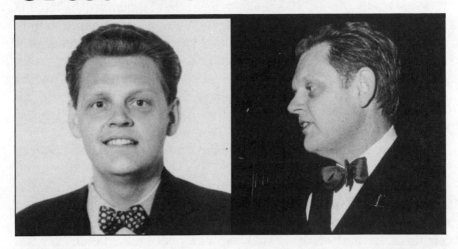

*I*n 1968, during the student occupation of Columbia University, one professor's files were broken into and his papers burned. The book of European history on which he had been working was never written. Professor Ranum now teaches at Johns Hopkins University in Baltimore.

I was a moderate, and moderates don't do very well in revolutions. I was quite familiar with the leadership of SDS. Our contact was friendly and kind of theoretical. We talked on theory about revolution quite a bit, and they gave me one of their copies of the Port Huron Statement.* I felt I was in the presence of some people who were really willing to go to rather extreme limits. Even after discussions like this we remained on speaking terms. But they were interested in my ideas, and I was interested in theirs.

The morning after the first occupation of the university buildings, I put on my gown—I usually lecture in a gown—and decided to go over there. The students were in the president's office already. There was no way to get in through the door, so I went into the president's office through the window. After a number of hours of going round and round talking to these students, I realized that there was no good way of

---

* The political manifesto of SDS, published in 1962 following a convention in Port Huron, Michigan.

negotiating. They needed their police bust, as they thought, to radicalize not only the campus but society.

Mark Rudd and the SDS really thought that Harlem would come in and support them. I remember saying, "You just don't have the right language. You talk Marxism and you've never made a sermon in your life. You've never listened to a black preacher. You don't know what the language of Harlem is." Mark had his Marxist discourse, and he thought that it was a universal language that other people would understand. He had no idea of what it was like to live in Harlem. I mean, they were ordinary people down there, and they didn't give a damn about what was going on up here. But the students were totally divorced from reality.

After I left them, I issued a statement making an analogy from American literature: that we were being led by an Ahab looking for a great white whale. There were only two ways out: rebellion against the leadership of the students in the buildings or a police bust. I didn't say this in a preachy way, I said it in a kind of social-scientific tone, and I think that pained the leadership in the buildings. That statement was spread everywhere, and I've always interpreted the decision to break into my office and go through my things and to select my materials to crunch up and put on desks and set on fire as a result of that moderate statement.

The night they burned my papers was the night when the first barricades were built in America. They tore up the blocks in the roads, on the paths of the university, and they attempted to make simple barricades to stop the police. They were carrying out metaphorically what had happened in Paris in 1789, 1848, 1870—the great moments of revolution. Their model was clearly European at that moment. They couldn't complete it, because they didn't have the masses, but they tried in a kind of metaphorical desperation.

The relationship between what people say and what people do is always interesting to historians. There had been threats for days of "We will burn this place down." There was very little to burn in the building. It was fireproof, it was made of concrete and stone, terrazzo floors, practically no curtains in it. What they burned was my papers. At some point my office was broken into. My file drawers were never locked. They simply took my research notes, lecture notes, off-prints, whatever papers there were—the things that you always find in a professor's office. They crumbled them all up, took them to one of the corner lecture halls so that they could try to maximize the notion from the outside that the building was on fire. They distributed these little piles of my papers, crumbled up on various desks, to make it look like the fire was bigger than it really was.

I was phoned the next morning by some university official, and I went over there. By that time the police were occupying the building, and I saw this sort of mess. I was just astonished. I mean I just couldn't believe it. I hadn't thought there would be any attempt to carry out the rhetoric about trying to burn down the university. I had never felt any physical danger or fear for anything that had belonged to me. There was just a deep sense of bewilderment, and I guess my pride was hurt, too. I mean, why me?

After the fire there was a very warm expression of support from other scholars, and I liked that a lot. The experts who had been working on the Dead Sea Scrolls at the Jewish Theological Seminary called and offered to help me with my materials, because they were experts in reconstituting burnt documents. I retrieved some of these materials, and since the papers were soaked, people offered to try to dry things out and copy them, but I just didn't go ahead with it. I didn't do that book then and I never will.

Nancy Biberman

*F*or the past thirteen years she has been a public-interest lawyer, working with low-income clients, primarily on housing and domestic violence matters. Currently on leave from her job, she has a fellowship at Columbia University, where she was one of the SDS members involved in the 1968 student takeover. The students were protesting the university's involvement in military research and its plans to construct a gymnasium in nearby Morningside Park.*

Columbia sits on a bluff. There's the river and New Jersey off to one side, and then there's Harlem off to the other. And Morningside Park is a strange kind of vertical park. It drops sharply down, and then you're in Harlem. Everybody understood that this park was like a border. This was the fortress that protected Columbia from the black and Hispanic community. On some level, the university had historically said, in a way, "Okay, the park is yours." White students didn't go in there. This was really the community's park. It was just one of those things that was unsaid, but understood.

So then Columbia devised a plan to build a gymnasium in Morningside Park, and people in the community were outraged. Architecturally, it was not well done. The design enforced the fortresslike sense about

* A city park, two acres of which were leased by Columbia University.

it—security, big walls. And to start this thing, the university erected a huge chain fence around the construction site and started digging. So SDS claimed the gym as an issue.

I don't think taking over a building was ever anything that was articulated. You sat in, you demonstrated, you picketed; but the taking of a building just hadn't happened before. It was just not in our arsenal of things to do.

When it finally happened, it was not the white SDS students who initiated it. It was the black students. All of SDS's planning and plotting to do something big, and then when the shit finally hit the fan, it was nothing that SDS had planned at all.

In April, to stop the gym being built, the black students seized Hamilton Hall, which is the main building, both administrative and classrooms. Once the occupation of the building started, SDS followed suit. When the black students left Hamilton Hall, white students came in, and it developed a momentum of its own. One by one we just sort of spread into other buildings.

Clusters of people started forming in buildings. A lot of people emerged as leaders who had never been involved in activism before. SDS was just a small fragment of the people who wound up in buildings. It was really amazing. Something had taken hold of some deep, pent-up discontent. And it took off.

Each of these buildings kind of took on a character. People from SDS, militants, were in Low Library, the main administrative center of the campus. They took over the president's office, chained themselves in, barricaded all the doors. The mathematics building was also a building that militants were in, but not necessarily SDS. Hamilton was sort of a mix. And Fayerwether was the building where the graduate students were—more liberal types.

The buildings that were taken over had no particular relationship to the war machine. Had it been more organized, perhaps we would have targeted a building where defense research might have been going on. But the takeover of the buildings was genuinely spontaneous.

It was a counterculture event, as well as a political action. There were elaborate feasts in some buildings, socializing, music, dancing. There was a wedding in Fayerwether, and the two people who were married called themselves Andrea and Richard Fayerwether. In Low Library, there was this guy who was sort of a literary type on campus, not an activist. And the events just sort of captured his imagination. Someone took pictures of him sitting in the president's lavish mahogany office, smoking his cigars, his feet up on the desk. He was a real character: long black hair, long black mustache, an arty type. It was a great picture. And it *enraged* the university. This was the ultimate degradation, this dirty character sitting in the president's chair.

At about the time that the first building was taken, there was a call for a student strike, and the purpose was to end the university affiliation with the Institute for Defense Analysis and to stop the university from building the gym in Morningside Park. We said, "It's wrong that there should be business as usual while these things are going on."

I was on the strike steering committee, so I wound up being a leader. From that point on, it's all sort of a blur. People worked around the clock for the two weeks that this thing lasted. There was simply no sleep.

What the steering committee did was bounce around all the buildings to share with people what other folks were doing. Inside the buildings there were endless meetings, sharing newspaper clippings, sharing rumors, discussing the issues, figuring out what the demands were. And then, of course, there was the amnesty question: How could something like this ever end if there was no guarantee from the university that students weren't going to be prosecuted criminally or through disciplinary proceedings?

The university didn't want to talk about anything until the buildings were empty. And of course we said, "Listen, we're holding the cards now. If they're not going to talk to us now, they're never going to talk to us." They just said, "This is unacceptable, this campus has to return to normal, and then we'll talk about the issues." And there was always the pretty explicit threat of bringing police in, but I know that the faculty fought that to the bitter end.

Different groups got organized, and people walked around campus with different-color armbands indicating which of the groups they were in. There were red armbands. Red meant you were militant. There was another armband that meant you were on the other side, people who weren't supportive. I'm not sure what they called themselves, but we called them the jocks. The kinds of things they would do were preventing food from getting to the people in the buildings.

We had devised elaborate ways to get food in. The doors were always guarded and barricaded, but in some buildings it was easy to get food in, because Columbia has a tunnel system under the buildings. Once you got into the tunnels, it was easy to learn your way around. People knew enough to barricade the tunnel entrances so that police couldn't get into the buildings, but that was also a source of food.

There were some buildings that, for some reason, couldn't use the tunnels, particularly in Low Library. So people in Low set up a pulley mechanism from a window to a place down on the ground to send up baskets of food. The jocks organized a line around Low Library, so that nobody could get through, so that food couldn't be sent up. I remember there being fights, students trying to bring food being physically stopped, people being beaten up. Sometimes the campus police would try to break things up, but they were obviously pretty pissed off at what was happening, too, so they weren't exactly going to intervene on behalf of feeding students who were occupying buildings.

There was a lot of fighting. This is where the third group of students came in. They were the pacifists, who would put their bodies between the militants, who were taking over the buildings, and the jocks, who wanted to rout everybody out by their hair. A lot of faculty fell into that group also. Their message was, "We don't want violence." And the jocks just couldn't maintain the ring around Low Library forever. It dissipated and we could bring in food.

While people were in the buildings, there were a million different support activities going on. Community demonstrations would come up onto campus to support the students. There would be rallies, and singers would come. Pete Seeger and the Grateful Dead gave concerts. Rap Brown, Stokely Carmichael, other black militants came onto campus. And everybody in between. Everybody who was anybody in the progressive world, either politically or culturally or academically, came up and made an appearance. It was really sort of mandatory.

It's hard to describe, but there was an incredible exhilaration, that here we were making history, changing the world. We had done something that nobody else had done before, and, who knows, maybe we were going to *make the revolution* at Columbia. This was the beginning of the end. Everybody believed that this university would never be the same, that society would be irrevocably changed, that there'd be a revolution in the United States within five years, and a whole new social order. This is really what people believed, and I did, too. It was that kind of heady experience, it really was.

Needless to say, every magazine and newspaper in the country had enormous spreads on this. They wanted to interview everybody. The role of the strike steering committee in large measure was to provide communication between the buildings and the outside world, to let the press know what was happening. Plus we wanted this continuing coverage. We felt that in a way it protected us. Though it didn't.

The police had been massed around the border of the campus for a number of days—along 116th Street, along Amsterdam, and along Broadway. There were hundreds of them, loads of police buses and those big vans. They had been requested by the university, but told to just stay there. They loomed there as a threat, and clearly they had gotten angry and pent up, because they had been sort of kept at bay outside the campus for so long.

In the middle of one night, the university called the police in. I guess they figured it had to end somehow. When students heard that the police were coming on, they erected makeshift barricades at the entrances to the campus and then set them on fire, so there were huge fires at either end of the campus.

And to make a long story short, the police just went on a rampage. There were so many of them. Teams went to different buildings and into the tunnels, and then groups of them went randomly around the campus. They broke into all the buildings and beat students up, beat up anybody they could see. They just came on and rioted.

In some buildings people had made decisions about how they were going to leave. Some said, like in Fayerwether, "We'll just go out peacefully. We don't want anyone to get hurt." And people in other buildings, like math, said they were going to fight to the death. The police didn't exactly play along. They didn't know that Fayerwether said they would go out peaceably. So they just came in and emptied the building.

Once things started happening, everybody came out to just watch. It was so incredible. There were thousands of students milling around the campus. And the police didn't know who to beat up and who not to beat up, so they beat up loads of people who had nothing to do with what was going on in the buildings. So everybody was running around, ducking the police and looking for cover or a place to watch what was going on.

No place was safe. The police would go into dormitories, literally chase students up flights of steps—students who were just running back to their rooms for safety—beat them up, and drag them out of the dorms. And a lot of people were outraged, yelling and screaming and cursing at the cops, so the cops would beat *them* up. It was a genuine riot.

It was out of control for hours. There was bloodshed everywhere. There was no gunfire, but there were clubs and blackjacks. Medical students from Columbia came on campus, had first aid teams to deal with injuries. I wasn't hurt, but I vividly remember a number of male friends who were really beaten up: blood all over the faces, bandaged heads, broken arms, battered legs, terrible pain.

They arrested a thousand students that night and beat up hundreds more. People were just being dragged off continually. They drove police vans right onto campus, put people in, drove them out, brought new vans in, put people in, all night long. And eventually people who had been running around realized that it was simply not safe to be outside. So once the campus was cleared of both people who were in the buildings and people who were outside observing, that was the end. It was dawn.

Everyone was just devastated. The day after that the university officially shut down. They forgot about exams. They just gave pass or fail grades. And that was that.

I'm spending a year now at Columbia on a Revson Fellowship. The purpose is to award stipends and tuition to mid-career professionals who are involved in different ways in municipally focused public-interest activities. I'm in the school of architecture and planning, studying ways to develop new forms of housing for the elderly, single mothers, and the disabled. For two semesters now, I've been immersed in zoning and other land-use issues, real estate finance, and architecture and social history.

I'm having a great time! When I was younger, I didn't want to be in the university. I wanted to be out in the real world where everything exciting was happening. And now I *love* being here. I really appreciate the ivory tower.

One of the things I can't get over is the durability of the institution. Columbia is an architecturally imposing place. It's a very beautiful campus. The buildings are forever. You walk onto the campus and you say, "This institution will endure." Somehow I thought the place would never be the same after '68, but the fact of the matter is that it's exactly the same. Through thick and thin, nothing has changed. It really has endured. And there's a piece of me that feels good about that, in spite of everything that happened.

The gym was never built in Morningside Park. There was a gym eventually built at Columbia, but what they did was build it underground, right smack in the middle of the campus, which was a smart idea. One of the ironies of my life is that now, during my fellowship year at Columbia, I'm spending more time in the gym than any other place on campus.

The
Yuppie
and the
Yippie

Jerry Rubin

George Tames/NYT Pictures

O ne of the original Yippies, organizer of the 1967 March on the
Pentagon, codefendant in the conspiracy trial of the Chicago Seven,
and master of political theatrics, he was a symbol of youth protest in
the Sixties. Today he lives in an impressive Upper East Side apartment
building in Manhattan, complete with two doormen. Together with his wife,
Mimi, he runs the very profitable Network Parties, a series of glorified
singles gatherings for young professionals held at the Palladium nightclub
in New York. Recently, as the self-proclaimed spokesman for the Yuppies,
he debated his former activist ally Abbie Hoffman at colleges across the
country.

I was always a sort of mainstream person. The only Reds I knew until
I left Cincinnati were the Cincinnati Reds, and they were very important
to me. All the time I was in elementary school and high school and
after I went to work as a sports reporter, they were the Reds that
counted.

I wasn't a red-diaper baby like so many people in the Movement.
My anger was a genuine anger and my realizations were born of curiosity, not out of loyalty to family or anything like that. I was more
influenced by the Lone Ranger than by Mao or Che or Lenin.

I went to Oberlin College and later to the University of Cincinnati,
and while I was there I worked as a sports reporter for the paper. And

when I graduated in '61, I continued to work there. In 1963 I went out to Berkeley and enrolled as a graduate student in sociology. I became involved in a lot of the civil rights demonstrations going on then and in the Free Speech Movement out there—but only as a participant on a low level, not as a leader of any sort.

Berkeley at this time was a kind of a left-wing community, and there was a left-wing culture there. You were an oddball if you didn't have this point of view at that time. I mean, normalcy at Berkeley at that time was to ask the question, "What do you think of Leon Trotsky?" That was a loaded question to them. There were actual Trotskyites and Communists out there, and they were yelling and screaming at each other about something that happened in 1935. But it was all on an intellectual level at that time.

Then when the bombs started dropping in Vietnam—this would have been in '64, '65—it seemed to me that there was an absolute imperative for people to do something about it: stop careers, stop their lives, do whatever was necessary to make a symbolic statement.

The process that I envisioned was that we would start with making statements and then go into direct disruption, and then from Berkeley we would organize the entire country against these policies in Vietnam. I had read a lot of Gandhi by that time and I was very influenced by him, and I sort of thought that people should really fill the jails of America until America stopped oppressing people around the world. It wasn't so much the nonviolence of Gandhi that influenced me as it was the moral urgency of action.

The first thing was to organize a teach-in on Vietnam. We did it out of my apartment, and we worked for about six months on it and ran up a huge telephone bill. We invited people from the State Department to come and talk, and we had antiwar professors, and we got the university to ban the event. Then we used the publicity of their banning the event to attract crowds through the media. And then the university backed down, and twenty-five thousand people attended.

It was a huge historical accomplishment. All the energy of the Free Speech Movement was channeled into the antiwar movement. We were trying to attract as much attention as possible, and when General Maxwell Taylor came to town, we went down and threw paint on his limousine and were all arrested, and it became a front-page story. Since I was an ex-newspaperman, I was very aware of the media and how through the media a little thing can be blown up to be a big thing, and I knew how to get that front page story.

Then we discovered that the federal government was sending troop trains right through Berkeley to the Oakland Army Terminal, and we began having rallies down at the train tracks. We would lie on the tracks when the trains came through, and the police would come. It was really wild. The police would try to drive us off the tracks, and we would just lie there. These demonstrations started getting a lot of publicity, and Berkeley became a kind of a national focus.

Then we began to organize a thing called the National Committee Against the War in Vietnam. I went to a conference where I made a speech saying that we should have national demonstrations against the war. So when the House Un-American Activities Committee held hearings on the opposition to the war, I was a logical target for it.

As I say, I knew the media and what would get its attention, and so I was thrilled when I got the subpoena. In fact, more than thrilled. I was really hoping I'd get one, and the day the subpoenas came out, I called up the FBI to ask if I'd got one. It was like calling up to see if you've been accepted at a university or for graduate school. [*Laughs.*] It really was. I remember I was in a drugstore when I called the FBI, and they said, "Oh, yes, they're looking for you." And I said, "Yay! They're looking for me!" I would have been really crushed if I'd been left out.

Actually, the FBI were dumb. If they'd just played psychic warfare and left me out, I would have been so depressed that I think it would have made me inactive for a year. But instead, they walked right into my hands when they handed me the subpoena, and they gave me the platform I needed.

I had a month or two to prepare before my appearance before the House Un-American Activities Committee, and I gave a lot of thought to what I would do. I wanted to do something arresting, something shocking, something that would really make a statement.

Everybody in Berkeley kept telling me, "Say this," "Say this," "Make this argument," "Point this out." I was writing down all the things they told me, and I said to myself, Well, who's going to listen to all these arguments?

You know, most of the people subpoenaed were ideological Marxists with the Progressive Labor Party. They wanted to make all these points and wanted to talk about the working class, and it was like garbage, like gobbledygook. Who's waiting to hear this message, you know?

I was talking with one of the theater people at Berkeley, and he said, "Well, why don't you wear a Revolutionary War hat to the hearing rooms?"—the theater approach, you know. And I said, "What a good idea, an American Revolutionary War hat. . . . But that's not enough. Why not wear the whole uniform? That's *it*!"

But when I started asking around, everybody thought this was a terrible idea. You have to remember these were all Berkeley intellectuals who would never do anything but sit around and debate and argue all their lives. They kept telling me, "Don't do that. You're going to embarrass the antiwar group if you do such a thing."

Remember, this was before theater became a way of life in America. This was before gays went marching through the streets saying, "We're proud we're gay." This was before streaking. This was before pies in the face. And although the New Left was politically radical, it was still very conservative culturally.

But I knew it was a good idea. I went to a costume store and for twenty-five dollars I rented this Revolutionary War uniform, and I tried it on. It looked *great*. It was the perfect message. It said, "We're the revolutionaries. This country was founded on a revolution. You're violating your own ideals. You're violating your own traditions." It was a visual statement.

As a concession to the Berkeley intellectuals, I had a little picket sign made with a verbal message saying something like, "In Vietnam the United States has violated the Declaration of Independence, which says that governments have the right to be overthrown," or words to that effect. It was an argument on a picket sign, and it was my concession to the intellectuals.

I wanted to be effective and I felt the costume was the way to be effective, because America is primarily a visual society. What could I possibly say that would be noticed as much as this image?

When I went to Washington I had a bit of so-called opening-night jitters, and I wavered and considered that maybe I shouldn't do it. After all, I was the only one. It wasn't as though I had a group. I was just a little scared of what might happen and I thought maybe I'd be laughed at by everybody, and nobody likes to be laughed at. I kind of felt ridiculous getting into this very hot, wool uniform on a sweltering August day in Washington, D.C., but I went ahead with it anyway.

When I walked in, everyone's mouths kind of just dropped. I knew immediately that I'd done the right thing, because there was that "Aha!" look in their eyes, that "I see what he's saying" look. It was obvious, my message. So I was right. The medium was the message. This was before McLuhan's book, but I was acting it out.

Everyone at the committee hearings kind of played their roles. The Progressive Labor people called the right-wing congressmen Fascists, and the right-wing congressmen started banging down the gavel and calling them Communists, and they got into fistfights and were ejected as predicted.

I just kind of sat there in my Revolutionary War uniform, and pictures of me in that uniform went all across the country. Many people have told me that that picture is what motivated them to become activists. Abbie Hoffman says it's probably the best thing I've ever done—which I guess is sort of a putdown.

It worked perfectly. They fell into my trap and decided not to let me testify. My purpose there was not to testify but to be seen. But when they canceled the hearings, I screamed, "I came to testify! I want to testify!" And the chairman said, "Sit down." When I didn't sit down, they arrested me. And when the marshals dragged me out, it was like dragging Thomas Jefferson, Thomas Paine away from the House Un-American Activities Committee as they tried to testify. It was kind of like the church would arrest Jesus if he arrived today. I was being prevented from testifying by being dragged out, and the whole thing was A-plus theater.

So everything worked out perfectly. I thanked the federal marshals, I thanked the media, I even thanked PL for being nuts and creating their own excitement. When I went back to Berkeley all the left-wing intellectuals said, "You were right. The coverage was perfect. You made your point. You were right."

At about that point, the hippies from San Francisco began coming to Berkeley, and they invited the Berkeley radicals to come to their Be-In in Golden Gate Park. When the day of the big Be-In arrived, I went and I made a political speech, and it went over to a resounding ho-hum from the audience. I became very influenced by this. I thought maybe the real battle of America is not politics, it's lifestyle. And lifestyle determines politics. That's what these people were saying. My life up to that point was built and based around confrontation and the idea that the truth comes through confrontation. But after the Be-In I was changed.

I started smoking a little marijuana myself then. I was probably one of the last people to smoke marijuana out there. I was not particularly a sexual libertarian, and I was personally sort of conservative. I actually lived with one woman all through the whole Sixties. I went on the first march with her, and I went on the last march with her. That was an achievement in the Sixties, I think. When I did start smoking pot, everyone else was doing it by then. I was almost forcing myself to do it. In the beginning I was almost humiliated into doing it by all these people who were smoking all the time. I think I was kind of scared of getting stoned at first. Of course, then I became a fierce marijuana advocate and a daily smoker. I was a square becoming a hip, and I was fighting the square inside of me.

And I was intrigued by all this creativity that was coming out of the hippie movement—a lot more than was coming out of the political movement. There were the Diggers and their free food in the streets and the theater of the streets, and I thought, If there was some way to politicize this energy, could it possibly be contained? If one could combine the new culture of the young people with the frame of reference of politics, one would have an explosive combination that would challenge America to its foundations. It would steal the children of America. The young people would choose us, because we had excitement and they had boredom. I felt that the more outrageous we were, the more effective we could be.

You know, without the war, it would have been hard to stimulate the crisis that we created. We would never have been able to match what we were hearing on television—what America was doing in Vietnam. There's nothing we could have done and nothing we did to match that.

I mean, *if there hadn't been a Vietnam War, we would have had to invent one.* It was a way to talk about America, about the racism in America, the militarism in America, the mechanical anti-Communism. It was an opportunity that we weren't, you know, happy about, because people were dying, and that was a tragedy. But after all, America had created it, and in a way America revealed itself by creating it. Vietnam was the lightning rod that changed American society.

The National Mobilization on the War in Vietnam was planning a march on Congress in 1967, and Dave Dellinger called me up and asked me if I was willing to become the project director for the march. I was getting pretty tired of Berkeley, and I was just thrilled that Dave Dellinger and the steering committee had voted to bring me there as a project director. I think later they all regretted it, because they had no idea how militant or how hippie-oriented I had become by then. I packed my bags and was on a plane to New York City in two days.

The first night I had dinner with Dave Dellinger, and when Dave described the planned march on Congress, I said, "You know, this march on Congress, Dave, doesn't really make sense to me. People don't see Congress as the enemy. They elect Congress. There's no point to be made by doing that. We should march on the *Pentagon*." I saw things in media images, in terms of good versus evil, and the media image would be the Movement versus the Pentagon. That's all we had to do. Nothing else. No words. You don't need words.

Dave said, "But look, it's impossible to march on the Pentagon. There's only one bridge from Washington to the Pentagon; we'll never get there." I said, "Well, they'll stop us on the bridge then." Dave said, "Well . . . let's send a group of people to Washington to look over the geography of it." So we flew down to Washington and walked all around the Pentagon and looked at the bridge, and we said, "Hey, it's perfect." And from then on it was the March Against the Pentagon.

I met Abbie for the first time in New York and what happened I guess was kind of a merger. He was more into cultural change at the time. What I immediately saw was here was this guy who was so funny and clever and brilliant, and the thing to do was to take that energy and direct it against the war in Vietnam, like an enormous weapon. I saw someone who had the potential to be a mass leader, and I said, "Abbie, why don't you get involved at the March on the Pentagon?"

He was intrigued by the idea. At the next meeting Abbie proposed that what he'd like to do was to exorcize the Pentagon. He meant that we were going to surround the Pentagon with hippies. By making a complete circle around the Pentagon, which was a five-sided object, they would make the Pentagon rise from the ground a few inches. And all the evil was going to leave.

Did he really believe this?

Heh, heh, heh, heh. Yes, I guess he really did believe this. You know, Abbie was the guy who brought the whole idea of the put-on into the Movement. Of course, I had a similar thing to the exorcism. I said we were going to close down the Pentagon. Did I really believe that? That was my own form of put-on. Abbie's put-on was that we were going to exorcize the Pentagon. So we were both putting-on.

I think my put-on was taken more seriously. Lyndon Johnson responded, "I will not allow the peace movement to close down the Pentagon." By saying that he wasn't going to allow us to close it down, he gave us the power to have that possibility. So in a way, just by announcing it, we created a victory.

The straight left, which played a role in the coalition to end the war, was very anti-us. The older people, the more established people in the peace movement, were outraged at the whole thing that we were doing. I remember there was one meeting at which Bella Abzug stood up and pointed at Stu Albert, who'd been working with me, and said, "If I was your mother, I would take you home and put you over my knee." Oh, she went into a rage.

Then began the weirdest thing: We began *negotiating* with the General Services Administration, which has a responsibility for the Pentagon, as to how near the Pentagon we would be allowed to get. What we were negotiating was civil disobedience. They agreed to let us go over the bridge and come up to within a certain number of feet of the Pentagon. Then all the while people around the country started getting involved: militants from SDS, splinter left groups, everybody. It became a big story.

I think it was probably the best demonstration in the Sixties. On the day of the march, thousands of people assembled in Washington. The march over the bridges was beautiful. There were Ben Spock and Norman Mailer leading, and thousands of people in a very festive environment, and there were the Fugs playing outrageous music, and the hippies. It was just a great big beautiful be-in demonstration, you know.

The militants of SDS started throwing things, and the police at the Pentagon beautifully played their role by putting up a line of National Guardsmen with their rifles there. That's when they got this real famous picture of the hippie putting a flower into the muzzle of one of the rifles.

We gave lots of speeches saying, "Join us, join us," to the National Guardsmen, telling them, "We have music, we have drugs, we have happiness, we have women"—we were sexists then. "Everything is wonderful here. What are you playing that role for? Come on, you guys." It was just great.

We were throwing red paint on the Pentagon. People were breaking into the Pentagon. They were running into the sides of it. People were getting clubbed, and it was bloody. When night fell, they attacked and started arresting people. There were mass arrests, and I got arrested. My feeling was that the arrests played into the Movement's hands and helped us become a cause célèbre.

I'd been in jail before a number of times—for throwing blood on

General Maxwell Taylor, for some of the marches, for demonstrations—but this was really great. It was great because we were all together. They had to set up makeshift barracks. We felt like we were prisoners of war, because we weren't in jail cells, but in a big field. We were just going around organizing and talking and singing and having conversations with each other and strategy meetings, and we really felt at that time that we were making history. We were at the center of action. Our lives were *relevant*. America would come to its senses and get out of Vietnam. I guess Abbie was right. We hadn't physically levitated the Pentagon, but we had spiritually levitated it. The government would have been smarter if they had just ignored us.

Daniel Ellsberg, by the way, who is a friend of mine now but was an official at that time, says he watched the whole demonstration from the top floor of the Pentagon. He was standing with Robert McNamara, and he said it was while watching this demonstration that he decided to release the Pentagon Papers. He thought, If they can do this, I can release the Pentagon Papers. You never know the ripple effect you have.

And all the kids who were in high school at the time of the Pentagon demonstration watched it on TV and said, "I'm going to do that." *We'd become role models.*

About that time, the Yippies were born—the Youth International Party. It was forged from the merger of the political radical and the hippie that was born at the Pentagon, and it describes that restless youth tying in to a political movement. We decided to go to Chicago, we hippies as Yippies, and we announced it in the press, and the media just loved it. I mean it was like delivering meat to an animal. We became the entertainment of America.

We spent a year-and-a-half organizing for the Chicago demonstrations, and I think we saw them as a cataclysmic event that was going to be a historical trial of America in the streets. All the players were going to have their alloted roles, and it turned out to be just amazing how everybody played their role: Mayor Daley had to play his role, the Chicago police had to play their role. Had any of them broken out, they would have broken the theater, they would have won. That's what they didn't understand. But we wrote their roles and they played their roles. The image of those blue-hatted police slugging and beating up kids just radicalized an entire generation.

One of the things we decided to do for the convention was to run our own pig for president. We were going to call him "Pigasus," and we were going to make a point that both parties were the same. So Abbie went and got this little, cute, shiny, tiny pig. I thought that was the wrong image. I didn't want it to be cute, I wanted it to be ferocious. So Phil Ochs and I got into a car and drove out to rural Illinois, and we bought the ugliest pig we could find and tied him up in the back of the truck and stored him in Chicago overnight. I'm not a farm boy and how we pulled this off, to this day I can't imagine. But it worked. It was mission accomplished.

The only moment of levity between Chicago policemen and Yippies that week occurred after we were arrested and were in jail and went in to be booked. One of the Chicago policemen came in and shouted out all our names and then said, "You guys are all going to jail for the rest of your lives—the pig squealed on you."

The demonstrations at the Chicago convention were the story of the decade. America was willing to beat up its own children. . . . But you have to realize that the violence that took place in Chicago was very symbolic. There were no permanent injuries, there were no deaths. Somebody was killed a few days before the convention, but during the demonstration itself there were no deaths. People were clubbed, but the stitches healed. As Abbie says, "All the violence of the Sixties put together doesn't add up to a weekend in Beirut."

After the demonstrations and the fiasco of the convention, it took eight or nine months before the Justice Department made the huge mistake of putting the symbols of a generation on trial in the most publicized trial at that time in history. Of course, if they'd wanted to destroy Jerry Rubin, the smartest thing would have been to indict everybody but him.

I remember when I got my indictment I was thrilled. Oh, I was thrilled. Thank God! I called it the Academy Award of protest. We burst out the champagne and had a champagne party in my apartment to celebrate the indictment, because what the government was saying was, "How big do you want your platform, Jerry?"

It was the most photogenic trial ever. It was just perfect. We'd spend all day at the trial, and every night we'd fly out to another college with thousands of people screaming and yelling, and we'd give a talk. We were doing it to raise money for our defense, but we were also doing it because we wanted everybody to hear our story. It was perfect political poetry. Everything gelled. The whole message came together.

They couldn't get enough of us in the colleges. The youths were pouring over us. The sons and daughters of the Nixon White House were coming over to us—Kleindienst's son, Hickel's daughter. It was clear that we were dividing the country right down the line.

In the end we were found not guilty of conspiracy, but guilty individually of crossing state lines to incite a riot. I got one of the heaviest sentences: five years in jail. But the higher court of appeals threw it out eventually, so the only time we served was a few weeks in jail before we got bail. But we went around for a couple of years with all these sentences hanging over our heads, and we did believe that at a certain point we would go to jail. In the end the Seventh Circuit Court of Appeals showed that democracy does live in America.

Do you now think you were innocent or guilty?

Were we guilty of having a conspiracy? Well, conspiracy is a plan to do something, and we did plan in our own way all of us to go to Chicago and create the biggest demonstration possible, but we didn't conspire to have a riot. We were guilty of achieving a successful demonstration, but I don't think we deserved to go on trial for it or to go to jail for it. If we were guilty, we were guilty under a law that was illegal, a law that has since been thrown out.

All during the trial we were just fired up. It was like we were on speed. We were *electric*, you know. I don't think I'll ever achieve the energy peak that I had in those periods of time. But the Seventies were kind of a burn-out. I had to recharge my adrenaline batteries that had been overloaded by the Sixties.

The Movement began to turn violent. Every six months there had to be another escalation in tactics, because of boredom. I mean, you're sitting in. "Well, what else is new since you sat in last week? You're not on page one anymore, you're on page ten." "Okay, then we'll block the dean's office." So you get headlines for blocking the dean's office, but next week you don't get headlines for that, so now you have to blow up the dean's office at three A.M.

In a sense, we fell into a very American trap: We had to produce more and more. The Movement had to produce more and more stimulation for society out there to keep the Movement going. And where do you go after you're bombing? I mean there's nowhere to go from there. Some of our best people went underground, and some of them haven't been heard of yet.

I wasn't the kind of person who would enjoy going underground or who was built to go underground or who even felt that it was a useful thing to do. I kind of said to myself in the Seventies, "Now, wait a minute. There may not be a revolution, and maybe I'd better get healthy." I wanted to prove that there was a "me" that existed outside of politics. So I began studying all sorts of forms of experimental psychology. I got rolfed—that's a kind of deep body massage that relaxes your body. I started doing yoga every day.

By then I was living in San Francisco—a kind of very moderate life based on low expectations. The idea of making money or becoming successful in the economic sense was just odious to me. It struck me that the only way to make money was to sell your soul. I was kind of part of the lost generation of the Seventies. I didn't know what I wanted to do. I still saw myself as an outsider, and I was just passing the time, you know, just passing the time.

Then around 1977 I started coming out of it. I moved to New York, and I decided that I wanted, above everything else in life, an intimate personal relationship. Nothing else was as important. I said to myself, I'm going to have a personal successful relationship with a fantastic woman, and I described her. I had fifteen points, and I described Mimi without ever having met her. She was to be a successful person, not someone from the Sixties who thought that to complain and to fail were signs of moral superiority. She was to be tall, blonde, from a wealthy family, have a sense of security about herself, and a sense of taking success for granted. And there were a number of other points.

I asked everyone I knew, "Do you know someone who fits this description?" I was going to four parties a night and heavily networking to meet this woman. And then I was invited to a party with an old Movement friend, and I thought to myself, Oh, God, I'm never, never going to meet a woman at this party, because it's just going to be a whole lot of old political graybeards sitting around talking about the has-been in their lives.

But I went and *boom!* out of nowhere, there was Mimi at this party. She was exactly the person I was describing and for me it was a beginning. . . . You know, some people have said that Mimi made me more capitalistically oriented, but that's not true at all. I began that before Mimi. Mimi was actually a hippie in the Sixties, and wrote a paper about me and Abbie when she was in college. She wasn't a political activist, more of a cultural one, but she went to the demonstrations and she was influenced.

By the end of the Seventies, I had come to the decision that the way to change America is by amassing as much power, financial or otherwise, as one could, and *then* to create a new establishment. America is not going to be changed from below. Either you live on the edge of society and say, "I'm not playing the game," or you go in and you say, "Well, how do you play the game? I'll play it, and I'll play it better." This is really going underground. This is the *real* underground.

You know I've been debating at colleges around the country with Abbie as "Yuppie versus Yippie." I basically did these debates with him out of economic necessity. I was in debt a little bit, and I heard that Abbie had said that he was a Yippie, not a Yuppie, and that the word Yuppie was created because of my networking parties. So he'd give the Yippie point of view, and I debated as a representative of the Yuppies.

The word Yuppie has gotten a lot of abuse. I think it's been misused as a symbol of greed, and I don't think that's right. In a way the Yuppie point of view is, "It's okay to enjoy your life, and you can *also* change things." Let's make America work, you know.

Abbie says to me in the debates, "You don't really want to change things, you just want to become the establishment." Of course, he has to say that, because otherwise his position falls apart, and who has Abbie's point of view but a tiny clique of Sixties leftovers? That's not the debate of the Eighties.

The debates were like wrestling matches. I'd come with my Perrier water and my blue suit, and I'd be booed, you know, because the audience consisted of old or new radicals. There were some middle-of-the-road students, but basically the audience was loaded. Abbie thinks he won, and I think I won. He certainly started out with the audience pretty much on his side. I think I swayed most of them toward me, but Abbie would disagree with that emphatically.

But so what? I was making money doing it, and Abbie was making money, and it was a profitable enterprise for both of us. But now I've got to where I'm making more money in my business than I was doing the debates, so I'm concentrating on that. In America you've got to follow the dollar, right? And as I said, I've always been a sort of mainstream person.

Abbie Hoffman

Nacio Jan Brown/Black Star

© Robert K. Morrison

*E*verything *he did in the Sixties seemed designed to inspire youth to revolt and outrage the traditional establishment: leading a levitation of the Pentagon, wearing an American flag shirt, publishing* Steal This Book. *Like Jerry Rubin, he was a controversial Yippie leader and a defendant in the Chicago Seven conspiracy trial. In their recent debates he has defended his role as unreconstructed full-time activist, focusing his attention now on the environment and U.S. policy in Central America. He divides his time between a cottage on the St. Lawrence River and a modest rent-controlled apartment in New York City.*

I go out and debate Jerry Rubin, and the deck is stacked. He's coming as a Sixties radical who sold out. You don't get a lot of points for that in any league. It's like a little morality play: two people who were idealistic when they were young, and one hung on to his idealism and the other one hasn't. Now who wins? [*Laughs.*]

Basically, it's about what kind of value system do you hang onto as you grow old? How much money do we need to live a secure life? What's the definition of a good life? And how much ass do you have to kiss? How much do you have to render unto Caesar's palace that which is Caesar's palace? These are all my phrases. He's not that poetic.

Jerry says we were young and foolish, but now's the time to get new toys, to get serious. And getting serious means careers, working from within—not challenging the establishment, but *becoming* the establishment. We have the brains, we have the numbers, we have the technology on our side. The young, upwardly mobile professionals, the entrepreneurs, are the shining white knights leading the world to change.

And what's your argument?

That he's full of shit. [*Laughs.*] There's a big difference between a social phenomenon and a political movement. In a way, he's continuing the youth class idea. You know, in the Sixties, if you didn't have your long hair, if you didn't have all the countercultural attributes, you were out of it. We used that need for identity with the Yippies. We created a myth. We confronted the parent culture to get across our political ideas. We knew we couldn't get Archie Bunker, so we went for Archie Bunker's kids.

Well, now, in a way, if you're not young, urban, upwardly mobile, and professional, you don't count. But that's not connected to any political program. The Yuppies are a myth created by the media to push overconsumption. That's no political movement at all. And the Baby Boom generation is not all Yuppies by a long shot. For every dashing entrepreneur, you've got eight mothers with kids; they're sucking the glue off food stamps, but they don't make the glossy magazines.

Any political opinions that Jerry might have are opinions for a cocktail party. So he's against apartheid. Tell us about it, and then he can talk for thirty seconds before he has to shift to another subject. I say, "What are you *doing*? Americans don't want to know what you think. They want to know what you are doing." If you figure it out, you're going to say, "Well, he's helping corporate executives in New York City get laid." And I say that's part of the problem, not part of the solution.

The audience can see really clearly how superficial that lifestyle is. Because it's hard to get emotionally worked up over credit cards and Perrier, see? So it's a demonstration of the shallowness of gearing your life solely around the upwardly mobile drive for material success. I present myself to the students as someone who wasn't that much different from them when I was their age. I just decided that working for E. F. Hutton or J. Walter Thompson or IBM was going to be a pretty boring way to run my life. That you don't have to give up your altruistic impulses. That a person can make a difference. You can go out, and you might get hit on the head a lot and knocked around, but, you know, here I am, alive, relatively happy. So they like that.

In the Sixties, you know, I wanted all the students out the next day after I had gone through, taking over buildings, taking over the student government. If not, I felt it was, like, a disappointment. I mean, it was, like, civil war. In eleven states I was banned from even speaking. I go to schools now and they call me "Mister." I'm venerated. I'm part of history. I guess I get points for believing in something and sticking with it for a long time. And my hope is that I'm triggering the questioning mechanism, so that they'll get the sense that maybe all's not right, here in the Garden of Eden—to get people to be active, as opposed to apathetic.

I lay out political organizing as the best game in town. I say, "Look, I got tired of beating everybody at Monopoly and Ping-Pong and Trivial Pursuit and all the other games. Now I'm taking on the utility companies. I'm taking on the Pentagon. This is the most fun. Winning these battles is the most fun."

I tell them it's fun to act out your fantasies, and if it's in a social context, then there are extra points. I mean, you get sort of teary-eyed. You feel kind of gooey inside. You feel nice and warm. You feel like you're doing God's work or something. It's happening, and you are a part of it. You have not accepted the general notion that nothing changes, that no one listens, that you can't fight city hall. You haven't accepted that, and you've gone against it, and you've been proven right. That's a really good feeling. Every time that happens, I get a good buzz. This is how you change the world.

That was the difference between the Yippies and the straight Left with its language of antihedonism and austerity. I thought it was extremely counterproductive. I couldn't stand it.

You see, I accept American culture, its demand for entertainment. Europeans who observed the period of the Sixties tell me that my contribution to revolutionary theory was to come up with the idea that revolution could be fun. Only an American could have done that.

Desperate Measures: SDS, Weathermen, Black Panthers

Carl Oglesby

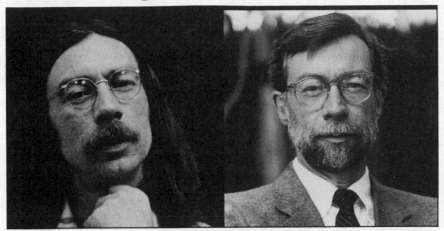

*F*rom a small community-oriented grassroots organization, SDS grew
tremendously in popularity on college campuses across the country
as the escalating Vietnam War fueled student activism. Carl Oglesby
became president and theoretician of SDS at the beginning of its burgeoning
growth in the mid-Sixties—and watched the transformation of many of its
members into the militant Weatherman faction. He is now a free-lance
writer and lives in Cambridge, Massachusetts, with his second wife.

I was ten years older than the SDS kids. I was running the technical
publications department at Bendix Aerospace Systems Division of the
Bendix Corporation in Ann Arbor: pure defense work, rockets and
missiles and electronic subsystems, some moon stuff, some supersecret
Vietnam stuff. I had fifty people working under me. I was on the softball
team.

I had a little red car, and my wife had a little blue car, and we jollied
around town. We had three kids. The school was very advanced and
clean and middle-class and white, with enough black kids and Chinese
kids in there so that you didn't feel too terrible politically. And I was
also taking a full class load at Michigan. I worked, I went to school, I
wrote my plays. That was what my life was going to be. I was going to
be a playwright. A very high-powered bourgeois life-style. I loved it.

The reaction at Bendix to the Kennedy assassination really blasted me loose. I was at work, of course, like most everybody else. It was Friday, and a half-hour or forty-five minutes or so after the guy was announced dead, I wandered down to the personnel office to talk to my pal, the personnel manager, Tony, and I said, "Tony, we should take the flag down."

He didn't want to do it. He said, "Well, when we get word. When we're told by corporate headquarters to put the flag at half-staff." And we got into a big argument in the hallway about that, about whether or not we needed to hear from corporate headquarters about putting the flag down. Did the flag belong to corporate headquarters? Was that what that was about? That Bendix owned the flag? Did it own the country? Big fight.

Then I went up to Mahogony Row, a couple of floors up, to check it out with some guys I knew up there, who I thought would be more reasonable, and in this one office they had the Scotch out. The ripple of excitement, the *thrill* that ran through Bendix Systems Division when the word came of Kennedy's death, and with it the implicit word that now we got Johnson. It was like—I don't know how to describe it. It was almost a physical tremor.

Before, there was gloom, because for one thing Kennedy had canceled out a big contract we had. We were building something called the Eagle missile that was supposed to go on a certain airplane. Well, the airplane didn't exist, and it wasn't *going* to exist, either. So Kennedy logically figured why build the missile? But this didn't seem reasonable to "corporate headquarters," which was real pissed at having lost the Eagle missile system. Well, that was the mood people were in.

The next minute Kennedy gets popped. A minute after that, the Scotch is out, because the contracts are coming back. And they did! By God, they did. I couldn't shrug that off.

There was a little enclave of liberals at Bendix. In early '64 they started thinking about backing a candidate to unseat the fourteen-year Republican incumbent in that district, the First District in Michigan. And would I have something to do with this? Would I do some writing for them? I knew something about writing, so it was appropriate that they asked me. I said, "Sure," and one thing led to another.

One day the candidate drew his staff around him, and I was now part of that staff, and he said, "What if Vietnam becomes an issue in this campaign?" This is 1964. He said, "What's the right position? I've got to have a position paper on Vietnam. Who's going to write it?" We drew straws. I got the straw. So I immediately realized that I didn't know anything about Vietnam. And I panicked.

So I went to this one guy, an archconservative at Bendix, a former Army colonel by the name of Joe, ramrod-straight guy, a real disciplinarian. I said, "Joe, I got to write this thing about Vietnam, and I figure I should attempt to understand the cold war in order to get it in the proper setting, and I've looked in all these books about the cold war, about Vietnam, and about China, and I'm just dismayed. Is there one book that I can rely on from your standpoint that would be factual, as a kind of encyclopedia of the events?"

He said, "The only book that comes anywhere near being that book is an excellent book by D. F. Fleming, called *The Cold War and Its Origins: 1917 to 1950.*" Just right away. He didn't have to look it up.

I later discovered that this guy Fleming was the idol of the Left, that he was regarded as one of the major forces in the revisionist cold war literature. I didn't know that at the time. I got Fleming's two-volume book out of the library and, you know, there are certain books in your life that really do blow your mind. When you spend all night saying, "What? We did that? No! It can't be!" Page after page after page, a thousand pages of this stuff—my first education into the fact that there was another version besides the American myth of the cold war. It was incredible. I was a pretty grown guy, I was twenty-nine years old at the time, and fairly well educated—three years at Kent State, two years at the University of Michigan, good grades—what the heck. I didn't know any of that stuff.

I just couldn't believe the crap about why we were in Vietnam. The Vietminh had been our buddies in 1944, 1945, 1946. Our OSS [Office of Strategic Services] guys couldn't say enough good about them, that Ho Chi Minh was a grand guy, loved the United States, wanted to institute a kind of American democracy there. And then the next thing you know, he's the villain. He's the focus of evil.

It was just a matter of the facts. And from simple assumptions, that America is and should be in favor of democracy and independence, I thought you came to certain conclusions about the war. To find ourselves in alliance with the Diem family in Vietnam seemed more or less the same as going into the lines with the Nazis. We were fighting on the wrong side.

I gave the critique I wrote to the candidate, who was successful by the way, and he said it was too radical. Radical? It didn't seem radical to me. I mean, a former Army colonel had given me the book to read. How could it be radical? He said it was not going to be his position paper. Well, that sort of made me kiss him off.

But then there I was with this position paper on my hands. What to do with it? I had a play being produced at the University of Michigan theater called "The Peacemaker," a melodrama based on the Hatfield/McCoy feud. It was being produced, I think, in December of '64. Some people from SDS, which I didn't know anything about, came to see the play. They enjoyed the play, and they therefore bought a copy of *Generation* magazine, which was being sold between the acts and had the script in it. It also had in it, as an open letter, this statement on Vietnam that I had written for the candidate, because my buddy who was editing the magazine had seen it lying around and said, "What are you going to do with this?" So he printed it.

The SDS people found this statement on Vietnam, and they said, "Who is this guy?" They thought they knew all the radicals around campus. The reason the SDS folks kind of needed me was the SDS chapter in New York had printed up a subway poster, which showed a very searing photograph of a Vietnamese kid burned on the shoulder and with a touching look on her face. And the poster said, "Why are we burning, torturing, killing the people of Vietnam? Write to SDS and get the true facts." Well, they fought to get it into subways. It became an issue. People saw the poster and started writing to SDS for the true facts, and they didn't have anything to send back. And this thing of mine that they had found in *Generation* seemed to be just the ticket.

Well, the phone rang one day, and a guy said, "Hi, I'm from SDS." And I said, "SDS?" He says, "You mean you don't know what SDS means?" I said, "Why should I know?" He said, "Let me get this straight—are you the author of a certain article?" "Yeah, that's me." "And you don't know what SDS is? Have you got a minute?"

I was intrigued. He came out on his motorcycle to Sunnyside Street, which was just like it sounds, and we talked, and he told me what SDS was. It was the first I knew that anybody was trying to make a student movement. And he said did I have any more of that stuff? I said, "Well, I was thinking of pulling all my research together in kind of a monograph." Various SDS people came out to encourage me to do this, and I did it. It came out as a sixty-page paper called "Third World Revolution and American Containment," and SDS adopted it as its position paper. That was my first touch with SDS.

There was an SDS conference in Ann Arbor, and we put up a bunch of the kids at our place and got to know a lot of them and really fell in love with SDS as a group of people. It was easy to do. They were just knockouts. I mean, so serious and intent, and yet they had the best parties, the prettiest girls. It was the sexiest show around.

They were a bunch of whippersnapper middle-class white kids animated by this passionate sense of "Why not? You can do anything!" They had gone out into the real world, picketed the war or gone South to one of the "Freedom Summers" to help SNCC organize. It imparted a glow that was unmistakable. It just singled out the SDS bunch. It gave them a charisma, I guess the charisma of the "real."

You know students. They hang around thinking, "Who am I? What am I? What should I be? What is my destiny? What's my identity today? I just ate an orange; am I happy?" And here were kids who had stopped being obsessed with themselves, and were taking active steps to address very real and obvious and dangerous injustice and were putting their bodies and their lives where their mouths were.

Then there was the teach-in. The teach-in grew out of an attempted faculty strike to protest the war, which was going to be called by a very small number of professors. It was just a strike of a dozen guys, but the state legislature came down on Michigan like the sea behind Moses. They were *not* going to let these guys strike on a political cause like this. They were going to get fired. This quickly polarized the academic community and added to the numbers of guys who wanted to make some statement about the war.

As they grew in numbers to fifty or sixty professors, they basically lost the leadership to more moderate people. There was one guy in particular who was on the side of the antiwar people, but didn't want violence, didn't want relationships to break down in the university; so he proposed a compromise. They wouldn't have a strike, but they would teach classes at night. And the university said that seemed like a good idea. "We'll give you some lights, we'll set up buildings and microphones and stuff." And suddenly it became a blessed event. It was really shrewd of this guy.

In the beginning, though, the guys who had started it all felt they'd been gypped, because now there was just going to be this senseless little confab in the middle of the night and maybe a hundred people would come, and the impetus would have been lost. Well, famously, it wasn't like that. Several thousand people came to the thing, and it was like a transfigured night. It was amazing: classroom after classroom bulging with people, hanging on the every word of those who had something to say about Vietnam. I mean, we had the pull. There weren't many people who knew a lot in those days, and we had to pull from all our resources.

I got involved because I was one of the few people who knew anything about Vietnam, because I had just done all this stuff before, for the candidate, and then the monograph that I was working on at that time for SDS. So it was logical and reasonable that I be asked to be on one of these panels. Suddenly it awakened this whole thing, which was to speak in front of a crowd and think on my feet and more or less enjoy doing it and communicate.

So at that point, I decided that that's where my role was going to be. The Movement needed people to talk about Vietnam, and somehow a series of coincidences had given me enough information that I was in a position to do that. I decided that was really what I should do. There are times when you feel things come together, and you go with that flow.

It was in the winter of 1964–1965 that I declared my intentions over at Bendix to leave for the purpose of going into SDS and doing antiwar work. Friends said, "Well, you shouldn't do this." And I said, "Well, I'm going to do it anyway." "There are other ways you can work." "But this is what I'm going to do." "You've got a wife and three kids." "No, I'm going to do it anyway. She wants to do it too." It wasn't just my decision, it was a family decision.

I remember the last day at Bendix was sometime in June, and the day after that I left for the national conference of SDS, which was in upstate Michigan that year. That was where I got elected president, which was a big surprise to everybody, including me, because I'd just come into the damn organization. I just barely made it as president before turning thirty, in the year that the slogan was "Don't trust anyone over thirty." At the time it seemed very strange to me that somebody like myself, new to the organization, should be pushed to the front this way. And at the same time, I was moved by it, because I had fallen in love with the SDS kids and utterly trusted their political instincts.

The conference was like fresh-air camp with enormously intense political discussion. I mean those kids could talk the ears off a stone, just endless dialogue. You know what it's like when you're twenty, twenty-one: The whole world is a word. And you've found the power to unlock its mysteries by sheer speech. The meetings would start early in the morning and go until late at night. People stayed so attentive, and so far as I could see, were really exclusively interested in trying to find the right answers.

It was an incredible growth period on the campuses. I mean our membership was just going through the roof. It was three or four thousand at the time of the conference, and by the end of my term it had gotten up to ten times that, at least. We couldn't keep students away. They came. They wanted it. They felt that SDS was saying something to them. Pretty soon there was just no question about whether you were going to have an antiwar movement. You were, and SDS was going to be in it, whether it wrote position papers or not. It would be right in it because its people were in it. These guys faced getting drafted.

One evening in '67 Staughton Lynd called me and said that there was this thing happening in Europe, the International War Crimes Tribunal on Vietnam, and he thought I should be part of it. So I was a member of the tribunal. There were three of us from the U.S.: me, Dave Dellinger, and Stokely Carmichael.

There were two sessions. The first one was in Stockholm and the second one was in Copenhagen. It went on for a total of about a month, and it wasn't an open-and-shut proposition. At each session we heard a lot of witnesses. The Vietnamese took it very seriously, and it made a lot of difference to European opinion. I don't think it had much of an impact in the United States, but it did develop a good amount of information.

We broke the story of the antipersonnel bombs that were being dropped by the U.S. in population centers, mainly in North Vietnam. The Vietnamese called them guavas, because they were about the shape of a guava fruit. Really they looked like a baseball, but with flanges on them. When the mother bomb, which was a big cannister, would open up at a certain altitude, its sides would split apart, and thousands of these little baseball bombs were released and just strewn out over a broad area. The flanges on them made them spin and get level to the horizon—a gyroscopic effect—and they were triggered to then spray BB-type shot over a large area.

The fantastic discovery was that this weapon was designed to produce casualties, but not fatalities, in order to overload the medical system. People get hit with these big BBs, and you could put phosphor in the BBs so that the BB goes inside and starts burning. It's very hard to treat that kind of wound, and you tie up the civilian populations and their resources when you introduce a lot of wounded: just more to be done, more hassle, more pain, more agony.

It goes back to World War II, where there was a powerful group within the U.S. Army who thought that you could terror-bomb populations into forcing their governments to surrender. A lot of the bombing of Germany was rationalized in that way. Then after the war it was found that it didn't do much good, except it stiffened the people's will to resist and made them more dependent than ever on the central government. So it was totally counterproductive. Yet they were such gorgeous weapons, right?

And the targets in North Vietnam . . . The U.S. bombed their Catholic cathedrals, and they even bombed a very famous leprosarium in North Vietnam, with huge red crosses painted on the roofs of the building, and then strafed the lepers as they were running out.

You saw through the tribunal what it looked like to be in the Vietnam War from the Vietnamese side. Our movies over here were taken by cameras up in the sky, looking down on the village and coming down—*baboom!*—and then flying off. The movies we saw in Stockholm and Copenhagen were taken by Vietnamese cameramen. They showed the planes coming in—here's what Hanoi looks like after a bombing raid: fires that burn, people who scream. It got to you.

Sixty-eight was such a critical year. Bobby Kennedy was the payoff to SDS politics that was snatched out of our grasp by the assassination. The student antiwar movement would have moved in behind Kennedy to support him for the presidency, and it would have assumed its proper place in American politics, on the left wing of the Democratic Party, well *inside* the party. The war would have ended. I knew damn well that I would fight like a maniac to bring SDS into the Bobby Kennedy coalition if he got nominated, because to me anything else was silly. So I was all gung-ho about it.

After the assassination, SDS people and others were organizing for Chicago, and I was against that. I didn't want to go to Chicago. I thought we should evacuate the place, declare it a dead city and nobody go near it, put a quarantine around it, if anything—but not go there and yell in the streets for a week and get into stupid fights with cops and Mayor Daley. I didn't see any reason to fight fights that we couldn't win.

But somehow it was my turn to go. My wife went to the Pentagon one, and I was always bugged that I had missed it. Somebody had to stay home with the kids. The Pentagon was a major episode. It sounded terrifically novelistic, and as Norman Mailer later showed, there were great scenes to be witnessed and described. Chicago was my turn.

I didn't take a leadership position at all. I was in the streets. I didn't hang around with the leaders or talk to them. The closest I got to the leaders was in one of the cops' nighttime charges through Grant Park or Lincoln Park, I even forgot which. A weird scene: helicopters overhead and lights shining down and the cops running like shadows through the trees. I was hiding behind some bushes while a bunch of them ran through, and then up the sidewalk right behind their line came a former SDS president with some friend, discoursing on the power of the media to determine the meaning of political events, talking about the applicability of So-and-So's concepts of alienation.

It was one of my happiest moments. The cops are charging, the helicopters are roaring, the lights are shining, the battle is going on, the smoke, the tear gas floating in the wind, and here they are strolling along like it's just a night in the park. It was so SDS.

There were plenty of times when the cops were getting mad. Kids throwing bags of shit, screaming, "Pig! Pig! Pig!" You know, even in these kinds of confrontations, there is a kind of code. There is a method to what the cops do, so that you can predict their responses. Like one part of the code was: If you don't go after them, they won't go after you. If you stay where they tell you to stay, it'll be all right.

But then there were moments of irrationality on the part of the cops that were really scary. They got us into the band shell by false information being sown in the crowd that we were supposed to go over there to hear somebody speak. The band shell was somewhat removed from the hotel and the park, and the media people weren't over there, for some reason. There was not a camera to be seen. A few hundred people collected over there, and some more or less routine boring speeches were being made. And the cops charged this group, just did a number on people. Moved in a single line into the heart of the crowd, clubbing on both sides like a machine, for no apparent reason that I could see.

Oh, it was all a mess. I hated it. I saw people panicked and screaming and running home and feeling that they had been exposed to themselves as cowards. And that was no good. These helpless kids, some trying to actually get into fights with cops, would begin to think that they had to organize in a paramilitary way.

Later on, the Weathermen were doing this. They came back in October 1969 for the Days of Rage, as they called it, when they put on their little helmets and their shit-kicker boots that they had bought from L. L. Bean and ran down the street ululating like women from a Greek chorus, thinking that this is going to scare away the cops—that they had the physical ability to contend with the SWAT forces in a metropolitan area.

It was sad. Especially to see them try it in Chicago, where that was just what Mayor Daley's cops wanted. Like, "Make my day!" It was madness. But the middle-class kids were afraid of being afraid. They thought they didn't have physical courage, and they needed to test themselves. That's what it was about. It was just a game of kids.

There were mutterings of Weathermanitis before that, but it was always young buck stuff, guys scratching their antlers on each other. But after the assassinations of '68, there was no answer for the objection to moderate politics. And the objection to moderate politics was, "You can't win, and even if you do win, they won't let you."

Given the assassination of King and Kennedy, there was no more basis for a big-party coalition on the left. In came Hubert Humphrey, with his incredible debt to Lyndon Johnson and everything that was corrupt and sick about the Democratic Party, and then we had Nixon. We were supposed to have Bobby Kennedy! We had set everything up to get Bobby Kennedy and blinked our eyes, and we got Nixon. Holy smoke! We got the Empire. The militarists have total control.

I was still hanging out with this group that was forming the Weathermen caucus, trying to bring them back to moderate politics. It was the Bernardine Dohrn group. She was a good speaker, a fiery person, a meteor flashing across the sky. The Weather people were certainly authentic. There were no interlopers in that crowd. They were real people trying to do what they thought was best.

For them, there was a revolution sweeping the whole Third World, and if you were on the side of justice, you had to support that revolution. There was no more America as such. They were members of the revolution who happened to be living inside the belly of the beast, and they felt they should behave as though they were Vietcong.

What would a Vietcong cadre do if it landed in Chicago with great disguises? Blow up the Loop. Why? Because it's going to help win the war? "Well, I don't know exactly, just blow it up." *That* was the analysis. Maximize the disruption of the domestic rear to convince the power structure that it can't safely pursue its objective in this war.

There may have been something powerful and effective in a strategy that suicidal. And to tell the truth, I wasn't full of alternatives about what to do after '68. I fooled around with them as long as I could, and then I couldn't handle it anymore.

At the same time, my marriage was breaking up. I think the terrible thing that happened in 1968 and 1969 was that I felt defeated. And when you're a defeated man, when you feel inside that you've given your best and it all came back on your head, you're not a terrific companion for other people. Especially if you've been a little macho—and I guess I was a little macho—then you look all the more ridiculous. It's as though you made a claim like Babe Ruth pointing to the fence. I was feeling that I had taken a big whiff with the bases loaded, and now the game was over.

We were out of it, those of us who had predicated our political action on the assumption that the system was still straight. We had nothing left to say. I could bitch and moan about the incongruities of the Weatherman manifesto, but that didn't mean that I had an alternative. That made me feel very, very impotent. I think that was part of what went wrong with me, with my marriage, and with a lot of guys who had based their political action on some premise of credibility and realism. Now they were twisting slowly in the wind.

So I decided that it was a good time to burn out and, really, it was a great burn-out. It was one of the Movement's better burn-outs. It was nice and slow. I wound up in Vermont on a farm, and there I stayed, living in a chicken coop which had been cleaned out and insulated, with a bunk bed in it and a place to work and a little potbellied stove and a view of the Vermont country.

It was a terrific winter. Deep, deep cold and a sense of something pure and ironlike in the ground. There were a lot of good, righteous people showing up in places like Vermont and New Hampshire in those days. Lots of parties, great reefer, good acid. Lovely friends. It was an excellent burn-out. I remember it with great fondness. It was almost the best part of the struggle. The best part of the struggle was the surrender.

Jeff Jones

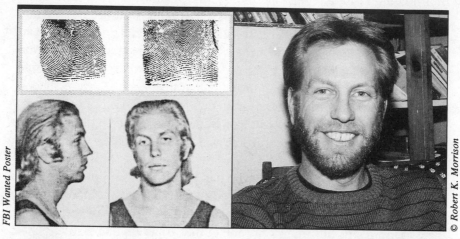

*B*orn a Quaker, he was one of the Weathermen who participated in
the Days of Rage in Chicago. He later went underground as a
fugitive for eleven years. He now writes for the Guardian, a national
radical newspaper, and lives in New York City with his wife, Eleanor, a
law student, and their two sons, Thai and Blue Jay.

The very first I heard of SDS was after I had graduated from high school
in 1965. I read a *Newsweek* article, an interview with Carl Oglesby,
and something in it really appealed to me. Within six weeks after I got
to Antioch College in Ohio, I realized that politics and SDS were all
that I was really interested in.

The first antiwar demonstration I went on there were sixty-five of us
at the federal building in Cincinnati, and the counterdemonstration was
equally large and very hostile. The threat of violence was there all the
time. That was the first time I ever heard "traitor" and "Commie" and
"go back to Russia."

I threw myself into SDS. In May of 1967 I moved to New York and
for the next two years was the coordinator of the SDS regional office
in New York. Things were changing. We became increasingly militant.

Militancy in and of itself is very scary. That's the way I've always
felt about it. Especially coming from a Quaker background, both my
parents pacifists, it was unnatural. But I became fairly militant because

I was so upset by the things that were happening in Vietnam and in the U.S.

I remember the Pentagon demonstration in the fall of '67 as the most significant in my life, where the drama and the seriousness of the confrontation represented an escalation on such a large scale. Thousands of people broke past the boundaries that had been set up for a peaceful demonstration, and we surged about as close as we could to the Pentagon. Some people got inside, and then the Eighty-second Airborne and the military police came out from inside the Pentagon. But they couldn't even push us back twenty or thirty feet from the entrance to the Pentagon. Then this standoff was played out all night long, with them arresting people one at a time and taking them away.

Everything was very spontaneous. It wasn't like someone sat down and said, "Now we have to raise the level of confrontation." Within the forces who were demonstrating were some people who believed in provoking confrontation, and what happened was that those people, who had been previously viewed as crazy or provocateurish, began to represent more and more the natural sentiment of militant anger. It had a very powerful impact on a lot of people.

Then two weeks later, in New York, there was a very militant demonstration against the Foreign Policy Association's awarding some award to Dean Rusk at the Hilton Hotel. It was one of those demonstrations in which the elite came in their limousines to see Rusk get this award, and we made them all run the gauntlet of hatred, baggies filled with red paint. There was fighting with the police, and demonstrators moved out into the street, and traffic was tied up. It was sort of the first of that series of confrontational demonstrations that went on for the next couple of years.

That night, in particular, I remember finding myself in the street with people whom I had previously considered nuts and running side by side with them. Their level of militancy and their level of anger were higher than mine, but eventually it reached some stage that we all shared, and I've been friends with some of them ever since.

I was in the SDS office when I got a phone call telling me that the Columbia SDS chapter had occupied Low Library. We pulled together and for a couple of days maintained a support demonstration of non-Columbia SDS members over on Amsterdam Avenue, because it was hard to get on campus then. Then, about three days into it, a bunch of us, who couldn't stand being outside any longer, just moved in and took over our own building.

I was in the mathematics building until the arrests. It had some Columbia students in it, but it was the building for the militant outside forces who just could not be denied participation. A group from the Lower East Side called the Motherfuckers was there. They were very militant and very ideological anarchists who were a white parallel organization to the Black Panthers.

There was a rumor that the math building would resist arrest in a more dramatic way than any of the other buildings, which in the end wasn't true, because it was such a losing situation to be inside a building and try to defend it against the hundreds of police. So we built a tremendous barricade and everyone sat down and waited for the police to come through the door, and then they dragged us out. There wasn't a big fight.

When the mathematics building was shown to reporters the next day, it had been totally destroyed. And the truth is that it was destroyed by the police, other than the fact that we took tables and chairs for the barricades. There was one person who avoided arrest by hiding under a sink, and he said it was the most terrifying twelve hours of his life, as he listened to the police destroy the building on the inside—I mean with axes—after we were all taken away and arrested. Before they let the press in, the police destroyed the building. Then they let them see what the "students and outside militants" did.

At a national leadership meeting the week before the Chicago Democratic Convention of 1968, it was clear to us that thousands of young people would come. The people we represented and the people we were trying to organize, mainly the students who were supporting McCarthy, were coming, so SDS should go and get involved. So we did. We put out a newspaper every day called *The Street Wall Journal*, and we organized a couple of demonstrations, but mainly we just got involved.

The Chicago authorities had made the decision not to allow demonstrators to spend the night in Lincoln Park, which had been claimed as the rallying point for the demonstration. So every night, just after dark, the police would attack the park, and then we would all run for it, and they would beat the people they caught. And as we would leave the park, roving bands of cops would attack roving bands of demonstrators. You would basically just try to keep moving. The police would try to isolate people, hit them with the sticks, and they'd throw them in the wagons and hit them again. So by the time people were getting to the hospitals, they were needing a lot of stitches in their heads.

Everybody had bruises and welts from getting hit with the nightsticks.

At one point I was in a crowd of people moving through some back alleys several blocks away from Lincoln Park, when a police car came screeching up about a hundred yards away and a couple of cops jumped out. I remember them firing three to five shots in our general direction.

I have a very vivid memory of myself and the woman I was with running as fast as we could across a deserted gas station, with an enraged police officer chasing after us. My girlfriend was wearing high heels—God only knows why—but the cop weighed about two hundred fifty pounds. He couldn't move any faster than she could in high heels, so we got away.

I don't know how it came about, but on the really dramatic night, the famous night, we all found ourselves down on Michigan Avenue in front of the Hilton Hotel with all the TV cameras there. It had begun earlier with this confrontation in the park, and then we were occupying the street in front of the hotel and chanting things that would be unpleasant for a policeman to hear. By then the word *pigs* had begun to enter the vocabulary, and the cops were responding to all this with incredible violence. I also remember, following McCarthy's defeat, all of the McCarthy kids losing their faith in the democratic process and sort of coming over to our side.

After Chicago, the people I was closest to in SDS were beginning the process of forming our own faction, which became the Weatherman faction. I began periodically flying to Chicago, mainly for these long grueling meetings where we hammered out our political ideology, and then went into the SDS national convention of '69 with that political program.

It never was a completely clarified ideology, and I don't agree with big parts of it. But at the time, the primary thing that seemed valid was that people like the Vietnamese and, in this country, people in the black community, especially people like the Black Panther Party, were in a state of revolutionary warfare. The question was: Were we going to join that war on terms equal to what black people or Vietnamese people were doing, or were we going to continue to use our privilege as white people as an excuse for not accepting the same level of risk? That's what motivated us for the next year or so.

In that summer I moved to Chicago and we began to plan what we called the National Action, which is now known to history as the Days of Rage. In the course of that we had a lot of dealings with the Chicago Panthers. We were both on the West Side of Chicago. Fred Hampton was the very young, very articulate, very charismatic leader of the Chicago Panthers, and someone with whom we worked fairly closely. It was a stormy relationship, but a supportive relationship for me personally. I gave him and his wife or girlfriend a ride home after a meeting, and three days later he was dead. He was shot to pieces by the Chicago police.

Those kinds of experiences are very profound. It confirmed everything that we believed, that enraged us, and made us all the more determined to avenge him and raise the level of struggle. So what I'm trying to do is paint a picture of ever-escalating militancy. The war is escalating. The assassinations of Panther leaders—including people we knew personally—were escalating. What was very much on everybody's minds in the fall of 1969 was: Just how much are you willing to risk? And most everybody was prepared to die.

We began organizing for a confrontation in Chicago. We had this slogan: "Bring the War Home." So through August and September, those of us in the national office of SDS traveled around the country organizing people to come to this demonstration. In the end, we organized about fourteen or fifteen centers of people who agreed with our politics, maybe anywhere from ten to thirty people in each one of those centers. These were the most committed people, and in most cases they lived together in large collectives.

Each collective was in a different place, all over the country, a lot in the Midwest. Their primary purpose was to bring people to the national action, but there was also an internal process of what was called "criticism, self-criticism," which borrowed heavily from our reading of Chairman Mao's Little Red Book. This resulted in very long, very painful internal meetings, the upshot of which was that nobody was really good enough yet to be a revolutionary. People were constantly demanding of each other higher levels of commitment to prove how revolutionary they were. And in order to do that, the action became increasingly confrontational.

Like we jumped in the car and drove from Chicago to Milwaukee, and five of us entered a high school in the middle of the afternoon and went through the high school chanting, "Jail break!" Our politics were that the schools were jails, so break out of jail, join us for a rally outside your school, and join us in October in Chicago for the demonstration.

You would find that a couple of people were interested but most people thought you were nuts, and you would try to get out of there before the cops came. Sometimes you wouldn't make it. I was arrested in Pittsburgh in a situation like that. So there were a lot of those little actions, little confrontations, arrests, jail, court appearances. That's what life was about.

The one demonstration that was aggressively violent, the Days of Rage, was politically a failure. I don't want to equivocate on just how big a failure it was because it represented the extreme anger and rage that we had come to. But as a political program it was a failure. It was something very real in what it demonstrated, what produced it, but it was not a way for other people to show their anger. Violent, aggressive fighting with the police and property destruction just wasn't something that was going to mobilize masses of people. The people who came to the demonstration were basically the core groups that we had organized and nobody else, between six and eight hundred people.

The demonstration itself was intensely frightening, because the police had the Chicago Democratic Convention under their belt a year before, so they were battle-tested. And this time, instead of trying to block traffic or run away from them, we were charging them. We weren't trying to fight them, because they were armed and everything, but there was some fighting. Mainly what we were trying to do was prevent them from stopping us.

I was a leader of the first night's demonstration, which started in Lincoln Park. When it got dark, we looked at the crowd, and it was much smaller than we had hoped for and anticipated, but we said we were going to march to Judge Hoffman's apartment in the Gold Coast, the rich part of Chicago. Judge Hoffman was the judge in the Chicago conspiracy trial, and these demonstrations were timed to coincide with the beginning of that trial.

We marched out of the park, and we started in the direction of the Gold Coast. I was with a bunch of people at the front of the march. All of a sudden, the only sound you heard was the sound of breaking glass. I mean people in this march, psyched as they were, began breaking windows in stores and cars, and it very quickly became a quite destructive procession of people, at least as far as glass was concerned. We went about ten blocks, and the police responded by throwing up a barricade. We made the decision to run toward them, and basically what happened is that a bunch of us in the front lines ran into the crowd of cops and tried to run past them.

I was grabbed and thrown to the ground, about six cops jumped on top of me, and then someone stuck a can of Mace right in my face and Maced me right in the eyes. It was incredibly painful and frightening, because I couldn't open my eyes. During this time I was being kicked and hit. And they drove me to the central Cook County jail. But people behind us got past because we tied up the cops. I don't think anyone ever made it to Hoffman's apartment house, but there was a series of these confrontations.

I was bailed out the next morning, so I participated in the march through the Loop. We were against business-as-usual while the war was going on and while the repression of black people was taking place, so we were going to march through the Loop and disrupt people's normal shopping activity. Because the Friday night thing had been such a confrontation, the police were really psyched again, and everybody was psyched.

Very quickly confrontations developed in the intersections. People in the demonstration were wearing football helmets and motorcycle helmets, and some people were carrying signs on sticks and were capable of hitting back. So there was fighting with the police, and in the course of that fighting a couple of cops drew their guns. Several of our people were shot, but I personally did not see any of the shooting. We got pretty spread out, and in a lot of ways what it boiled down to was sort of a run through the Loop. Then once we got past a certain point, we melted into the crowd. I eventually changed jackets or turned the jacket inside out and sort of disappeared into the crowd of shoppers.

Then everyone regathered for a meeting and an evaluation in a big room that we had reserved up at Northwestern University. There was a lot of debate about whether or not the action had been a success, because the turnout was so much smaller than what had been expected, and there was a lot of chaos. A lot of people didn't like the action.

At the time, I was very much wrapped up in it and feeling good about it, good about myself, and so I took the position that it had been a success. There was a position to the right of me, which was, "It was a failure. We shouldn't have done it." And there was a position that was to the left of me, which was, "It was a failure. We have to escalate." So I kind of had a middle position at that particular historical moment.

What eventually happened was that the position to the left of me won, and became the position that we have to end being an above-ground organization, because you can't fight openly like this. You have to fight from underground.

One month later, after the Days of Rage, a half a million people came to Washington. I have often referred to that demonstration as one of the most important of the whole antiwar period.

It turned out years later that Kissinger and Nixon were, at that point in time, on the verge of deciding to possibly use tactical nuclear weapons in Vietnam, which would have killed hundreds of thousands of people. The decision not to do it came when they saw the size of this demonstration in Washington. I believe Kissinger is quoted somewhere as saying that they realized that the country could very well be plunged into civil war if they went ahead with this plan. And so they shelved the plan.

People went home from that demonstration feeling demoralized, and it was a demoralization that lasted for quite a while, because they said, "Half a million mobilized in Washington, and it has no effect on the war." But years later we realized that, in fact, it was significant.

The Weathermen were irrelevant in that demonstration, because we'd put all our energy into this thing in Chicago. Now, I say we were irrelevant, but we were a factor. We were an alternative. We were an alternative that people were overwhelmingly not accepting.

I don't want to just put it down. It was based on wrong political ideas, and there was a very limited effectiveness, but how old were we? We were nineteen, twenty, and twenty-one. We were living in this incredibly violent period of history, trying to respond to it in a principled way, in a moral way. And this is how we responded to it.

Bill Ayers

*H*e was a schoolteacher when he quit work in 1968 to work full-time for SDS. Now, after eleven years as a fugitive in the Weather Underground, he is a doctoral candidate at Teachers College, Columbia University. He lives in New York City with his wife, Bernardine Dohrn, a lawyer, and their two children.

My father was a very successful businessman, and I grew up in the suburbs of Chicago, went to prep school, and led a sheltered and privileged life. My parents were not political in any sense of the word, except that they had a humanistic philosophy and they were concerned that we have an ethical outlook on life. They stressed fairness both within the family and within the community, and I think that I took those values very much to heart. And I came of age at a time when taking those values to heart drew you into political activism. . . .

With the Columbia rebellion and then the rebellion in Paris of workers and students in the spring of '68, I had a tremendous sense that a lot of political activities we were involved in were all coming to a head. Great changes were in the air.

I also think that I felt the need to take more drastic action. We had done everything we could think of in our liberal, radical, anarchist, socialist framework. We'd organized a large antiwar movement. We'd gone door to door. We'd built up organizations. We'd done it all, but still it wasn't enough. It didn't make any difference in the conduct of the war. It didn't stop the killing in Vietnam. It didn't stop the system that was chewing up lives.

In '69, the opposition to the war had become enormous. And Richard Nixon let it be known that he was watching football instead of paying attention to half a million demonstrators outside. Now what? Where do we go? There were as many voices answering that question as you could imagine, so there was a fracturing tendency going on through all the movements. And there is no question now, looking back through Freedom of Information files and so on, that our most paranoid fantasies were mild compared to what was happening. They had police agents in every organization. These agents didn't just look for who was doing something illegal. They played the role of splitting up organizations. It's amazing not only how many phones were tapped, but how many organizations were torn up. And '69 was when SDS split in two, and then split some more. One of the things about splitting is that once you start, it's hard to stop.

For the previous couple of years, the Progressive Labor faction within SDS was growing in strength. They had a very Marxist orientation, they were very disciplined, and they had a lot of appeal to people who were serious about their politics. But to many of us, the rise of PL was alarming. They took the position that nationalism was reactionary, so they opposed the Vietnamese national liberation. We would be trying to convince students on campuses to support the Vietnamese struggle, and there was PL saying, "Ho Chi Minh is a sellout." So we found it very difficult to live in the same organization.

They kept growing in strength, so I felt like we had to know some Marxism in order to talk to the Marxists. We tried to do a lot of catching up, studying, trying to have a coherent, compelling opposition to their coherent, compelling position. So we became Marxists ourselves, even though we were the silliest, least intellectual group of Marxists ever.

In the summer of '69, we showed up at the SDS national convention in Chicago, and ten of us had written a paper with the title "You Don't Need a Weatherman to Know Which Way the Wind Blows," based on a line from Bob Dylan's "Subterranean Homesick Blues." The title was ironic, because a close reading of the Weatherman paper would drive you blind, it was so dense and so complicated and so impossible to read. It was an internal document directed at all real and imagined political tendencies that might oppose it, and so it had that kind of ingrown quality that makes it impossible to understand unless you have a program and know all the players by name.

But the things that still ring true to me in the document were the notion that the world was at war, and that you could characterize that war as a war of the Third World for its liberation—the efforts of people in Latin America and Asia and Africa to take control of their own destinies and define their own freedom. It went on to argue that the responsibility of white Americans, who enjoy the benefits of living in the most powerful imperialist power that's ever been known in world history, was to join forces with the Third World and struggle for the end of the system of imperialism. I still think those things are basically true, but I've conveniently forgotten the other six hundred fifty-two pages.

PL had built up so much strength that they came to the convention with a practical majority. It appeared to everybody that PL was going to take over the national office of SDS. They were a coherent, disciplined bloc, and the rest of us were just not organized. SDS tended to run the gamut from serious Marxists and intellectuals to anarchists and crazies and freaks and clowns, all kinds of people. So we could never figure out how we were going to oppose PL. We were meeting constantly. Nobody slept, everybody tore their hair out.

One day Bernardine Dohrn expelled PL, spontaneously, on her own. I think she had probably talked it over before with a couple of people. She was giving a speech, and she was being booed by the PL contingent. And she said, "Anybody who agrees with these principles can come over here, and everybody else is kicked out of SDS." The principles were things which would cut a certain way—such as support for Vietnamese victory.

There was total turmoil. "How can she do it? By what right can she do it?" And yet, she did it. She walked out, and all the strong anti-PL groups walked out. PL claimed that they were the real SDS and set up a national office in Boston. We claimed we were the real SDS and kept our national office in Chicago. And both of us withered away.

Then some of us started to build an illegal underground component. We were called Weathermen for a while, from our paper at the Chicago convention. And when we felt that was too sexist, we started calling it the Weather Underground.

Being illegal didn't strike us as being a great obstacle. In some ways it struck us as a necessary part of everything we believed in and everything we did. Certainly to help people escape the draft or escape from the U.S. Army seemed to us a highly moral thing to do, and we knew places where we could hide people. We had houses and things like that from 1966 on. And we'd done several illegal things at the Democratic Convention in Chicago. I know a couple of women got right up next to Hubert Humphrey's suite in this fancy hotel and wrote in lipstick on the satin wallpaper, "Stop killing Vietnamese."

It seemed to us that the repression against us was growing. We were being arrested constantly, had lots of charges and court appearances. Several of our people were being picked up on the street and beaten up in Chicago and Detroit. We felt that we were exposing ourselves unnecessarily to the worst of repression and spending all of our time in the most narrow kind of legal defense, and that what we should do instead was hide ourselves from the police and carry out the kind of actions that would be painful to the United States if they continued the war.

We didn't have a particular plan for when to go underground, but then the townhouse explosion happened. A group of people who were with the Weathermen group were living in a town house on West Eleventh Street in Greenwich Village, and they were apparently making bombs in the basement. A mistake was made, somebody crossed the wires incorrectly while they were teaching each other how to do it, and three of them were killed.

We realized that many of us would be arrested as a result of this. We were all so closely identified, and we were all doing the same types of things. So we made a decision not to appear for our next court appearances, which were about a week later. And at that point, we were officially listed as fugitives. Bernardine was put on the FBI's Ten Most Wanted list.

So I stayed underground for eleven years; the Weather Underground organization existed for six years. We carried out bombings. We organized groups of people to carry out other kinds of clandestine action, like draping banners from university towers opposing the war. We had an underground press and put out a newspaper. And we survived. We felt that our survival was an important blow against the government's claims to omnipotence and omniscience.

We felt that being able to do things like the bombing of the Capitol and the bombing of the Pentagon would wear them down. They were related to when the United States government bombed Laos and when they invaded Cambodia. We felt that they would have to pay a price for those kinds of crimes. Our point was that we live in the mother country of imperialism and that we have access to places and technology, so if you make the world unsafe for everybody else, we'll make the world unsafe for you.

We played up the fact that we are the children of the system. We are your children, and we can penetrate you. We're not some alien force. We're not Russian agents. We're not Cuban agents. We are American homegrown, many of us from middle-class families, some of us from very wealthy families, and many of us from working-class families. We are absolutely the apple pie of our generation.

All that time we lived under false identities in communities of people who didn't know who we were, we worked at jobs, we just settled into life in the youth culture. And we felt that the kinds of things that we were doing were broadly supported by people who opposed the war— and that was most people.

The political organization broke up in 1976, largely because of the lack of a compelling vision of what we were trying to do. For the next four years, our lives were simple and ordinary. Bernardine had just gotten pregnant and I was working, and so we had our child. And then we had another child. We had friends, we had a community, and we didn't really want to leave it.

We surfaced in 1980. We had decided that it was too difficult and counterproductive to continue living underground without the kind of compelling purpose of being part of a political organization. And it was difficult for our children. That's why we surfaced. Had there been a compelling purpose, we may well have stayed. There was not.

We turned ourselves in in Chicago. We had thought that we could do it somewhat quietly and that our community would not be affected by it, but in fact it was a big deal in the media. People who had not known who we were were extremely supportive and extremely welcoming. So we came back to the Upper West Side, the community that we'd been a part of. I worked in a day-care center, and our kids got older and went to school.

Nobody was ever charged for any of the bombings. The Weather organization took credit for them, but there was never any evidence, and nobody took specific credit. I had been charged with conspiracy to riot, the so-called Rap Brown Act, and conspiracy to make bombs, but both of these conspiracy indictments were dropped in the early

Seventies because the government had done so many illegal things in trying to develop the indictments.

You have to put what the Weather Underground did in the context of the times. If you read FBI documents from 1973, say, there were tens of thousands of political bombings in this country. Every draft board, every ROTC building, every recruiting station had problems in those years. It was really a phenomenon that was quite widespread.

So the fact that the Weather Underground took credit for twenty bombings was in that context. Some of it was undoubtedly misguided, but in no way does it measure up to the crimes that were committed by this country, when you look at what the United States unleashed against Vietnam. The Weather Underground never killed anybody, we never hurt anybody. Three of our own people were killed, and we certainly felt devastated by that loss but also felt that the loss recommitted us to a course of taking greater risks and making more of an impact.

If we have any criticism of ourselves, it's that we didn't do enough, that we didn't know enough, that we didn't think enough about it, that we didn't try harder, that we didn't find ways to put a more serious obstacle into the path of this onrushing machine of destruction. That's a long way of saying I don't apologize for it. I don't advocate it. I don't recommend it to anybody particularly. It was risky. It had lots of loose ends that we didn't think through, lots of consequences we didn't understand. But I'm still not sorry we did it.

Eldridge Cleaver

AP/Wide World Photos

© Barbara Beirne

A *uthor of the best-selling* Soul on Ice, *Cleaver became Minister of Information for the Black Panther Party after serving twelve years in California state prisons. In 1968, he fled the country with his wife, Kathleen, when he faced a return to prison because of his presence at a Black Panther gun battle with the Oakland police. He returned to the United States in 1975, surrendered to the authorities, and was released to do community service. Now a born-again Christian, he lives in Berkeley, California, where he has declared his candidacy for the U.S. Senate as a conservative Republican.*

I got out of prison in 1966. I had some very clear ideas of what I would like to do about the black struggle, and it involved armed activity. My attitude was very violent and murderous. I felt there needed to be some killing. The cops needed to be killed, the capitalists needed to be killed.

But it wasn't a racist attitude—I was against racism. One of the things that was so disappointing about the Black Muslim organization was that it was a racist ideology. It put you in the same moral category with the Ku Klux Klan in a way. By the time I got out of prison I was free of all that.

I looked for people to work with when I got out, and I encountered many people of the Black Panther Party, people like Bobby Seale and Huey Newton. They had also been attracted to Malcolm X and when he was killed, they felt that they needed to carry on his work. So we put our marbles together and jumped in the middle of the whole thing.

Everybody had their own contribution. In prison I'd begun to study all the classic Communist literature, Mao Tse-tung's works, Che Guevara, people who had practiced guerrilla warfare, Communist Party structure. So I had some concept of what needed to be done with what was really at first just a militant band, with no structure, united around a charismatic leader, Huey Newton. So I was writing the Black Panther Party newspaper, organizing rallies, organizing party machinery, political education classes.

It was a period of a lot of revolutionary ideas floating around, Fidel Castro coming to power in Cuba, guerrilla warfare going on, and I began to see that the Marxist-Leninist ideology was inadequate for America because it did not address the racial or sexual problems, which to me were more powerful than class in America.

I read Simone de Beauvoir and Betty Friedan—*The Feminine Mystique*—and I began to think about the plight and grievances of white women against white men. As a black man, I also had a head full of resentment over slavery. Black Muslim rhetoric had a lot to say about the white slave masters sexually exploiting the slave women and creating the North American "coloreds"—the people here that we call "black" who have mixed blood coming out of that whole experience. Everybody's status was connected in the way that the white male had organized everything to his convenience.

In my book, *Soul on Ice*, I analyzed the relationship between the black man and the white man and the black woman and the white woman, and the dynamics in their relationships. There's a lot of energy in that resentment against the white male, so the revolutionary task became targeting the white male. And I found it struck fire with a lot of people, and particularly it influenced the women. It was the white women who made *Soul on Ice* a bestseller.

A lot of the ideas that we brought into the Black Panther Party came from prison. And I think we brought a certain spirit also. We were familiar with working conspiratorially; it was just second nature to us. And we knew the cops. When we came out, the main confrontation point became police brutality.

A lot of what we wrote was propaganda lies. For example, we pretty effectively stigmatized the police department. We labeled them "pigs" and gave them the image of being reckless aggressors against us. There would be those shootouts, and we always denied that we did any shooting or that we started anything. Many times we were lying, and the result was a distortion of information to the public. Plus the cops would know that we were lying, and we would know that we were lying, so it would just make them more angry. My function was motivating people, and a lot of people didn't know that they were being manipulated deliberately.

Those distortions were vicious weapons—and in a revolutionary struggle, they were *meant* to be. If you are a revolutionary, you feel that you're dealing with the evil, bourgeois, capitalist dogs. Then whatever you can take from them or whatever you do to them doesn't matter. It's not a crime. We used to say that when we'd steal something we'd "liberated" it. When you do this for a long time, this becomes your morality.

Then, in getting involved in the Panther shooting, I left the country in 1968. I think it was fortunate that I had that opportunity to leave the country. I had never really been in America; I had always been in jail looking at America. They say that travel broadens you, so I traveled a lot throughout the world. I lived in Algeria. I got to know the Arab world. I traveled extensively in the Communist world. I lived in Cuba.

I ended up coming to some conclusions about Communism in practice—to see the dictatorship of the proletariat in action. I found out about corruption, people enriching themselves on a personal basis. The Communists always gave me a red carpet, invited me to their parties, and that gave me a chance to see their living standard compared to the people's. It's quite criminal. I don't think anyone knows how to live as royally as the Chinese. Maybe Mao Tse-tung and his guys came from peasants, but they ended up in the palaces. And there was a spiritual element to man that was being neglected by Marxism.

I wanted to come back. I was a fugitive and I was sitting in France and I couldn't stand it anymore. I used to think Socrates was being melodramatic when he chose hemlock instead of going into exile. I thought, "Heck, if I could go somewhere else . . ." But after going out in exile myself, I really understood that it's another form of death.

You become frozen in time in a way. I'll just give you an example: There are a lot of expatriates in Paris, France—a lot of black Americans, a lot of white Americans—and you can almost tell what decade they left America by their language. You get those guys from the Fifties, and everything is "Cool, man," "Hey, Daddy-o," and all that. And then in the Sixties you get the hippies. And I saw myself frozen there.

America was my home. My heart was here, everything I knew about was here. Also, I became a father. My son was born in Algeria. My daughter was born in North Korea. For all those reasons I wanted to come back.

I surrendered. I wanted to be here, and I was willing to pay the price by going to jail. I believed that I'd get out of jail, and it's been proven that I had nothing to fear. I felt that I was full of hotshot ideas. I knew that I had information about Marxism in practice that American leftists didn't have, and I felt that once they heard it, they'd really appreciate it. But I found out they didn't want to hear it. People were still suspicious, even though I wasn't captured, that I was saying what I was saying just to get out from under some charges.

America had changed. A revolution took place, but in a very civilized manner. If this whole revolution had taken place in another country, it would have been real bloody. Hundreds of thousands, maybe millions would have had to die to bring about the kinds of vast changes that have come about in America.

Basically I still think we were justified. I'm talking about what the Panthers did: the shootings and all that. I think America feels that way. Not that America wants blood, but I think America agrees that black people should have struggled to get their freedom. It's not an issue anymore.

It's a strange feeling. For the first time in my life I'm completely free, and I feel good about that. I can't think of a better place that I'd rather be than exactly right here on College Avenue in Berkeley. It's the best cell I've ever had.

I had eight years out there, and I came to the conclusion that democracy is better than Communism. I despised the political institutions that I saw in the rest of the world where there were dictatorships. So the result was that I went from being determined to bring about a revolution in America as the only way to bring about change to seeing that we don't have to do that at all—that in fact we should preserve our institutions. They're precious.

Coda:
Kent State

Tom Grace

Washington Post Photograph by Frank Johnston

O *n Thursday, April 30, 1970, President Richard Nixon made a tele-*
vised speech announcing an "incursion" into Cambodia by U.S.
troops. Because this appeared to many to be a widening of the war
in Indochina, it sparked protests at universities across the country. Students
at Kent State University in Ohio took part in a series of actions over the
weekend that included the breaking of windows in the business district and
the burning of the Army ROTC building on campus. The Ohio National
Guard was ordered in and began policing the campus. On Monday, May
4, 1970, Tom Grace, a Kent State sophomore, was scheduled to take a
history exam.

My first class of the day was at nine-fifty-five and my girlfriend was in
the same class. Because of all the tumultuous disorder that had gone
on for the preceding days, the professor, being an understanding man,
gave people the option of leaving and taking the exam at another time
if the events had interfered with their studying, or going ahead and
taking the test. My girlfriend chose to make an exit; history was not
her strong point. As far as I was concerned, I had no problem taking
the test. So she left and I stayed.

I recall promising her that I wouldn't go anywhere near any demonstration. I assured her that I had no intention of getting involved in

rallies or demonstrations that day, that I simply was going to take the test and stay for one more class and then I would see her later.

So I took the examination, which I later found out I got an A on, and then I had a class in the same room at eleven o'clock. There was a ten- or fifteen-minute interval between classes. I filled up my blue exam book and handed it in, and then just stayed put. I might have gone out to get a drink of water. The next class was political science. Appropriately enough, the entire class discussion was devoted to what had gone on in the preceding days. The vast majority of the students, whether they had previously held antiwar sentiments or not, seemed to be opposed to the presence of the National Guard on the campus.

The term "outside agitator" was used considerably at the time, not only at Kent, but throughout the nation, to suggest that there was a hard core of protesters that would travel from one campus to another initiating and provoking disorder. I never gave much credence to that. The way we looked at it, if anyone was an outsider, it was these guys who came onto our campus with rifles and bayonets. We looked upon them as an occupation army that had invaded our campus, and we wanted them gone.

Toward the end of the class, I recall a student standing and saying that there was going to be a rally on the commons as soon as the class was over. I sat there for a few minutes deliberating as to whether I should go or not, and I remembered my earlier assurances to my girl-friend.

Then I thought to myself, This is too momentous; it's too important for me to stay away. Certainly I couldn't see any harm in my going over just to watch. So I went over there really with the intention of more or less surveying the scene, not knowing what I was going to find.

It was only a short five-minute walk to the commons. I found several hundred students, and some of my roommates, Alan Canfora and Jim Riggs, had flags, black flags, I believe. Alan had spray-painted "KENT" on it, and the other one was just a black flag, and they were waving these things about. So I was drawn to them right away. There was some chanting going on: "One, two, three, four, we don't want your fucking war" and "Pigs off campus."

The crowd had grouped around the victory bell, which had been historically used to signal victories in Kent State football games, and the bell was being sounded to signal students to congregate. There were at the very least another thousand or so observers and onlookers ringing the hills that surround this part of the commons.

At that point, a campus policeman in a National Guard jeep ordered the crowd, through the use of a bullhorn, to disperse and go to their homes. The policeman was riding shotgun, and I believe a National Guardsman was driving the jeep. "All you bystanders and innocent people go to your homes for your own safety," is what we heard. I think he had the best of intentions in terms of asking the crowd to disperse, but it did nothing but whip the crowd into a further frenzy.

We have to remember here the mind-set of people and everything that had gone on. A very adversarial atmosphere existed, and we felt that this was our campus, that we were doing nothing wrong, and that they had no right to order us to disperse. If anyone ought to leave, it's them, not us. That's how I felt.

I was standing there yelling and screaming along with everyone else, and then someone flung either a rock or a bottle at the jeep, which bounced harmlessly off the tire. I don't think it was necessarily meant to bounce off the tire; fortunately the person was not a very good shot. That, of course, alarmed the occupants of the jeep. I think they realized at that point—because of the crescendo the chants had reached, and also the fact that people were pitching objects in their direction—that we weren't going to leave.

So the jeep drove back to the National Guard lines which had formed on the other side of the commons in front of the remains of the burned ROTC building. Then the National Guardsmen leveled their bayonets at us and started to march across the commons in our direction, shooting tear gas as they came.

I was teargassed along with perhaps a thousand other people. Unlike some of the students, who delayed to throw rocks or tear-gas cannisters back in the direction of the National Guard, I chose to leave the area as fast as I could. I retreated to a girls' dormitory where there were some first-floor restrooms. The female students had opened up the windows and were passing out moistened paper towels so people could relieve the effects of the tear gas. So I went and I cleansed my eyes to the best of my ability, and that seemed to take care of me at the moment.

In the meantime, one group of National Guardsmen had advanced the same way that I had retreated, but they did not chase the students further. But another troop of the National Guard had gone right past and proceeded downhill onto the practice football field. There was a rather abrupt drop-off and a chain-link fence where some construction had been going on, and on the other three sides the National Guardsmen were ringed by students.

I cautiously moved a little closer and watched. Some students were throwing rocks at the National Guard, and some of the National Guard were picking up the rocks and throwing them back at the students. I didn't see any National Guardsmen hit by rocks. They seemed to be bouncing at their feet.

Then I remember that the National Guard troop seemed to get into a little huddle before leaving the practice football field. They reformed their lines and proceeded back up the hill. It was almost like the parting of the Red Sea. The students just moved to one side or the other to let the National Guardsmen pass, because no one in their right mind would have stood there as bayonets were coming.

A lot of people were screaming, "Get out of here, get off our campus," and in the midst of all this were some students, oddly enough, who were still wandering through the area with their textbooks, as if they were completely unaware of all that was taking place. I felt that I was still keeping a safe distance. I was 150, 165 feet away. I know that because it's since been paced off.

When the National Guardsmen got to the top of the hill, all of a sudden there was just a quick movement, a flurry of activity, and then a crack, or two cracks of rifle fire, and I thought, Oh, my God! I turned and started running as fast as I could. I don't think I got more than a step or two, and all of a sudden I was on the ground. It was just like somebody had come over and given me a body blow and knocked me right down.

The bullet had entered my left heel and had literally knocked me off my feet. I tried to raise myself, and I heard someone yelling, "Stay down, stay down! It's buckshot!" I looked up, and about five or ten feet away from me, behind a tree, was my roommate Alan Canfora. That was the first time I had seen him since we were down on the other side of the commons, chanting antiwar slogans.

So I threw myself back to the ground and lay as prone as possible to shield myself as much as I could, although like most people I was caught right in the open. I couldn't run, because I had already been hit. There was no cover. I just hugged the ground so as to expose as little of my body as possible to the gunfire.

It seemed like the bullets were going by within inches of my head. I can remember seeing people behind me, farther down the hill in the parking lot, dropping. I didn't know if they were being hit by bullets or they were just hugging the ground. We know today that it only lasted thirteen seconds, but it seemed like it kept going and going and going. And I remember thinking, When is this going to stop?

So I was lying there, and all of a sudden this real husky, well-built guy ran to me, picked me up like I was a sack of potatoes, and threw me over his shoulder. He carried me through the parking lot in the direction of a girls' dormitory. We went by one body, a huge puddle of blood. Head wounds always bleed very badly, and his was just awful.

The female students were screaming as I was carried into the dormitory and placed on a couch, bleeding all over the place. A nursing student applied a tourniquet to my leg. I never really felt that my life was in danger, but I could look down at my foot and I knew that I had one hell of a bad wound. The bullet blew the shoe right off my foot, and there was a bone sticking through my green sock. It looked like somebody had put my foot through a meatgrinder.

The ambulances came. Some attendants came in, put me on a stretcher, and carried me outside. The blood loss had lessened because of the tourniquet that was on my leg. I remember having my fist up in the air as a sign of defiance. They put me into the top tier in the ambulance rather than the lower one, which was already occupied. I remember my foot hitting the edge of the ambulance as I went in. From that moment on, until the time that I actually went under from the anesthesia at Robinson Memorial Hospital, I was probably in the most intense pain that I've ever experienced in my life.

They had the back doors closed by this time, and the ambulance was speeding away from the campus. I looked down and saw Sandy Scheuer. I had met Sandy about a week or two beforehand for the first and only time. She had been introduced to me by one of the guys who lived downstairs in my apartment complex. They were casual friends, and she struck me as being a very nice person.

She had a gaping bullet wound in the neck, and the ambulance attendants were tearing away the top two buttons of her blouse and then doing a heart massage. I remember their saying that it's no use, she's dead. And then they just pulled up the sheet over her head.

The ambulance got to the hospital, and it was a scene that's probably been played out any number of times when you have a big disaster. There were people running around, stretchers being wheeled in, and I was just put out in a hallway because the medical personnel were attending to the more severely wounded.

I had the tourniquet on my leg, so I wasn't bleeding all over the place, but the pain kept getting more excruciating. I was screaming by that time, "Get me something for this pain!" Then I was wheeled into an elevator and brought up to one of the other floors. I remember receiving some anesthesia and being told to count backward from ten. I didn't get very far, and then I was out.

The next thing I remember was waking up in a hospital bed. I looked up at the ceiling and then all of a sudden it came to me what had occurred. I didn't know how long I had been out, and I sat up as quickly as I could and looked down to see if my foot was still there. I could see the tips of my toes sticking out of a cast. I just lay back, and I breathed a big sigh of relief. . . .

Today, if I engage in any strenuous exercise, I'll have a noticeable limp for a couple of days afterward. But on the whole, I consider myself to be rather fortunate. I could have lost my foot; I could have been killed. Four people had been shot to death: Sandy Scheuer, Jeff Miller, Allison Krause, and Bill Schroeder. My roommate Alan Canfora was struck by gunfire. He was among the least injured of the thirteen people who were either mortally wounded or recovered.

Eventually federal indictments against enlisted men and noncommissioned officers in the Ohio National Guard were handed down. But, as it turned out, the judge ruled that the Justice Department failed to prove a case of conspiracy to violate our civil rights and dismissed the case before it was ever sent to the jury. That was the end of criminal proceedings against the Ohio National Guard. They got off scot-free.

But I think there are some guardsmen who are sorry for what happened. One guy in particular seemed to be genuinely remorseful. I remember his testimony. He has very poor eyesight, and on May 4 he couldn't get the gas mask on over his glasses, so he had to wear the gas mask without glasses. He was blind as a bat without them, and he admitted he just knew he was shooting in a certain direction. That was a startling admission. There was a guy out there who could hardly see, blasting away with an M-1.

. . . Every year from May 1971, which was the first anniversary of the killings, there has been a commemorative ceremony at Kent State that has attracted anywhere from one thousand students to eight thousand. So the issue has been kept alive there, and I'd say that the main focus now is to erect a proper and suitable memorial to the people who were killed there. The university has finally agreed to do that. They have commissioned a study as to what the memorial should look like, and what it should say.

I'm more concerned about what it says than what it looks like. Ever since I was young, I've been an avid reader of history, with a particular focus on the American Civil War, and for that reason I have more than the usual interest in the subject. When I go down to the Gettysburg battlefield or Antietam, I can read on those monuments about what took place there, what the casualty figures were, and I can try to envision what took place. Somebody should be able to do that at Kent State as well.

I think the memorial should state: "On May 4, 1970, units of the Ohio National Guard—Company H, 107th Armored Cavalry (Troop G) and Company A, 145th Infantry Regiment—shot and killed four student protesters and wounded nine others during a demonstration against the U.S. invasion of Cambodia." Straight-out, simple facts.

Leone Keegan

In 1970 she was an eighteen-year-old freshman at Kent State University. On the evening of May 3 she was returning to school from a weekend visit to Columbus.

Sunday night I went back to Kent State, and when I got there, it was just unbelievable. There was so much tension. There was the National Guard, and there were helicopters flying at low altitudes with spotlights all night long. It was like a war situation. You could see that all the stores were busted out, windows broken. It was just chaos, chaos. We heard on the radio that the ROTC building had been burned and everybody was supposed to be off the streets. I went back to my apartment and went to bed.

Next morning I got up to go to my art history class. Going onto the campus, I saw all these young men in uniforms standing on the street corners with their rifles, and I was thinking, What is this? When I got to the building where the class was held and went in, I was told, "There's no class this morning. It's been canceled." I said, "Why?" "Because there's been a bomb threat in this building."

So I went back to my apartment that morning. I was still tired from the weekend, and I remember I lay down and sort of dozed off. One of my roommates came in and said, "Come on down, Leone, there's going to be a rally at twelve o'clock." That's what she called it—a rally.

And I said, "Okay, okay, I'll be down there." So I lay back, thinking about going, and I fell asleep.

A couple of hours later I woke up to the sound of gunfire. It sounded like—you know, when you sit in your backyard and fireworks are going off on the Fourth of July? That's what it sounded like. A few minutes later, my roommates came back in, and they were bawling their eyes out. They were very upset, and I said, "What happened?" They said, "There was a shooting on the commons. People were killed." All they knew was what had happened as they were running off. They didn't know any of the details. They were scared, and they were crying.

A few minutes later we heard the police coming through with their megaphones, saying, "You must leave the campus immediately. Leave within an hour. Don't take anything. Just get out of here." It was like a police state. Later we learned that the dorms were searched and they confiscated a lot of weapons. They put it in the press that they found weapons, but they didn't find revolvers, they didn't find machine guns. They found knives, things like that, and, of course, they found a lot of joints, and the press made a big issue of that. They wanted to make us out to be radicals. But we weren't radicals at Kent State. They were radical at Berkeley, you know, but Kent State was just a mild school.

The roads were so crowded with kids leaving that although it usually took only an hour to get home from Kent to Cleveland where I lived, it took four or five hours because of all the traffic. Everybody had to leave at the same time, you see.

All the parents were worried, of course. They'd heard there were four dead, and no parent knew who it was. They couldn't reach us because all the lines were busy. They were all trying to call and find out if it was *their* kid who had been shot.

Of course, we couldn't finish the year after we were ordered home. We had to finish our courses at home. Later, my father drove me back to pick up what was left of my apartment. We went into a restaurant, and they weren't very kind to us when we got something to eat. Everybody was really giving us the cold shoulder because they said we'd ruined their town. They were even giving my father the cold shoulder because he was with me. It wasn't a comfortable position to be in then, to be a student from Kent State. I was remembering my father's words to me when he drove me to college the first time the fall before. He said, "Remember, Leone, that everything you learn isn't out of books. It's life experience, too." Well, he was certainly right. I learned a lot that year, and most of it wasn't from books. . . .

About a month after the shooting—I think it was June—Crosby, Stills, Nash, and Young gave an outdoor concert in Cleveland. It was the first time they'd sung that song "Ohio" live, and it was chilling. People were on their feet, you know, clapping their hands, moving their bodies, crying. Everybody was just sort of shaking. . . . You listen to music now and it seems so candyish. . . . Then, it seemed to have a purpose. I'll never forget that night. . . . [*Sings softly.*]

> ". . . This summer I hear the drumming,
> Four dead in Ohio . . ."

Chronology of the Sixties

1960

- Lunch-counter sit-ins begin in the South.
- Birth control pills approved by Food and Drug Administration.
- U-2 "spy plane" is shot down over Russia.
- Castro confiscates American property in Cuba.
- Kennedy defeats Nixon for U.S. Presidency.

1961

- Kennedy is inaugurated, calls upon Americans to "ask not what your country can do for you, ask rather what you can do for your country."
- Peace Corps is established.
- Russian Yuri Gagarin is first man in space.
- U.S.-sponsored invasion of Cuba ends in disaster in the Bay of Pigs.
- First U.S. "advisers" are dispatched to Vietnam and Laos.
- "Freedom Riders" begin to test segregation on interstate bus routes in the South.
- Sino-Soviet split begins.

1962

- 12,000 U.S. advisers arrive in South Vietnam.
- Supreme Court bans prayer in public schools.
- Cuban Missile Crisis threatens world peace.

- *Silent Spring* by Rachel Carson is published.
- James Meredith is the first black to enroll at University of Mississippi.
- Cesar Chavez founds United Farm Workers union.
- Bob Dylan releases "Blowin' in the Wind."

1963

- Voter registration drives in South begin.
- Nuclear Test Ban Treaty is signed.
- Martin Luther King gives his "I have a dream" speech at a massive civil rights march in Washington, D.C.
- *The Feminine Mystique* by Betty Friedan is published.
- President Diem is killed in coup in South Vietnam.
- President Kennedy is assassinated.

1964

- President Johnson calls for a "Great Society" to fight poverty, prejudice, and ignorance.
- Surgeon General's report, *Smoking and Health*, links cigarettes to cancer and other health problems.
- The Beatles arrive in U.S.
- First federal civil rights bill prohibiting discrimination in public places is passed.
- First antipoverty bills are passed, funding youth programs, job corps, community action programs.
- Gulf of Tonkin incident off coast of Vietnam is followed by congressional resolution giving additional power to president.
- Free Speech Movement begins at Berkeley.
- Barry Goldwater loses presidential election to incumbent Johnson.

1965

- Johnson sends 170,000 U.S. ground troops to Vietnam.
- U.S. begins bombing North Vietnam.
- Malcolm X is killed in New York.
- Martin Luther King leads civil rights march from Selma to Birmingham, Alabama.
- Medicare bill is passed.
- Federal voting rights bill is passed.
- Antiwar teach-ins and demonstrations start.
- Miniskirts became fashionable throughout the U.S.
- New immigration bill ending national-origins quotas is passed.
- Color television sweeps U.S.
- Watts riots occur in Los Angeles.

1966

- Head Start program is established.
- Antiwar protests spread on college campuses.
- Race riots erupt across country: Cleveland, Chicago, Baltimore, New York.
- Timothy Leary tours campuses, urging listeners to use LSD to "turn on, tune in, and drop out!"
- American troops in Vietnam total nearly 400,000 by end of year.
- NOW (National Organization for Women) is founded.

1967

- "Great Easter Be-In," a celebration of the counterculture, fills Central Park in New York City.
- The "long hot summer" of race riots in major cities across the country ends with 26 dead in Newark, New Jersey.
- "Summer of Love" draws thousands of young people to San Francisco.
- Nguyen Cao Ky becomes premier of South Vietnam.
- Antiwar demonstrators march on Pentagon.
- U.S. troops in Vietnam increase to 474,000 (over 13,000 dead).

1968

- Tet Offensive imperils over 100 cities in South Vietnam, including Saigon.
- Lyndon Johnson withdraws from electoral race after Eugene McCarthy's show of strength in New Hampshire.
- Martin Luther King is assassinated; race riots follow in over 100 cities.
- Students occupy buidings at Columbia University.
- *Hair* is big success on Broadway.
- Robert F. Kennedy is assassinated in Los Angeles after California primary victory.
- Dr. Benjamin Spock, Reverend William Sloane Coffin, and others are tried for conspiracy to evade the draft.
- Troops in Vietnam reach 500,000.
- Chicago Democratic Convention is scene of bloody turmoil; many demonstrators and bystanders are injured.
- *Soul on Ice* by Eldridge Cleaver is published.
- Student unrest spreads in universities over curriculum control, hours, etc.
- Richard Nixon defeats Hubert Humphrey in presidential election.

1969

- Students strike at Harvard to end ROTC and support black students' demands.
- Black students carry guns on Cornell campus after occupying student union building.
- Scandal ensues when secretary is killed in Edward Kennedy's car accident at Chappaquiddick bridge.
- Americans Neil Armstrong and Nelson Aldrin are first men to walk on moon.
- Woodstock music festival draws 450,000.
- The Chicago Seven go on trial for conspiracy to incite a riot at Democratic Convention.
- Weathermen split from SDS at tumultuous convention.
- Nationwide antiwar Moratorium and massive antiwar demonstrations in Washington take place.
- American massacre of My Lai villagers is revealed.

- Draft lottery begins, eliminating student deferments.
- President Nixon orders bombing of Cambodia.

1970

- The Beatles disband.
- First Earth Day is celebrated.
- Nixon orders "incursion" into Cambodia.
- National Guard kills four Kent State students during protests over Cambodian action.
- Hard hats attack antiwar marchers in Wall Street confrontation.
- 448 universities and colleges are closed or on strike following Cambodian action and Kent State deaths.
- Two black student protesters are killed by police at Jackson State College in Mississippi.

Glossary

bad paper: less-than-honorable military discharge
Charlie: Vietcong
C.O.: conscientious objector
CORE: Congress of Racial Equality
DMZ: demilitarized zone; the border between North and South Vietnam
fragging: intentional wounding or killing of a military officer by his own soldiers
KIA: killed in action
lifer: a career military officer or long-term enlistee
medevac: medical evacuation of wounded soldiers, usually by helicopter
MIA: missing in action
the Movement: a catchall term for the political activism of the Sixties that includes all civil rights and antiwar activists, as well as others working for social change
NCO: noncommissioned officer
NLF: National Liberation Front; political organization of the South Vietnamese Communists often used loosely to refer to Communist soldiers
OD: overdose on drugs
PL: Progressive Labor Party
ROTC: Reserve Officers Training Corps
SDS: Students for a Democratic Society
SNCC: Student Nonviolent Coordinating Committee
Vietcong; VC: South Vietnamese Communist guerrillas
VVAW: Vietnam Veterans Against the War
Weathermen: a militant faction of SDS, later known as the Weather Underground
Yippie: a member of the Youth International Party

Index